The Modern Condition

ESSAYS AT CENTURY'S END

THE MODERN CONDITION

Essays at Century's End

❆ ❆ ❆

DENNIS H. WRONG

Stanford University Press

Stanford, California

1998

Stanford University Press
Stanford, California

© 1998 by the Board of Trustees of the
Leland Stanford Junior University

Printed in the United States of America

CIP data are at the end of the book

Preface

The essays in this collection were written between 1978 and 1997, a span of twenty years. They were produced for a variety of occasions; some appeared in academic journals, some in nonacademic "intellectual" journals such as *Dissent* and *Partisan Review*, a few in more widely read weeklies such as *The New Republic* and *The New York Times Book Review*. Several essays were invited presentations for conference panels assigned particular discussion topics. Still others I was independently moved to write. Two essays in the second section, Chapters 9 and 12, have not been published before; another, Chapter 11, appeared only in an internal university newsletter. Chapter 4, on the concept of power, was an introduction to a reissue of an entire book of mine on power originally printed in 1979 (Wrong 1995). Despite the presumption, which I share, against reprinting what had been straight book reviews in collections of essays, two reviews have been included here. I used a review of a book about Hannah Arendt on totalitarianism as an occasion to reassess the concept and pay tribute to her famous work on the subject. A review of an essay collection by Daniel Bell gave me the opportunity to survey his long intellectual career. The essay on Christopher Lasch begins with a review of his last non-posthumous book, but incorporates sections from both an earlier article of mine on his cultural criticism and my review of another of his books. In view of this diversity of origin, it might seem

even more difficult than usual to find a common theme unifying
the individual essays. All such collections, of course, may be pre-
sumed to express the sensibility and intellectual style of their
single author.

I believe, however, that I have identified at least two broad
themes permitting the grouping of the essays into two distinct
sections. The first section, which I have entitled "Concepts and
Realities," includes essays that explore the ambiguities and shifting meanings of a number of fundamental political and sociological concepts or ideas. Several of these—"capitalism," "totalitarianism," "alienation," "cultural relativism"—have loomed large in
both intellectual debate and political conflict in the "short" twentieth century, the century that opened in historical as distinct
from chronological time with the Great War of 1914–18 and ended
with the collapse of Communism in 1989–91. It is unlikely that
these concepts will be anything like as prominent in the new century, let alone the new millennium. (The same probably applies to
"new class" and "intellectual," the subjects of essays in the second
section from which the section title is adapted.)

The worldwide successes of capitalism render it less meaningful to identify (and/or oppose) it as one of two or more alternative
systems of modern economy, although political contestation over
the nature and degree of state interventions in capitalist economies will certainly continue. The term "capitalism" has in a sense
become obsolete as a result of the successes of the entity it de-
notes. Totalitarianism and alienation, on the other hand, seem
more closely tied to failed political regimes or ideologies distinctive of the bloody and tumultuous twentieth century that are unlikely to have much of a future. In addition to its Marxist origins,
alienation has been widely used to describe the situation in modern society of "the intellectual," whose identification as a social
and psychological type barely predates twentieth-century conditions that have ceased to exist, as I argue in one of the previously unpublished essays in the second section. Possibly but by
no means probably, the subjects of two of the other essays in the
first section may also turn out to have had their greatest relevance
in this waning century: the spatial metaphor of left and right as
the basic coordinates of politics, and the indiscriminate use of

"culture" to cover all group differences regarded as "socially constructed." The essays on rationality and power, by contrast, deal with concepts that are obviously of a more transhistorical character, although they are often defined in new and changing ways. I subject them to the same process of delimitation and disaggregation I have applied to the more timebound concepts.

The second section deals less with concepts as such than with substantive social phenomena. (A philosopher I know once mocked sociologists for their utter dependence on the word "substantive," and he may have had a point!) The relation of intellectuals to social classes and institutions, indeed to society in general, describes fairly accurately the essays in this section, so I have entitled it "Intellectuals and Middle Classes." The first essay critically assesses the notion of a "new class" in which intellectuals have been alleged to play a particularly prominent role. The second essay (previously unpublished) discusses credentialism and controversies over "affirmative action" in education as well as intellectuals and their institutional affiliations or lack of them. The third and fourth essays deal with the impact of the ideas and language of academic sociology on the wider off-campus American public. The fifth essay, also not previously published, discusses the relation of a particular group of intellectuals to a painful and discredited period in recent American history. It was originally presented at Brooklyn College of the City University of New York on a panel with Nathan Glazer and Arthur Schlesinger Jr. discussing "The New York Intellectuals and McCarthyism." The next four essays treat individual intellectuals. The four men discussed—David Riesman, Daniel Bell, Christopher Lasch, and Allan Bloom—in addition to their indisputable status as intellectuals, were themselves acute analysts of intellectuals, the shifting fashions of cultural life to which they contribute, and their relation to the general culture and class structure or social stratification of contemporary society. The essay centered on Bloom was the lead article in an issue of *The New York Times Book Review* featuring paperback books. In addition to discussing Bloom's influential philippic, it used the occasion of his book's publication in paper to review the general phenomenon of works of social criticism that had become trendy paperback bestsellers.

Except for minor corrections and updating, all of the essays with three exceptions have been reproduced as they were originally printed. The first exception is "The Politics of Left and Right," first published as long ago as 1979 as a chapter in my book on power, to which I have added later published qualifications of the original theory in response to the conservative politics of the 1980's as well as more recent observations written especially for the present volume. A section of the chapter had been published in slightly different form even earlier and was included in my previous collection of essays (Wrong 1976c), the only duplication, though a partial one, in the present collection. The essay on the late Christopher Lasch, as I have previously noted, melds together three separate discussions or reviews of his work. Finally, the autobiographical statement that closes the book has been re-titled and expanded in several places, with additions mainly from another shorter published autobiographical piece.

I am grateful especially to Laura Bloch and also to Muriel Bell of the Stanford University Press for their sage editorial advice. I owe a particular debt of gratitude to Deena Weinstein for her very thorough critique and suggestions for revision of an earlier, much more baggy version of this book. She contributed far more than her limited responsibilities as a reader of the manuscript required. I also appreciate the helpful suggestions of Axel van den Berg, Jacqueline Conrath, and Jaya Mehta.

Contents

The Modern Condition

ESSAYS AT CENTURY'S END

I

CONCEPTS AND REALITIES

CHAPTER I

Disaggregating the Idea of Capitalism

The term "capitalism" did not become widely used until the beginning of the present century when, as Fernand Braudel (1986: 237) writes, "it fully burst upon political debate as the natural opposite of socialism." Werner Sombart was mainly responsible for launching it in academic circles where it very shortly afterwards received an additional impetus from Max Weber's famous essay (1930), originally written in criticism of Sombart, and the debate over the Protestant ethic thesis that ensued. Although often believed to have been the major formulator and disseminator of the idea of capitalism as a historically distinctive economic system, Karl Marx never used the term, usually describing the social order shaped by the economic processes that were the subject of his most voluminous and influential writings as "bourgeois society." Nor did Adam Smith ever use the word. The Russian Revolution of October 1917 was largely responsible for securely establishing "capitalism" as the name of the dominant order in the West that the Bolsheviks aspired to overthrow and replace with "socialism," pictured as a vastly superior and radically different alternative.

This record contains many ironies and paradoxes. Most obviously, the common name for the old system doomed to perish came into general use nearly a century *after* the invention and spread of the name signifying both the social movement striving to overthrow it and the new order designed to supplant it. This might be regarded as an instance of Karl Mannheim's claim that conservative thought only achieves articulation in response to a prior ideological—in his terminology, utopian—assault upon the existing order it wants to affirm. However, "capitalism" was never a concept favored by its defenders. It has nearly always been used pejoratively. The historian Fritz Stern (1987: 235) recently wrote: "The detractors of capitalism are legion, its defenders few and uncertain. Stereotypes prevail: Capitalism involves alienation, exploitation, class conflict. Historically it is seen as the triumph of a corrupt and spineless bourgeoisie, ruthless in its pursuit of profit and in its repression of the class it lives off." Reviewing the much earlier seventeenth- and eighteenth-century use of "capitalist" to describe rich men and financial manipulators, Braudel (1986: 235) remarked, "The word is never, the reader will have noticed, used in a friendly sense." Braudel went on to recount how, converted into an "ism," it became a "political word" readily "incorporated into the Marxist model," ultimately giving rise to a "post-Marxian orthodoxy" in which "we are not allowed to talk about capitalism before the end of the eighteenth century, in other words before the industrial mode of production" (Braudel 1986: 238).

I remember C. Wright Mills in the late 1940's commenting on an article in *Fortune* that urged spokesmen for American business unapologetically to call the system they upheld "capitalism" instead of resorting to euphemisms like "free enterprise." Mills saw this as an example of the growing realism of those he then described as "sophisticated conservatives," an early approximation as a group to what he later named the "power elite." Mills overlooked that the article was probably written by one of several Trotskyist intellectuals on the magazine's staff, who undoubtedly saw himself as engaged in subtle ideological subversion in offering such terminological advice to the class enemy.

Even if Marx neither invented nor used the term, the essence of his work was to insist, against the classical economists, that the mode of production dominated by the use of money as capital was not simply equivalent to political economy as such; it was, on the contrary, no more than a transitory product of history rather than the embodiment of timeless natural laws analogous to those of Newtonian mechanics. But, though transitory, economic systems, or modes of production, generated classes in conflict over material interests that were the prime movers of history itself. Everything else in a society, its legal, political, religious, and cultural institutions and values, constituted a superstructure shaped by the base of the economy, or the forces and relations of production.

The idea of "capitalism" as a specific kind of economic system distinct from primitive communism, slavery, feudalism, and the future prospect of socialism and full communism attracted comparative historians like Sombart and Weber. Yet these scholars were primarily interested in exploring the complex links between capitalism as an economic system and class structures, religious beliefs, legal systems, and forms of government, as well as such relative cultural intangibles as moral outlooks and mentalities (*mentalités*). Paradoxically, if they borrowed the notion of capitalism as a particular kind of economic system from Marxism, they also enlarged it into a more comprehensive entity by aggregating it with noneconomic, even primarily psychological, social and cultural phenomena. At the same time, they criticized or denied the causal priority ascribed by Marxists to economic forces, giving at least equal weight to such noneconomic factors as the Protestant ethic, Roman law, urban political autonomy, or an underlying rationalizing spirit or *Geist* pervading all spheres of social life, in accounting for the genesis of capitalism itself. Capitalism as a generic term for modern society owes as much to the historians and sociologists who were critics of Marxism as to Marxism itself.

An additional paradox is that Marx's preferred term for the post-feudal era, "bourgeois society," essentially referred to a correlate of capitalism, namely, the class that became its historical carrier and achieved social dominance under its aegis, rather than to the mode of production itself. Bourgeois society is, therefore, an aggregative concept. Of all the various "post" labels that have been so popular in recent years—postindustrial, postmaterialist, postcapitalist, postmodern—postbourgeois is the only one that is not unavoidably controversial because of a vagueness verging on vacuity that lends itself to arbitrary interpretation. Postbourgeois at least suggests the disappearance of a bounded, residentially located, historical social class with a cultural profile of its own. But the disappearance of the class in no way entails the

disappearance of capitalism, the mode of production associated
with the rise of the class and both reflecting and shaping its style
of life. The bourgeoisie dissolves, its distinctive values are partly
negated and even reversed, partly diffused to everyone, but capitalism expands into a world system and with the collapse of communism overcomes the most formidable threat to its survival.

Apart from the overall issue of economic determinism or the
economic interpretation of history, the changing historical context of capitalism necessitates continual consideration of which
noneconomic values and institutions are compatible with it,
which limit or even threaten it, and which constitute necessary or sufficient conditions for its birth, growth, and survival.
The emergence of highly successful capitalist economies in the
non-Western societies bordering the China Sea gives added importance to such assessments. Peter Berger (1986: 15–31) devotes
much attention to the new East Asian capitalisms in a book whose
declared purpose is to disaggregate *modernity* as the central historical experience of the West over the past two centuries by
analytically separating from it capitalism as an economic system,
granting that the latter's rise was part of the great transformation
that created the modern West.

At the beginning of the century Max Weber (1930: 181–82) maintained that the persistence and future development of capitalism did not depend on the waning spirit of religious asceticism
that had contributed to its birth: "Victorious capitalism, since it
rests on mechanical foundations, needs its support no longer."
Whether capitalism complements, or even undergirds, democratic
government and the civil freedoms basic to the liberalism of the
great eighteenth- and nineteenth-century political revolutions, or
whether it undermines them by concentrating power in the hands
of a new ruling class, has been the subject of intense debate ever
since socialist ideologies and movements became leading con-
tenders for political power. "Socialism" was originally coined as
the antithesis not of capitalism but of "individualism," which was
coined at roughly the same time in the early nineteenth century. Individualism as a general moral and cultural outlook has
long been regarded as both a cause and a consequence of capitalist economies. Recently, however, the existence of any necessary

association between capitalism and individualism has been questioned, whatever connection may have existed at the historical conjuncture when capitalism as a new mode of production came into being. It has even been argued that "the capitalist mode of production does not have any necessary ideological conditions of existence" (Abercrombie et al. 1986: 190). (Ideological here essentially means "cultural.")

All of these interpretations amount to efforts to disaggregate the social wholes—social formations, as structuralist Marxists call them—that include capitalist economies in order to determine which links between capitalism and other phenomena are intrinsic and which are merely extrinsic or historically contingent. One is moved to insist that an economy is an economy is an economy: it is meant to put food on the table, not to advance the telos of history, measure up to an ideal, express the moral or aesthetic spirit of a people, function harmoniously as part of a larger integrated social system, or create modernity so that modish pontifications in bad prose about something called "postmodernity" can be turned out by professors.

The pairing of capitalism with socialism as its opposite leads to major misconceptions. The fundamental asymmetry between capitalism and socialism is often overlooked, especially at the level of political and ideological debate. Capitalism is not a theory —it is a condition. Both capitalism and socialism are conceptions of economic systems, but capitalism as a system was only discovered after the fact by the classical political economists, the last of whom, it has rightly been observed, was Karl Marx. Capitalism is a system of unintended consequences both in its origins and in its workings. Braudel once exclaimed, "The best thing about capitalism is that no one invented it!" Or, as Ernest Gellner (1974: 183) mordantly put it, "where it does not exist, no one will bother to invent it." Capitalism is what we have, what we got stuck with; socialism, on the other hand, is an ideal, an ideology or utopia awaiting realization.

It is remarkable how often these painfully obvious and banal observations are ignored by both the eulogists and the critics of capitalism. The rise of capitalism is sometimes described as if benevolent or malevolent men had planned and instituted it at a

determinate moment in history. Adam Smith is praised or blamed
for having actually invented the market rather than for merely
having first fully expounded how it worked to connect supply and
demand.[1]

But capitalism is nothing but an economic system which has
the palpable advantage but also the ideological disadvantage of
actually existing, warts and all. Socialism by contrast has from its
beginnings been a project, a shared ideal, something to be built by
strenuous political mobilization and collective effort. Socialism
possesses "mythic superiority" over capitalism, as Berger (1986:
194–209) puts it. It is seen—like freedom, democracy, nationhood
—as incarnating ultimate values, whereas capitalism is judged by
its inevitably uneven economic results as solely of instrumental
value. No one, as Schumpeter pointed out long ago, has ever died
for capitalism. To be sure, there have been visionaries of an ideal
or utopian capitalism—one thinks of Milton Friedman—but controversy over the merits of capitalism has always chiefly focused
on its actual failures and achievements.

The mythic or utopian aura of socialism was only very partially dissipated by the successful Communist revolution in Russia. Nevertheless, since 1917 and especially since Stalin's dictatorship socialism as an economic system has faced the same problem
of aggregation and disaggregation that capitalism has long con-
fronted. To what extent did Soviet totalitarianism result from the
centralized economy or from traditional Russian autocracy? Is it
possible to combine socialist economics and political democracy?
Long before the collapse of Communism in 1989, at the very least
since Khrushchev's famous "secret speech" of 1956, a majority of
socialists in the West have firmly dissociated their ideal from the
model of Soviet Communism. The New Left of the 1960's was
an effort to cleanse socialism of the taint of association with the
Soviet experience, although many of its partisans briefly invested
illusory hopes in the "actually existing" Third World socialisms
of Cuba, China under Mao, North Vietnam, and, somewhat later,
Nicaragua. Yet the very term "actually existing socialism" (*real ex-
istierender Sozialismus*) was the ironic coinage of a refugee from
East Germany on encountering the utter indifference of the West

German radical left to the regimes on the other side of the Berlin Wall.

The familiar contrast between capitalism as the status quo and socialism as the obvious alternative to it has been suddenly reversed with the collapse of Communism in Central Europe and the Soviet Union. As the joke has it, socialism is the longest route between capitalism and capitalism. The attempt by formerly Communist states to initiate a transition from a command to a market economy in which private enterprise plays a leading role is altogether unprecedented. Is it possible to "build capitalism" from the top down? How can a new entrepreneurial class of private owners of the means of production be created or recruited out of whole cloth in a short period of time? To what extent will a privatized *nomenklatura* form part of such a class? A few Marxists have already exhibited the stirrings of a tendency to invoke the capitalist aspirations of the delegitimated *nomenklatura* to account for the almost total lack of resistance, even of a nonviolent sort, to the popular uprisings against Communism in its entirety in Central Europe and the feeble and ultimately fruitless opposition to its final dismantling in the Soviet Union. There have also been voices on the left contending rather pathetically that the peoples of Central Europe may have wanted democracy and national self-determination, but they have not been clamoring for the "restoration of capitalism." True enough, but, as we have seen, with the doubtful exception of a few ideologues of neoclassical economics, no one values capitalism for its own sake. The rebels against Communism, however, have certainly wanted the economic results of capitalism in the form of a higher standard of living and greater consumer choice. Moreover, the manifest economic deficiencies of state socialism are what finally brought about its collapse.

As these recent events strongly suggest, capitalism as an economic system is not a uniform entity but a complex of interdependent attributes. In addition to detaching it from the changing historical contexts of noneconomic institutions and cultural traits in which it has been embedded over the several centuries of its existence, we must also disaggregate its strictly economic features and regard them as capable of independent variation. The almost universal declarations by leaders of the erstwhile Soviet bloc nations that they seek to establish a "market economy" suggest this, as does the fact that all member parties of the Socialist International in the Western democracies (and in Israel and Japan) now assert their belief in free markets and their rejection of such traditional socialist objectives as central planning and the nationalization of major economic enterprises. The Italian Communist Party, now renamed, has also followed this route to acceptance of a mixed economy with a strong private sector and abandonment of socialism as a goal representing a radical alternative to capitalism.

I shall eschew yet another formal definition of capitalism and confine myself simply to listing its attributes that should be disaggregated from the total complex with which it is usually identified. They are: free market pricing, production for profit, competition between independent producers, a free labor market, and private ownership of the means of production. The free market is obviously the most important. Doubtless, as asserted by a woman in a Jules Feiffer cartoon, "free market" is a "better-sounding name" than "capitalism," given the negative overtones that cling to the latter. But the use of market as a euphemism notwithstanding, the notion of "market socialism" is not a contradiction in terms, nor even an oxymoron. There is an intellectual tradition affirming it in economic theory and it has recently been advocated by a number of Polish, Czech, and Hungarian economists as well as by Alec Nove (1983) in his influential book *The Economics of Feasible Socialism*. In addition to his theoretical analysis, Nove assesses the experiences of Hungary and Yugoslavia, where reform-minded Communist regimes introduced elements of market socialism in the 1970's and 1980's.

Markets are, of course, an ancient institution, present to some degree in nearly all human societies. Adam Smith (1970: 117) was certainly correct in regarding as universally human "the propensity to truck, barter, and exchange one thing for another." (He was also correct in seeing it as a distinctively human disposition, presupposing "the faculties of reason and speech" and thus lacking in other animal species.) Markets, therefore, long antedate capitalism, as Marx recognized, although they are often equated with it in socialist or anticapitalist discourse. Such major theorists of socialism as Marx, Lenin, Kautsky, and Bukharin regarded socialism and markets as incompatible virtually by definition. More recently, Paul Sweezy (1971: 5) directly denied my previous statement in insisting that "the very term 'market socialism' is self-contradictory." One is reminded of Robert Nozick's (1974: 163) brilliant bon mot that "the socialist society would have to forbid capitalist acts between consenting adults." Rejecting the market/capitalism equation from the perspective of a historian, Braudel repeatedly deplored their conflation, maintaining that the market economy existed in the *longue durée* of history whereas capitalism is a relative newcomer. Not just markets but *free* markets, in which the rate of exchange or price fluctuates (within limits) in response to perceived magnitudes of supply and demand, are also, Braudel (1986: 227) pointed out, both ancient and widespread. Markets spring up spontaneously in a variety of different situations, often in the face of attempts by powerful authorities to suppress them. Black markets subvert wartime rationing, underground market economies have flourished in all communist countries, covert markets in scarce or illegal goods and services quickly come into being in prisons and detention camps, often improvising new media of exchange such as cigarettes.

Markets presuppose real competition between independent producers or traders. Nove recently observed that, economically speaking, the opposite of competition is not cooperation but monopoly, including state monopolies.[2] But the competing units need not be "private" individuals or groups owning their own means of production. Nove (1983: 200–201) distinguishes five distinct types of unit that might exist in his model of feasible socialism: large state-owned and controlled enterprises, autonomous state- or worker-owned enterprises, cooperatives, small private businesses, and self-employed individuals. The preponderance of the first three types justifies the socialist label given that private property is clearly a *sine qua non* of capitalism as conventionally understood. Nove's model is actually that of a mixed economy including different kinds of publicly and privately owned enterprises, combining some government planning with the market, and providing generous state welfare services.

From a pro-capitalist standpoint directly opposed to Sweezy's socialist view, Berger (1986: 187–89, 226) joins Sweezy in denying the meaningfulness of "market socialism." He explicitly defends as a "hypothetical proposition"—the 48th of 50 that he formulates —that "there can be no effective market economy without private ownership of the means of production" (Berger 1986: 190). Berger is narrowly empiricist in equating socialism entirely with the Soviet model. He readily accepts the terms of conventional ideological controversy in treating capitalism and socialism as stark, mutually exclusive alternatives. Although conceding that no pure case of either has ever existed, Berger (1986: 194–209) insists that an economy *must* be primarily one or the other without precisely specifying the meaning of "primarily." The whole notion of property and what it means to own it, and the relationship of legal ownership to control, raise exceedingly complex conceptual and substantive issues. Berger cogently disaggregates capitalism as an economy from modernity as such, but he accepts capitalism (and socialism, for that matter) as irreducible aggregates.

What of that old socialist saw favoring production for use over production for profit, or the Marxist goal of abolishing "commodity production" and "exchange value"? Production for profit presupposes that the product is useful; otherwise, the makers of pet rocks might be aspiring to enter the ranks of the *Fortune* 500. If exchange value were determined solely by the amount of labor required to produce a commodity plus the surplus labor appropriated as profit by the capitalist, there would be flourishing markets for immensely expensive pins with the Lord's Prayer hand carved on their heads and for ship models built inside narrow-necked bottles. Free markets indeed require that enterprises show a profit as a measure of their efficiency, but the profit need not end up lining the pockets of an individual owner. Both as a test of efficiency and as an incentive, profit can accrue to organizations as collective entities regardless of who, if anyone in any meaningful sense, owns them. Property relations, as Marxists like to call them, are just not of critical importance with respect to economic performance.

As for a free labor market, in practice labor has rarely if ever been treated as a "mere" commodity offered for sale by its owners out of sheer necessity, not even in the era of the "dark satanic mills" of early industrial England, as Marx and Engels themselves acknowledged. Denial of the status of labor as a marketed commodity like any other is the centerpiece of Lester Thurow's (1983: 173–215) critique in *Dangerous Currents* of the "equilibrium price-auction" model of the market, as he calls it, that dominates neoclassical economics. Independent trade unions and protective labor legislation exist, though notoriously not to the same degree, in all democratic capitalist countries.

I note with satisfaction the increasing use of the term "the market mechanism" to describe how contemporary mixed economies work. A mechanism is what it is and does what it does; it inspires neither love nor hate, incarnates neither good nor evil. It also suggests something operating within a larger established context that can be turned on or off, accelerated or decelerated, muffled or allowed free play. I think this is the way we ought to look at capitalism as an economic system, distinct from its historically contingent social and cultural supports, and capable of being disaggregated into its component economic elements.

Perhaps the very name "capitalism" ought to be confined to the dynamically expanding market, creating unprecedented economic growth and social dislocation, that contributed so greatly to the modernization process, the great transformation, the breakthrough to modernity, or whatever one chooses to call it, that began in Western Europe just over two centuries ago. So used, it would, as distinct from the concept of a market economy, constitute a "historical individual" in Weber's sense. I have considerable sympathy with Anthony Giddens's (1985: 289) rejection of the frequent substitution of "industrial" for "capitalist" on the grounds that "industrialism first emerged within the institutional nexus of capitalism, whose competitive pressures served in substantial part to generate it." Berger, despite his effort to dissociate capitalism from modernity, notes his own past failure, as well as that of others, even to identify it as a causal factor in the modernization experience undergone by the West. "Marxists," he writes, "have been obsessed by capitalism; 'bourgeois sociologists' have at times failed to notice it" (Berger 1986: 226).

The collapse of Communism and the ongoing globalization of

markets mark a historical divide. It is a good moment to divest the idea of capitalism of the penumbra from the past that still clings to it by treating it primarily as an economy and separating its various economic components. One would like to see sociologists and economists collaborate in this task.

CHAPTER 2

Is Rational Choice Humanity's Most Distinctive Trait?

The identification of Reason as the most distinctively human capacity or faculty, the *differentia specifica* of Man in Aristotle's sense, goes back to the Greek philosophers and was retained by the philosophers of the Renaissance and the Enlightenment. Man was defined as the *animal rationale* and when classified later as one of many species of living things he was named *homo sapiens*, the wise or knowing hominid. To define human behavior as essentially based on "rational choice" is unmistakably continuous with this classical intellectual tradition.

At the same time, the stress on "choice" linked to action rather than to thought or contemplation represents a particular post-Enlightenment version of Reason, one that sees it as an essentially practical capacity serving the purposes and aims of human actors whatever those purposes and aims might happen to be. Well before Darwin identified the human species as having come into being by the same process of struggle for competitive survival and natural selection as all other species, Hobbes wrote, "For the Thoughts, are to the Desires, as Scouts and Spies, to range abroad and find the way to things Desired." A century later Hume famously wrote, "Reason is, and ought only to be the slave of the passions, and can never pretend to any other office than to serve and obey them." Hobbes and Hume are the most illustrious ancestors of the tradition later known as utilitarianism that became in its special version dealing with economic behavior the foundation of classical and neoclassical economics, which is the most immediate precursor of contemporary rational choice theory.

Earlier thinkers influenced by Plato and Aristotle, including the Christian theologians, tended to regard Reason as the enemy rather than the servant of what they saw as the base passions or appetites with which an irrational or sinful humanity was also endowed. Reason was able to legislate what ends and purposes human beings ought to pursue and what social and political institutions were right and appropriate for them. This approach survives today in neo-Thomist theology and in the antimodernist classical social thought whose most prominent contemporary representatives are the late Leo Strauss and his followers. It has also been central to the neo-Marxist–Hegelian outlook of the Frankfurt School, which affirmed the tradition of "objective reason," encompassing normative ends and values, against the "subjective reason," specifically labeled and anathematized as "instrumental rationality," that was seen as dominating the fallen world of capitalist modernity. It has been lucidly articulated by Max Horkheimer in terms that would almost certainly be acceptable to classical conservative thinkers otherwise alien to the Frankfurt outlook: "When the idea of reason was conceived, it was intended to achieve more than the mere regulation of the relation between means and ends; it was regarded as the instrument for understanding the ends, *for determining them*" (Horkheimer 1947: 10; italics in original).[1]

The tradition that identifies rationality with effective action also presumes a psychology of egoistic individualism. Rationality lies in the choice of means to achieve ends dictated by individual self-interest. The utilitarians and their forerunners—Hobbes, Locke, Mandeville, Hume, and Smith—accepted a hedonistic psychology in which the search for pleasure and the avoidance of pain determined the choices of individuals. An individual might make many such choices, and the choices might vary widely among individuals, but a "hedonistic" or "felicific calculus" underlay all of them. These assumptions were converted by the classical economists into the postulate that the diverse concrete ends or "utilities" pursued by individuals were incomparable or incommensurate. However, since the material resources used to attain them were finite and scarce, their allocation among different uses could be precisely measured and calculated, most signally when they could be priced on a monetary scale. The ends of action were, accordingly, considered to be "given" as individual "preferences," while the plurality of ends individuals strive to attain can at least be measured in terms of the costs in scarce resources required to achieve them. The identification of rationality with the adaptation and allocation of means to ends on the assumption that ends are given and not subject to rational determination became so taken for granted that Talcott Parsons in his famous assault upon the utilitarian tradition in *The Structure of Social Action* described ends as "nonrational" choices not reducible to the rational/irrational dichotomy. He was affirming Pareto's concept of "nonlogical action," Pareto having been an engineer and an economist who drew a sharp line between the "logico-experimental" method of science, the sole locus of rationality, and the sentiment-drenched realm of ordinary human life in society.[2]

In conversation with a sociologist who is a leading proponent of rational choice theory, I once remarked that I shared his "methodological individualism" but not his commitment to "rational choice" as the defining quality of human action. He replied, "What's the difference?" I later repeated this colloquy to the late James Coleman, the leading advocate and representative of rational choice among sociologists. Coleman agreed with me that methodological individualism does not necessarily entail rational choice. Individualism, of course, comes in many different forms, and even its methodological version is understood in a number of different ways. All I mean in affirming methodological individualism is that the full understanding of any and all social phenomena requires reference to the beliefs and intentions of the individual actors, the concrete flesh-and-blood human beings who are the basic units composing collectivities and constituting "social forces." Such a view in no way presumes that individuals are self-moved movers, that their psyches are not influenced and have not been fundamentally, if not totally, shaped by the other people with whom they have been associated since birth. Freud was certainly a methodological individualist in this sense, but it would be incongruous to regard him as a believer in rational choice. The primacy of "irrational choice" in human conduct was surely the basic tenet of his theorizing.

Coleman has nevertheless contended that "what is ordinarily described as nonrational or irrational is merely so because the observers have not discovered the point of view of the actor, from which the action *is* rational."[3] This suggests that virtually all human actions can ultimately be construed as rational if we try hard enough to do so. "Rational" here becomes more or less synonymous with *explicable*. Action based on ignorance or error, even presumably ignorance or error dictated by unconscious motivations stemming from early childhood experience diagnosed by psychoanalysis, can be subsumed under the rubric of rational choice. In fact, psychoanalysts often speak of the inner or hidden "logic" underlying neurotic behavior. That *psychotic* behavior consistent with an actor's paranoid or delusional belief system could be described as rational is perhaps the reductio ad absurdum of such a position. Psychiatrists and psychoanalysts have often maintained that there is a continuum from "normal" through "neurotic" to "psychotic" behavior. This at least suggests difficulties in drawing a hard and fast line between rational and irrational choices. Perhaps "choice" should be the operative term: only sheer "unthinking" habit, as we call it, and "uncontrollable" manifestations of strong emotion would be excluded from rational action, for they do not involve any choice. They are not, in short, what we normally consider to be "voluntary" actions, and a criterion of rationality is therefore irrelevant to interpreting them. Distinguishing between actions that are voluntary and those that are involuntary is crucial in assessing legal responsibility, but it needs to be remembered that the line between them is notoriously fuzzy and debatable for the law as well as for psychiatry and in everyday life.

Psychoanalysis is based on the assumption that emotions and basic human motives grounded in them are *not* the products of voluntary choice, but are subject to a psychic determinism rooted in the unconscious and shaped by early childhood experience. The appeal of psychoanalytic therapy, essentially of all psychotherapy, is to restore voluntary choice by overcoming particular involuntary feelings and motivations of the patient—"where id was, there shall ego be," in Freud's famous statement. Feelings and desires are harder to conquer, transform, or eliminate than ideas or actions; they cannot simply be willed away or put out of mind by sheer determination, even if they can be blocked from direct expression in action. Emotions, desires, and affect-laden ideas and actions based on them that are experienced as compulsive or obsessive do not, therefore, fall within the bounds of rational choice. They doubtless exemplify, if often in idiosyncratic forms, the "appetites" of Plato and the "passions" of Hobbes and Hume. Psychoanalysis and other psychologies of personality have chosen to analyze and try to understand them in both their universal and their individual variants. Animals and humans, as Darwin noted, share most emotions and even the bodily forms and gestures in which they are expressed. It is not obvious why human nature as such should be identified with those traits and capacities—reason, language, voluntary choice, purposive action, instrumental rationality—that are peculiarly or distinctively human. In seeming to do so, rational choice theory resembles theories of a hermeneutic, culturalist, and pan-linguistic nature with which it claims in other respects to be at odds.

It is worth briefly noting, as I have done above, the kinds of actions of individual personalities falling within the purview of psychiatrists that would ordinarily be classified as irrational, because the debate over rational choice in sociology commonly overlooks them and centers on the status of the common values and norms that Parsons defined as nonrational rather than irrational. It is interesting to note that Max Weber, who is so often criticized by antimodernist thinkers for limiting rationality to the adaptation of means to ends,[4] specifically regarded action seen as normatively justified for its own sake as a kind of rationality differing from rational action defined by the use of appropriate means to realize a given end. Both *Zweckrationalität*, the instrumental rationality of fitting means to ends, and *Wertrationalität*, or value-rationality, are classified as rational by Weber, whatever the creative or merely arbitrary subjectivity he may have imputed to the initial choice of values. Parsons's "nonrational" deviates from Weber in this respect, perhaps reflecting the fact that Weber in his awareness of the antipositivist and antimodern outlook of the early-twentieth-century German academy stood closer to the ancient conviction that normative values were grounded in the nature of things despite his repudiation of its essence in insisting on the logical gulf between facts and values.

Critics of rational choice have for the most part focused on its preoccupation with self-interest, insisting that it neglects the "moral dimension" of human action or treats it reductively.[5] This has, of course, been the traditional line of sociological criticism of utilitarianism and economic individualism, with Durkheim and Parsons its most prominent exponents. At its worst, the debate degenerates into a caricatured contrast between a cold and calculating egoist engaged at the breakfast table in a cost-benefit assessment of the value of continuing his/her marriage and an oversocialized goody two-shoes programmed in early childhood to cherish the values and conform to the norms that sustain the social order by serving the common good. Coleman contrasts the basic assumption of "maximizing utility in rational choice theory" with what he contends is Parsons's equally basic assumption that "persons behave in accordance with social norms."[6] Coleman and other rational choice sociologists, including earlier "exchange theorists" such as Peter Blau, are nevertheless genuine sociologists in tackling as their central problem the issue of how common norms, values, and group solidarities (Hechter 1987) emerge from the self-interested pursuits of individuals at the micro level of action and interaction.

Coleman acknowledges that individuals can identify with external objects, most notably with other people, and incorporate them into an expanded conception of self—he calls it the "object self"—that produces an expanded sense of self-interest. He writes: "It can be argued that an important process that occurs throughout life is an expansion of the object self to include larger and larger sets of objects. . . . Acts of apparent altruism, acts which derive from sentimental attachments and appear to be against the actor's interests narrowly defined, are explicable through such an addition to the theory, the use of the notion of an expanded object self" (Coleman 1990: 517–18). Yet this entirely reasonable claim surely undermines the notion that all action is based on self-interest, although the references to "acts of apparent altruism" and "actor's interests narrowly defined" echo familiar efforts by proponents of universal egoism to assimilate behavior that is not obviously self-interested to their own fundamental assumptions, at the risk of tautology. Coleman, moreover, proceeds to assess the possible benefits that may ultimately accrue to the self from actions that appear manifestly to serve the interests of others (1990: 519–20).

This concession, if it be so regarded, comes late in Coleman's massive volume. In its earlier pages he more typically argues that rational choice theory necessarily assumes "persons who are . . . not only rational but also unconstrained by norms and purely self-interested" (1990: 31–32). But the very notion of "self" connotes an object of consciousness that is constructed by language, or "symbolic communication," as George Herbert Mead called it. The capacity to choose, to reflect on the possible consequence of different lines of action, also presupposes the prior acquisition of language. Both the cognitive identification with others and the emotional identification seen by Freud as the basis for the formation of the "superego" are effects of interaction with others that begins at birth. Persons rationally engaged in self-interested actions entirely unconstrained by norms certainly exist, but they are the exception rather than the rule. And even they—psychopaths or sociopaths, as they have been labeled—have at least undergone sufficient socialization to have learned language empowering them with the capacity to make rational self-interested choices in advance of overt action. To be sure, the self is a very special and crucially important object in experience; we lug it around with us wherever we go and can only partially rid ourselves of it in sleep or by chemical intoxication. Its desires and interests therefore are almost as insistent as sheerly biological urges rooted in the body. But we cannot even possess a self and differentiate between its interests and those of others, or between self-serving and self-denying normative prescriptions, without having undergone a process of socialization.[7] The ignoring of this and the drawing of an artificial distinction between self-interest and both the interests of others and normative demands are fundamental flaws of all rational choice theories.

In short, rationality, choice, the existence of a self, and even awareness of "interest"[8] as distinct from mere motive, all categories essential to and indeed definitive of rational choice theory, presuppose language and the necessarily social context in which it is learned. To deny this would amount to endorsing an atomistic *substantive* and truly unsociological individualism as distinct from the methodological individualism on which rational choice theorists rightly insist. Coleman's recognition of a self capable of identifying with external objects and Jon Elster's acknowledgment of the non-reducibility of social norms to rational self-interest maximizing behavior (Elster 1989: 15, 97–151, esp. 97–101, 125, 150) do credit to their good sense and realism in refusing to stick to a rigid and doctrinaire version of *homo economicus*. But they also open the door to the major considerations that most sociologists who are skeptical of the rational choice approach would raise in criticism of it.

Coleman contends that Parsons and other sociologists take for granted the existence of norms and then proceed to explain individual actions as determined by them. Rational choice takes the opposite standpoint in deriving norms from individuals pursuing their self-interested aims in situations where other individuals are doing the same. But criticism of Parsonian "normative determinism" for simply presupposing norms and ascribing causal priority to them is by no means confined to rational choice theory, for it has often been made by interactionist and phenomenological sociologists.[9] They have argued that norms often emerge initially out of a process of "negotiation" between actors, that the applicability and the exact prescriptive content of particular norms in concrete situations may be subject to negotiation, and that norms are regularly redefined and manipulated to the actors' advantage. I myself have advanced an account of how norms emerge from preexisting social interaction, sometimes crystallizing out of originally nonverbalized expectations, sometimes remaining at the level of implicitly understood expectations (Wrong 1994: 17–58).

Nor is the emphasis on self-interest peculiar to rational choice. It would be thoroughly questionable, to say the least, to maintain that Erving Goffman, for example, presents an oversocialized, passively conformist view of individuals in which self-interest has been entirely shaped by or subordinated to collective interests embodied in social norms. The presentation, protection, and projection of self are at the core of Goffman's work at the same time that he locates the self and its strategic maneuvers as arising out of and manifesting themselves entirely in social interaction. To be sure, all interactionist and phenomenological sociologies are excessively cognitivist and neglect or implicitly presume the motivations that set actors in motion in the first place (Wrong 1994: 59–69). But this is also true of rational choice, which simply postulates self-interested ends that are by definition incomparable as distinct from the means mobilized to pursue them. Neil Smelser (1990: 780) notes of Coleman's major book that "the terms 'affect,' 'feeling,' and 'emotion' appear neither in the text nor the index, nor do their specific manifestations—euphoria, anxiety, guilt, lust, greed, hate." In discussing the "internalization of norms," Coleman partially recognizes the inadequacies of rational choice in dealing with motivation: after arguing that theories presupposing the existence of "societal purposes or social norms" suffer from a deficiency at "the level of the social system," he concedes that theories based on rational action suffer from an "individual-level deficiency" in their failure to explain the process of internalization that contributes to shaping the ends of action. The assumption that individuals are always motivated by an undefined self-interest at most grounded in a generalized hedonism or pleasure/pain calculus does not allow for the fact that "individual interests do change and individuals do internalize norms" (Coleman 1990: 292–93). Elster, though also a rational choice theorist, asserts: "I believe that the emotive aspect of norms is a more fundamental feature than the more frequently cited cognitive aspect. If norms can coordinate expectations, it is only because the violation of norms is known to trigger strong negative emotions, in the violator himself and in other people" (1989: 100; see also 250–51).

Rational choice theorists typically justify their model on heuristic grounds, recognizing that it does not fully capture the nuances and complexities of human conduct. It is no accident that Coleman, for example, is probably the most prominent sociologist to have devoted much of his career to social policy. For a large, socially heterogeneous, and multiethnic population such as that of

the United States, the assumption of universally shared concrete
and practical ends realizable by the rational employment of the
most appropriate and efficient means obviously makes sense—is
itself rational—in devising or evaluating social policy. The need
for the "rational reconstruction" of social institutions in a complex, changing society that has undermined the "primordial" institutions of the past has been a major theme of Coleman's recent
work (1990: 584–87; 1993: 1–15). Max Weber regarded means-ends
rationality as the most universal and therefore most subjectively
understandable kind of action. The effort of the original Frankfurt
School philosophers to brand "instrumental rationality" as a de-
plorable cultural peculiarity of the post-Enlightenment capitalist
West (most fully in Horkheimer and Adorno 1972) is less than persuasive: it is hard to see how anyone anywhere could get through
a day or even a few hours without acting in an instrumentally
rational manner.[10]

Let us grant the usefulness of rational choice assumptions for
formulating social policies and explaining some kinds of action.
But can we really rest content with its pragmatic "black box" assumptions about human behavior and regard it as a self-sufficient
theoretical standpoint for the understanding of human nature in
society? Are we not likely at some point to be driven to ask, "What
are human beings *really* like and how do they get that way?" And
has it not often enough been the distinctive task of sociology to
try to answer these questions by criticizing the abstract and partial perspectives of other theoretical and disciplinary approaches
in philosophy and the social sciences? Is literature—at least great
literature—alone to be the place where we can look for representations of human beings and human nature in the fullness of their
complexity and contradictions?

Literary people used to express their contempt for the pretensions of the social sciences in general and sociology in particular
by declaring that "Dostoyevsky said it all before and better." I remember a friend of mine who had given up the "truancy"[11] of life
in Greenwich Village as a literary bohemian to attend the Yale
Law School telling me of a professor who had covered the board
in his classroom with an elaborate taxonomic schema intended to
encompass all possible human motivations. My friend raised his

hand and asked him what he would do with Dostoyevsky's observation in *Notes from Underground* that there is a perversity in man's nature that leads him sometimes to reject reason and even to act deliberately against his own self-interest. The professor looked puzzled for a moment and, light dawning, turned to the blackboard, pointed at it, and said, "Oh that, that would go here under my number 8d." What does the rational choice theorist make of the observation that "Man has that in him which sometimes rejects the sun or his neighbors, and vomits out the State, nature, all logic, and common sense"?[12]

CHAPTER 3

Hannah Arendt on Totalitarianism

Kafka wrote: "A book should be an axe that breaks the frozen sea within us." For some of us Hannah Arendt's *The Origins of Totalitarianism* was such a book when it appeared in 1951, and we have never recovered fully from the effect it had on us. Kafka may have had in mind works of literature, religion, or philosophy rather than historical studies or political treatises. However, the power of *The Origins* owed something to the visionary intensity it shared with outstanding works of the literary imagination as well as to its "unscholarly" use of such works themselves—by Proust, Conrad, Kipling, Kafka himself—to illuminate its major themes. In addition, the author's deepest intellectual roots lay in classical German philosophy and revealed what an English scholar once called "the tyranny of Greece over Germany," although all this became fully evident only in her later, less historical writings.

Stephen J. Whitfield, a young historian at Brandeis, has given us a book that reviews, with exemplary clarity and concision, the complex issues Arendt raised in her interpretation of totalitarianism. *Into the Dark* (1980) is neither a conventional intellectual biography nor an exposition and exegesis of Arendt's total oeuvre —Whitfield notes that there are already more than half a dozen of these—but belongs rather to a coherent but as yet undefined genre: the examination of an idea closely identified with a particular thinker and the debate it has inspired. Although Whitfield devotes a chapter to the relation between Arendt's theory of totalitarianism and her later writings on other political themes, his primary subject is totalitarianism as a specific historical phenomenon of the 1930's and 1940's and Arendt's contribution to our understanding of it. Accordingly, he largely confines himself to part three of *The Origins* and to *Eichmann in Jerusalem*, which he rightly regards as an addendum or case study exemplifying the thesis of the earlier book, something that was insufficiently recognized in the impassioned controversy following its serial publication in *The New Yorker* in 1963 as a report on the Eichmann trial. The first two parts of *The Origins*, on anti-Semitism in modern European history and on nineteenth-century imperialism, dealt essentially with precursors of totalitarianism or the totalitarian spirit rather than with its origins in any direct causal sense, whereas the third part presented us with the thing itself in its full and terrible reality. The American title of the book, as Whitfield points out, was therefore misleading compared to the British title, *The Burden of Our Times*.

The concept of totalitarianism is sometimes dismissed nowadays as the product of American "cold-war propaganda" of the 1950's; occasionally, Arendt is thought virtually to have invented it, or at least to have first introduced it into serious intellectual discourse on modern politics. Both contentions are nonsense. I remember encountering the term as a schoolboy in Canada as early as 1940. I even recall laughing with pitying adolescent condescension at a minister who, in a sermon, mixed up "totalitarian" and "proletarian" to form "protalitarian." (His coinage, come to think of it, has the suggestive ring of an Orwellian neologism.) Canada was at war and, significantly, this was the period of the Nazi-Soviet pact, which proved to be the incubator of political insights that were quickly forgotten with Hitler's attack on Russia, only to be revived in full force after the war when Stalin dictated a change in the world Communist line, secured Soviet control over Eastern Europe, and ultimately aroused American resistance to further Russian expansion westward.

The summer the war ended, I used the term in a conversation with a friend—I had been reading Arthur Koestler on the "Soviet myth"—who immediately complained that *totalitarian*

was a word favored only by people "who want to play down the
differences between Nazi Germany and Soviet Russia." He had it
exactly right, for that was just what it had come to mean, although
his political illusions led him to regard as a defect what others
discerned as the fundamental truth of the concept. Invented by
a court philosopher of Mussolini's as an approving adjective to
describe the Fascist movement and state, *totalitarian* was sometimes applied in the early 1930's to both Communism and fascism
as a synonym for one-party dictatorship. Whitfield mentions, but
does not sufficiently stress, the Spanish Civil War as the situation in which the term became charged with horror and revulsion
among such former Communists or sympathizers as Koestler,
George Orwell, and Franz Borkenau, who witnessed the "war
within the war" successfully waged by the Stalinists against the
other parties of the Left. In early 1940 Borkenau became the first
person to use the word in the title of a book. In 1944, in an essay
on Koestler, Orwell penned his famous indictment: "The sin of
nearly all left-wingers from 1933 onwards is that they have wanted
to be anti-fascist without being anti-totalitarian."

Totalitarian, then, already carried a freight of meaning forged
in bloody political struggle rather than in the taxonomic games
of scholars, and this was where Arendt started. Despite the later
shapelessness of the term once the politicians and the academic
industry had gotten hold of it, applying it at one time or another to
everything from old-fashioned military dictatorships to past social
orders such as Sparta or the Incas and even to industrial society
itself (Marcuse), it still finds its unassailable warrant in the unprecedented experiences of our terrible century. Arendt accepted
its core signification of underlying similarities between fascism
and Soviet Communism despite the convention, still prevalent
today, of placing them at opposite ends of an ideological left/right
spectrum, not to speak of the deadly war they fought against each
other.

Whitfield properly begins with an examination of the "fearful
symmetry" between Stalin's Russia and Hitler's Germany, defending Arendt despite a scrupulously fair assessment and occasional
partial acceptance of the negative evidence. Perhaps his most per-
ceptive supporting statement comes in a later chapter when he

remarks of Nazi Germany that "only one other society created the kind of fear and trembling engendered in the Soviet Union as Stalin consolidated his rule." The argument from "fear and trembling" is absolutely crucial and excludes the other pre-1945 candidates for totalitarianism such as Fascist Italy, Peronist Argentina, the Iberian dictatorships, and the pro-German regimes in Eastern Europe. Arendt eschewed the apparatus of formal definition so beloved of professors, but in successive prefaces to new editions of *The Origins* she increasingly seemed to fall back on a single criterion: a regime is totalitarian when, after having thoroughly defeated its active political opposition, it turns to the terroristic persecution of entire categories of persons who are ideologically proscribed despite having offered no political resistance whatever. She herself acknowledged a process of "de-totalitarianisation" after Stalin's death, although she had previously implied that totalitarianism was inherently driven to intensification and could only be checked, as in the case of the Third Reich, by external resistance. This was what made her views so congruent with the high point of American cold-war sentiment in the early 1950's, but they actually predated that period and had even been published in several articles later incorporated into *The Origins*.

Having read nearly all the discussions of Arendt's two books on totalitarianism at the time of their appearance, I am impressed by Whitfield's thoroughness in overlooking nothing of importance. He does not spare her for the "obtuseness" of her "disparagement of Jewish vulnerability and anguish" in *Eichmann in Jerusalem*, which upset some of her oldest and closest friends at the time. He notes her factual errors, exaggerations, misplaced ironies, and questionable claims on this subject as well as on the character of Eichmann himself. He shows that the "banality of evil," Arendt's phrase that has virtually passed into the language, may have been doubtfully appropriate to Eichmann personally, although he notes that other observers arrived independently at a similar description. Yet Whitfield sees that Arendt's aim was to show that the ultimate horror of totalitarianism was that it made ordinary, normal, mediocre men commit mass murder all in the course of a day's work. The system rather than the perverse motives of its individual servants was responsible for its deeds, a line of argu-

ment so familiar to social scientists that one might have expected
it to have been more readily understood even if Eichmann was a
more deviant and pathological personality than Arendt indicated.

Whitfield is essentially writing intellectual history rather than
exploring the possible continuing value of the concept of totalitarianism independent of Arendt's historical cases. He does not,
for instance, even mention China under Mao or the Khmer Rouge
genocide in Cambodia, which are surely relevant examples. Arendt
herself insisted that totalitarianism was a truly novel form of political rule, a twentieth-century invention that constituted the
sole new addition to Aristotle's venerable threefold classification
of forms of government, and one which was bound to survive as
a permanent temptation and possibility in the secularized poli-
ties of the modern world. Her account of it demands, therefore,
an evaluation going beyond its adequacy as an interpretation of
Nazism and Stalinism despite her claim that these were the only
two genuine examples of the phenomenon and her disinclina-
tion to return to the theme in any detail in the last decade of
her life. She was, in effect, presenting an ideal type or conceptual model constructed out of the particulars of the Nazi and
Soviet experience. The historical rootedness of her vision, its possession of what George Kateb has called the "amplitude of epic,"
induces hesitation about dissecting it into its elements. Nevertheless, more recent history—history in the sense both of events
in the world and of later scholarship on the Hitler and Stalin
regimes—requires that an effort be made to separate, or "disaggregate," the components of what Arendt fused into an apparently
seamless unity.

Arendt's concept of totalitarianism has three major components. First, there is the social crisis, including the breakdown
of constitutional democracy, that uproots masses of people from
their customary routines in a threatening world they can no longer
understand. Second, there are the pseudo-scientific ideologies pur-
porting to offer true keys to the understanding of history that
are adopted as mobilizing appeals by new political movements.
Having won state power, such movements proceed ruthlessly to
reconstruct society in the image of their ideological vision. Third,
the result of this reconstruction is that the party-state apparatus

subordinates all independent social groups to control from the center. This third requisite amounts to a "structural" definition of totalitarianism. The noun form of the word, the *ism*, should perhaps be confined to this "structural" result alone, as distinct from the aims, tendencies, or potentialities inherent in totalistic ideologies and the movements organized to promote them.

It is immediately obvious that only in Germany in the 1930's were all three components present in historical sequence. Stalin won power as Lenin's successor through intrigue and bureaucratic infighting under an established dictatorial but nontotalitarian regime. Thus Arendt's critics who have argued that her model fits only the Nazis are partially justified, but they minimize the extent to which Stalinism meets the other two criteria as fully, or even more so, than Nazism. In power for a much longer time, Stalin, and, for that matter, his successors, achieved far greater penetration of and secure control over Soviet society than Hitler ever attained in Germany. Structurally, the Soviet Union remained totalitarian through the 1980's, although the second criterion, ideological dynamism including the use of mass terror against its own population, no longer was applicable to the conduct of the Soviet government.

Whitfield points out that even Arendt herself, much better informed about Germany than Russia, did not develop fully the parallels between them. She laid great stress on the anti-utilitarianism of totalitarian behavior, governed as it was by bondage to the rigid logic of ideology in opposition to common sense. Nazi anti-Semitism, culminating in the death camps that diverted scarce men and resources in the middle of a desperate war for survival, epitomized this mad logic. But so did Stalin's purges, which gravely weakened Russia both economically and militarily. "Arendt's theory," Whitfield observes, "could easily have been made stronger and more symmetrical by analyzing not only anti-Semitism but also the *Yezhovschina* as an outrage against common sense." The Khmer Rouge's forced evacuation of Phnom Penh and slaughter of anyone with any skills acquired through a Westernized education, even the ability to speak French, exemplified the same carrying out of an ideology—in this case one learned from French Marxists in Paris—to its supposed logical conclusion.

So did the Cultural Revolution in China when it closed all schools for two years and compelled academic and technical experts to work as agricultural laborers.

The three components of Arendt's concept are related to three separate areas of research and scholarship, reflecting the fact that each has had an independent historical existence. Arendt's account of the breakdown of European bourgeois society is a version of the "theory of mass society," which has been subjected to much criticism. One major issue has been whether mass society preceded or followed totalitarian rule. Arendt herself claimed that Stalin's terror turned Russia into the kind of amorphous mass society created in Western Europe by the social transformations of the modern era. Even students of Nazi Germany have contended that it approximated a mass society only *after* Hitler's revolution, some of them arguing that it was precisely the "pluralistic" fragmentation of Weimar Germany which made possible Hitler's rise. Yet Arendt knew Weimar at first hand and anyone acquainted with Brecht's early plays and ballads, expressionist art, or the movies of Fritz Lang and others cannot doubt that she captured much of its antinomian and anomic atmosphere at a level deeper than voting statistics or formal descriptions of social structure. No doubt she overgeneralized to the rest of Europe. And certainly the concept of mass society is too vague to be of much use if it can refer both to the atomized and discontented citizenry of a crisis-ridden democracy and to the fully mobilized, tightly organized population of a totalitarian regime.

Her second component—the rise of movements driven by an ideological will to transform the world that is oblivious to considerations of self-interest, traditional normative restraints, and material obstacles—fits into a rich intellectual tradition that has grown up in response to the totalitarian experience. Ideologies altogether different at the level of manifest content have been diagnosed as sharing a "paranoid style," in Richard Hofstadter's term, making them susceptible to totalitarian uses. Arendt abhorred Freudian or psychiatric language and, while there is no reason why others should be bound by her prejudices, the freshness of her insights owed something to her refusal to fall back on it. The past has been ransacked for parallels to modern totalitarian movements, Norman Cohn's study of medieval chiliastic sects, *The Pursuit of the Millennium*, representing the most distinguished contribution to this branch of scholarship. Contemporary cults and sectarian movements have been interpreted as mini-totalitarian communities, Jonestown being the most obvious and notable example.

Arendt's most original insight was less her emphasis on ideology itself, or on organizational structure, or even on the boundlessness of revolutionary utopianism, than her grasp of the fusion of ideology and organization in the totalitarian movements to the point where the organization *becomes* the incarnation of the ideology, which is divested of its status as a canonical doctrine legitimating organizational goals and behavior and providing a standard by which to criticize them. Though they were writing only of Stalinism, this fusion has seldom been better expressed than by Irving Howe and Lewis Coser in their history of the American Communist Party when they refer to the mistake of many observers "in supposing that it was ideology as such which bound the members, whereas in reality it was *the organization as the faith made visible* which was the primary object of loyalty" (italics in original).

Nowhere did Arendt display more fully her "catlike facility for seeing in the dark" (a phrase Whitfield borrows from what Henry James once wrote of Hawthorne) than in her detection of this identification with the demiurge of organizational power in the pronouncements of leading Nazis and Communists. Her remarking on their practice of making predictions, ostensibly grounded in the "ice-cold" or "dialectical" truths of party ideology, but which are really declarations of intention or veiled threats, is especially noteworthy. The epistemological implications for the rationale of the social sciences, the Marxist doctrine of the unity of theory and practice, and the idea, so popular among sociologists since the 1960's, that reality is "socially constructed" have yet to be fully explored. Arendt, to be sure, touched on some of them in her more philosophical writings, although Whitfield notes that she "resisted the temptation to make *The Origins of Totalitarianism* the foundation of her entire thought." I confess that I find these parts of her later work more suggestive than her idealization of the Greek polis, her "Hellenic nostalgia" as one critic has called it, precisely because of the link to *The Origins*, with its master claim that totalitarianism remains an ever-present potentiality in the managed societies of the modern world.

Totalitarians do not, however, reduce ideology to a mere instrument in the struggle for power, for the power that is sought includes the power to establish a kind of collective solipsism by overcoming the factuality of common sense itself and controlling the very definition of reality. This is the essential difference between totalitarian rulers and Agathocles of Sicily, Cesare Borgia, Richard of Gloucester, Idi Amin, and other notoriously cruel tyrants of history. Here Arendt converges with the Orwell of *Nineteen Eighty-Four*, published two years before *The Origins*. She even once offered the same example of totalitarian power over cognition itself: the power to declare that 2 plus 2 equals 5 and make it stick. Like Bernard Crick, an admirer of Arendt and Orwell's biographer, I am pained by the imperious identification with German high culture that prevented her from ever acknowledging this paragon of down-to-earth Anglo-Saxon empiricism, this "plain Billy Brown from London town" whose voice and presence are still missed by some of us nearly fifty years after his premature death. Whitfield, too, notes her neglect of Orwell and attributes it to her "failure to nurture a sufficient appreciation for liberalism."

The structural aspect of totalitarianism, when considered in isolation from its other two components, has led to thoroughly promiscuous abuses of the concept. Intellectual historians have glibly discovered the germs of totalitarianism in the thought of such past philosophers as Plato, Hobbes, Rousseau, Hegel, and many others. Conventional defenders of "free enterprise" have condemned state intervention in the economy as totalitarian. Libertarians have invoked the label to attack any and all forms of authority. It has been seen as implicit in, even virtually identical with, both bureaucracy and technology, an impermissible loosening of the concept from which Arendt herself was not entirely free in her later work, especially in her more Heideggerian moments.

Yet the encroachment of the state upon society, of which totalitarianism is the most extreme manifestation, has been a general tendency since the nineteenth century. There are also the continuities, ignored by Arendt, between the Soviet state and tsarism with its historical links to Oriental despotism. In modern societies, the centralized power of the state and its growing involvement in more and more areas of social life offer a standing temptation to ideological movements to seek power in order to impose a "revolution from above." But *totalitarian* loses its original meaning altogether if it is applied to any expansion of state power or to any repressive nondemocratic state.

Arendt undeniably drew on an older elitist and anti-democratic tradition of fear of the brutish irrational masses, represented by such writers as Gustave LeBon, in her account of the social context favoring totalitarian movements. The theory of a totalitarian potential in mass society fell under suspicion in the 1960's as providing new dress for old conservative arguments against *any* protest movements seeking to rectify social injustices. I myself wrote of a "political hypochondria" induced by the totalitarian experience in criticizing the blend of anxiety and complacency underlying the "end of ideology" thesis. Radicals eager to restore the primacy of the left/right axis as the fundamental basis of political division carried the polemic a good deal further. Yet Arendt was surely right to affirm as "the most essential criterion for judging the events of our time: Will it lead to totalitarian rule or will it not?" If awareness of the murderousness of ideological politics leads to a mood of conservative caution, so be it. National Socialism, after all, was a *popular* movement drawing primarily on the symbols and slogans of the *Right*. Arendt's uncanny ability to feel herself into the skins of Nazis and their supporters should have forever discredited the recently revived Marxist theory that Hitler was a capitalist tool, itself, at least in its cruder forms, a specimen of totalitarian thinking in its obsession with conspiracies.

✄

CHAPTER 4

The Concept of Power:
Boundless or Delimited?

I wrote *Power: Its Forms, Bases and Uses* as a contribution to a series entitled "Key Concepts in the Social Sciences," edited by Philip Rieff and Bryan R. Wilson. Both of them were sociologists and, as I recall, they first invited me to write on "social class" or "inequality," two concepts of an essentially sociological nature. I suggested "power" as an alternative, a subject on which I had recently published an article in a sociological journal. Although it obviously has much wider connotations, at the time I thought of power primarily in sociological terms as a particular kind of relation between actors and therefore gave little attention to the wider implication of the series' focus on the social sciences in general. (Some of the "key concepts" treated in other books in the series were "rationality," "social change," "individualism," "ideology," and "revolution," concepts that are by no means specifically or even distinctively sociological.)

I now regret this limitation, for in the social sciences and political discourse, and even in sociology itself, it has since become if anything more common than formerly to use power as an exceedingly comprehensive term, one that virtually identifies it as the fundamental object of human striving and sees it as deeply ingrained in any and all human relations and social structures. I made an effort to take this more sweeping and inevitably ambiguous breadth of conception into account in my preface to the

1988 edition of the book, developing more fully the distinction between "power to" and "power over," which had not been entirely neglected but had been insufficiently emphasized in the first edition. The distinction remains a crucial one because conflation of the two senses of power is the source of many of the ambiguities, conceptual and rhetorical, that cling to the concept. I welcome the opportunity further to discuss the often promiscuous recent uses of the concept.

Power has always been one of those words that everybody uses without necessarily being able to define satisfactorily. It is treated both as a quality or attribute possessed by individuals, groups, or larger social structures and as an indicator of an active or interactive process or relation between individual or collective actors. Moreover, it is also applied to physical phenomena and processes. In recent years power has tended to become an even more diffuse and far-ranging notion in social and political theory, partly as a result of the influence of Michel Foucault and the Nietzsche revival his writings have helped promote. It has been argued that, like "freedom" or "justice"—those "big words which make us so unhappy," as Stephen Dedalus called them—"power" is an "essentially contested concept," meaning that people with different values and beliefs are bound to disagree over its nature and definition (Lukes 1974: 9). It is claimed therefore that there cannot be any commonly accepted or even preferred meaning so long as people differ on normative issues as they are likely to do indefinitely, if not forever.

"Power," however, does not seem to me to be an inherently normative concept. Undoubtedly, conservatives, liberals, socialists, libertarians, anarchists, ethnic nationalists, religious believers, and secularists endlessly dispute over who should have power and how much, how it should be organized and channeled, and a host of other issues pertaining to its distribution and exercise. Accordingly, its scope and pervasiveness, its involvement in any and all spheres of social life, give it almost unavoidable evaluative overtones. Positive or negative, benign or malign, auras come to envelop it, linking it still more closely to ideological controversy. Yet power as a generic attribute of social life is surely more like the concepts of "society," "group," or "social norm" than like such essentially and inescapably normative notions as "justice," "democracy," or "human rights." "Power" is no more or less abstract than the first set of concepts, but it bears more directly on realities that are central to the enduring moral and political differences centering on the second set. In this respect, it resembles "inequality" or "social class," also fiercely contested concepts that are nevertheless not by their very nature normative and value-laden.

The conflations and ambiguities to which the concept of power is prone have their origins in three uses where the concept blends into, merges with, or overlaps cognate terms and meanings:

1. Its most general use as a near-synonym for influence, control, rule, and domination results in its seeming to share some or all of the different shades of meaning of these terms.

2. As an attribute or quality possessed by individuals, power may be regarded as sought after, even as a fundamental object of human striving. It thus raises questions about basic motivations involving the very essence of human nature.

3. Since power is unequally distributed among groups in all large-scale, complex "civilized" societies, the cultures of these societies will reflect and express this inequality. The "hegemony," to use the fashionable term, of some groups over others is held to be encoded in all their modes of activity and expression, including language, the most distinctively human creation and possession of all.

I shall discuss each of these three areas in sequence in an effort to link them to prevailing arguments that cluster around the concept of power, emphasizing the versions that have become common in recent years.

The most general sense of power views it as an event or agency that produces an effect on the external world. It is therefore obviously relational, postulating something that acts on its environment and brings about some change in it. It also is of universal scope, applying to the physical world in general, including the human actors within it. Power as the capacity to produce effects may be imputed to the agency as a dispositional (in Gilbert Ryle's sense) property even when the capacity is not manifest in action. Power here resembles and includes physical force or energy, for example the explosive power seen as residing in a bomb. Power as a capacity stating a potential relation to entities in its environment is no less a relational term when it is not actually realized in overt action.

Writers on power have often complained that the word does not exist in a verb form, at least in English. The difference between "having" and "exercising" power—a version of the actual/potential distinction—is thought to be obscured by the absence of a verb form, a problem that does not arise with "influence" or "control." Yet these terms carry slightly different shades of meaning and are therefore not really satisfactory alternatives to "power." The most famous American "how-to" book was entitled *How to Win Friends and Influence People*; one might well doubt that it would have become a best-seller if it had substituted "to control" or "to exercise power over" people for the weaker, blander "influence." (As it was, the author, Dale Carnegie, was often accused of teaching a possibly sinister technique for manipulating innocent and trusting people.) In recent years, the noun "impact" has been converted into a verb, "to impact," apparently because a word stronger than "influence" that nevertheless did not suggest conscious purpose like "control" was sought. (That "impact" as verb has become a dreadful cliché of the mass media is another matter.)

The verb "to empower" and the noun "empowerment" have also become commonplace in political debate, but they refer to the acquisition rather than to the exercise of power. What is to be acquired is "power to" rather than "power over" others; indeed, the terms are typically used with reference to groups perceived as victims or at least passive objects of the power exercised over them by others. "Empowerment" sometimes appears to refer to the mobilization of previously isolated individual actors so that they achieve collective power through solidarity and organization. There may be a conflict between an individual or collective actor's "power to," here equivalent to "freedom to," and the constraints imposed by another actor's "power over." The escape from such constraints may be total, eliminating an asymmetrical power relationship altogether, or it may be partial, setting new limits to, or countering in some areas of activity, the power holder's power over the power subject. Politics in the broadest sense involves both a struggle *for* power and *against*, or to escape *from*, power (Hirschman 1970; Wrong 1995: 12–13).

When applied to human agents, the issue of intentionality cannot be avoided. My own definition of power as a human or social phenomenon, adapted from Bertrand Russell's broader definition is "the capacity of some persons to produce intended and foreseen effects on others." No feature of my entire discussion of power has aroused wider disagreement than my defining it as necessarily intentional.[1] The vastly consequential unintended and unanticipated effects of the decisions and actions of the powerful—statesmen, generals, bureaucrats, big capitalists, religious leaders, the media, scientific experts—immediately spring to mind and my definition is seen as ignoring all these unintended consequences. The ubiquity of unintended consequences, moreover, is widely and properly regarded as providing a major, if not *the* major, rationale for the very existence of the social sciences. Yet here I am in an excessively voluntarist fashion apparently limiting power to the shortsighted and confined effects of conscious human purposes. This can be seen as a kind of cop-out, implicitly complacent toward ignorance and resultant social evils in simply ignoring the tremendous and often malign ramifications of the unequal distribution of power in human societies. Structuralist "de-centering of the subject" provides an additional rationale for excluding the power holder's intentions from the understanding of power, but theorists who are not structuralists or poststructuralists have also challenged definitions that treat power as necessarily intentional.

My response to this argument has been to contend that for power to have important unintended consequences it must usually first be exercised in a social relation in which one actor, the power holder, produces an intended effect on another actor. I have recognized the scope and significance of "unintended influence" in *Power* (Wrong 1995: 24), distinguishing it from intended influence (equated with power). As one critic (Gaski 1995) has observed, my concept of unintended influence is indebted to Robert Dahl and Charles Lindblom's "spontaneous field control," advanced in their compendious 1953 volume *Politics, Economics and Welfare*.

But to treat "power" and "influence" as synonyms is to make

power, that is, the exercise of power, equivalent to the production of *any* social effect. All influences that actors have upon one another then become exercises of power. "Society" and "social interaction," the very idea of "social," become phenomena of power since they presuppose the reciprocal influence of individuals on one another. Society *is* in this view a system of power at both the macro-level of its major institutions and the micro-level of personal relations. This corresponds more or less to the Foucauldian conception of society. If "power" is thus considered equivalent to "influence," there would seem to be no need for a specific concept of power at all. "Influence" would do all the necessary work and has the advantage of existing in both a noun and a verb form.

The widespread tendency to define power as necessarily coercive is undoubtedly inspired by a wish to avoid so broad and general an implication. I reject the identification of power with coercion, with force or its threatened application. Instead, I differentiate power from the more all-embracing concept of influence by adding the criterion of intentionality. I confess, however, to a certain sympathy with critics who react to what they see as my apparent minimization or neglect of unintended consequences, which undeniably are crucially important in assessing the role of power in society. "Unintended influence" or "spontaneous field control" perhaps sound too residual, suggesting relatively secondary effects of power. Nevertheless, the distinction between unintended and intended influence remains vital: failure to recognize it in defining power simply collapses power into influence in all the latter's sweeping and diffuse generality.

The concept of power continues to possess, unlike influence, overtones of coercion even among writers who do not define it as necessarily coercive. Max Weber's definition, probably the most influential one of all, is an example: after identifying power with "the chance of a man or a number of men to realize their own will in a social action," which does not make power inherently coercive, he goes on to add "even against the resistance of others who are participating in the action." Despite the qualifying "even" in most renditions of Weber's definition, it is not surprising that many readers have assumed that he regarded conflict and resistance as inherent in relations of power. For writers who explicitly avoid any equation of power with coercion, the term nevertheless manages to retain something of a malign, sinister, even demonic aura. Indeed, it is often a rhetorical strategy to evoke just such an aura. Foucault is a case in point, which accounts for his popularity among post-Marxists anxious not to abandon a critical, adversarial stance toward modern society. A power relation always implies that the person subject to it does something he or she would not otherwise have done, but it need not be something that is or is perceived as against his or her wishes or interests.

The negative connotations of power are even more marked when it is treated as a fundamental motive or object of human striving as in familiar allusions to "will to power," "lust for power," or "power drive." A long tradition of political thought including Machiavelli and Hobbes that goes back to Thrasymachus in Plato's *The Republic* has treated these as antisocial motivations promoting hostility and conflict. I have criticized the psychological assumptions on which this tradition rests at some length in *Power*.[2] Yet many writers in the tradition who are conventionally classified as cynics or pessimists about human nature actually define power in a fashion that is neutral with regard to its benign or malign uses in relation to other human beings. Hobbes's definition of power as an individual's "present means towards any future apparent good" is the classic example. Nietzsche, currently fashionable because of his influence on Foucault and other poststructuralists and so-called postmodernists, initially equated his "will to power" with something like life force or the drive to preserve and enhance the vitality of the organism and its control over its environment. Like his contemporaries William James and Henri Bergson, he was writing at a time when the influence of Darwin on philosophy and psychology was new and at its peak. Such approaches to power begin with general statements encompassing a wide range of human motivations and then proceed fairly directly to discussion of the efforts to dominate others and the ensuing conflicts to which such efforts may sometimes give rise. What is involved is essentially a conflation or at least a slurring over of the difference between "power to," the more general category, and "power over." Only the latter, a special case of the former, suggests the potentiality of hostility, conflict, and oppression in human relations, though it is only a potentiality, as I have argued in contending that power is not necessarily coercive. To say that all humans seek the "power to" gratify their desires or realize their goals is to say no more than that they *have* desires and goals, that, in effect, they want to get what they want. Who could possibly dissent from such a statement? This innocuous claim nevertheless lends a specious plausibility to Nietzschean and Foucauldian assertions that humans invariably seeks to dominate and impose their will on others.

The recent tendency to see power as the most universal and pervasive feature of social life has to do with differences in collective power, or the unequal distribution of power among groups and social categories. One form this takes is to equate the unequal distribution among individuals of anything and everything that people desire and seek with inequality of power. A warrant for this may be found in Weber, who famously characterized "classes," "status groups," and "parties" as "phenomena of the distribution of power within a community." Power is clearly used here in the sense of "power to," or the capacity of individuals to satisfy their wants. To say that individuals are unequal in power is simply another way of saying that society is stratified, that some people have more income, property, status, leisure, and other desiderata than other people. This is in no way objectionable unless it is assumed that more is being said: that the identification of inequalities of all kinds with inequality of power serves somehow to *explain* social inequalities and class differences rather than merely to acknowledge their existence.

Yet this assumption is often made. It conflates the aggregated unequal power of individuals encompassing inequalities of income, status, and other sought-after things with greater collective power allegedly possessed by the beneficiaries of the unequal distribution, eliding the difference between a distributive and a relational conception of power. The further assumption is made that the beneficiaries, the "haves," attain and maintain their favored position by means of the power they exercise *over* the underprivileged "have-nots." By a process of double conflation, the aggregated "power to" satisfy their wants of the most favored individuals is equated with collective power presuming a degree of solidarity and social organization exercised by them as a privileged class over a less favored subordinate class. Thus, the mere existence of inequality, of social stratification, is seen as evidence of class domination in which one class secures its superior position by some combination of ideological indoctrination, manipulation, coercion, and economic exploitation. That the lower class at least covertly resents its inferior position is recognized. This class would, it is alleged, favor a different organization of society that allocated rewards more equally if persuaded of the possibility of such an alternative. These assumptions constitute the broad core of the Marxist conception of class society; they obviously contain a large measure of truth, but they need to be argued and often qualified rather than simply assumed by being read into the very existence of social stratification as a result of equating the aggregated "power to" of individuals with the collective "power over" subordinate classes of more cohesive social classes—*Klasse für sich* in Marxist terms.

The past few decades from roughly the late 1950's to 1990 were a period in which what might be called "late Marxism" was prominent in intellectual circles, including those of academic social science. Marxists accorded greater importance to ideological indoctrination through control of culture than to political and economic coercion in accounting for the maintenance—"reproduction"—of capitalism as a social and economic order based on the rule of the bourgeoisie. Gramsci's "hegemony" was only the most favored concept of "Western Marxists" and their academic followers who paid more attention to the cultural superstructure than to the economic base. Political and economic domination of the bodies of the subordinate classes by means of physical coercion and control over the material resources required to satisfy their vital needs was less emphasized than the shaping of their consciousness by control over the agencies of cultural transmission. "Legitimation crises" or "countercultural revolts" rather than cumulative economic contradictions or revolutionary political mobilization were seen as the major forms of vulnerability of capitalism to fundamental change.

The collapse of Communism in the early 1990's has discredited

Marxism, probably for good, primarily by destroying the credibility of socialism as a more egalitarian form of society that would nevertheless secure and continue the economic progress already achieved under capitalism. Yet the general schema of some groups exercising power to their own advantage over other groups has been extended to groups other than classes, most commonly to groups distinguished by race and gender. At the same time, the view has become popular among intellectuals that knowledge, far from permitting a reflective cognitive distancing from the constraints of social reality, is itself, as Foucault in particular insisted, simply a technique or instrument by which some groups claiming superior access to it establish and secure their power over others. The "linguistic turn" in social thought has suggested a far deeper penetration of culture in the form of language into human consciousness. If the power of some groups over others is regarded as the salient feature of society, and language is the major medium of cultural expression and transmission, then language must unavoidably reflect and reinforce social inequality. It becomes both a major medium for, and an effect of, the exercise of power. All language resembles George Orwell's "Newspeak": it cannot help but affirm the existing order and exclude the very possibility of even formulating ideas critical of that order. As a "dominant discourse" it maintains the "ideological hegemony" of the privileged by "foregrounding" them and their concerns while "marginalizing" subordinate—"subaltern"—groups. Power penetrates the very core of human consciousness. It is implicated in anything and everything that can be said, which makes everything "political" so that any lack of explicit reference to power and politics points to "silences in the text" that are held to reveal a presence confirmed by its very absence. Even Stalin, of all people, did not go so far as this when he intervened in 1950 in a controversy over linguistics in the Soviet Union to insist that language was independent of class determination grounded in the economic "base."

Whether the application of such a schema is more or less credible when extended as it is nowadays to race, gender, and other groups than in the Marxist version of the centrality of class domination need not be considered here. A prior issue is the value of this "power here, power there, power, power everywhere" perspective (apologies to Coleridge). The power reductionism that treats everything as an expression of power follows essentially from the conflation of the generic notion of "power to" with "power over," which is a social relation in which some persons possess and exercise power over others. The first is merged into the second and the concept itself acquires an oppressive, near-totalitarian ring while its diagnosticians appear to be bold rebels challenging the subtle, hidden tyranny of modern society over its subjects.

Perhaps my identity as a sociologist makes me particularly skeptical of this power reductionist or pan-power outlook, leading me to prefer a more limited conception of power.[3] A conception that sees it as one of an array or repertoire of concepts describing the diverse forms of social interaction that constitute society as a web or network constantly created and recreated in nonidentical forms is doubtless more congenial to a sociologist.[4] I shall close therefore by citing several non-sociologists who have made a similar case. The late J. G. Merquior, a political philosopher, observed that "the overbroadening of the concept of power corresponds to an equal loss in depth and specificity" (1985: 116). Lawrence Stone, the historian, has written in terms entirely congruent with my own argument: "Since man is a social animal, and since all of social life involves some form of influence, molding, direction, or compulsion, the reduction of all social life to issues of power renders it almost impossible to make the fine intellectual, moral, and material distinctions necessary for any serious evaluation of change in history" (1983: 44). I accept the Weberian view that sociology is "Clio's handmaiden" and I cannot improve upon Stone's exemplary statement.

CHAPTER 5

Myths of Alienation

The concept of alienation is less salient in contemporary discourse than it was some years ago, largely as a result of its excessive use in the 1950's and 1960's. In part, it has acquired a taken-for-granted character as shorthand for the mood of distemper, cynicism, and distrust believed to prevail in contemporary life and society; in part, synonyms or near-synonyms, such as "legitimation crisis," have taken on much of the rhetorical and ideological work performed in the past by "alienation." The term became too vague and shapeless, coming to serve as a sort of verbal talisman connoting just about any state of psychological discomfort or malaise. Yet its very popularity depended on its suggestion of something more than mere personal discontent, which is, after all, a pretty commonplace condition. "Alienation" was meant to convey either a sense of metaphysical melancholy about the human condition or a sociopolitical diagnosis of and protest against the failures and limitations of the social order.

The latter emphasis was paramount in the 1960's, when the term was fashionable among social scientists, political intellectuals, and radical youth. To assert one's alienation became a badge of honor, a credential attesting to superior moral sensitivity—in short, something to boast of rather than to complain about. This has never been true of such strictly subjective or psychological states as "unhappiness," not even as expressed in the more sophis-

ticated synonyms for them favored by the educated like "frustration," "depression," "anxiety," or "neurosis." When alienation was
imputed to or reportedly observed among ordinary citizens, supposedly exemplifying their attitude to politics or capitalism or
American life in general, the implication was usually intended
that these collective entities rather than the alienated individuals
themselves were responsible for their condition. Thus even in its
most clichéd uses the term was never quite reduced to individual
psychology but retained a latent sociological and even political
meaning.

I have no wish to survey once more the uses and abuses of
the concept, or to explore its origins in Christian theology, or its
venerable practical meanings, free of wider philosophical or sociological significance, in jurisprudence and early psychiatry. Nor do
I want to review yet again the concept's intellectual history in
Hegelian philosophy and Marxism: the complex conceptual links
among alienation, objectification, estrangement, and reification—
Entäusserung, Entfremdung, Verdinglichung, et al.—in the German romantic and idealist traditions. Neither am I concerned to
offer another account of the specifically sociological adaptations
of the concept, its differences from and frequent erroneous equation with anomie, let alone the various efforts to convert it into
an empirically testable and even "measurable" phenomenon. All
of these things have been done before quite adequately by competent and intelligent scholars.[1]

It should be noted, however, that "alienation" was already a
commonplace as long ago as the 1930's among the left-wing literary intellectuals associated with *Partisan Review.* Its ubiquitous
use in these circles long antedated its postwar appropriation by
existentialists, sociologists, and "humanist" Marxists. Yet this
early history is invariably ignored by academic commentators
and chroniclers, as in Walter Kaufman's assertion in his introduction to Richard Schacht's book, *Alienation,* that "in the fifties a
few refugees from Germany and Austria naturalized 'alienation'
in the United States" (Schacht 1970: 154; he specifically mentioned Herbert Marcuse, Erich Fromm, Erich Kahler, and Hannah
Arendt). In fact, in the anthology of the first ten years of *Partisan Review* published in 1946, the single selection reprinted from

the journal's first two years, when it was affiliated with the Communist Party, was an exposition of the concept of alienation in Marx's *Economic-Philosophic Manuscripts* entitled "The Philosophic Thought of the Young Marx" (Braunschweig 1946: 289–96). This article originally appeared in 1936, a mere four years after the first publication of the famous Paris Manuscripts in Moscow. So at least one influential group of American intellectuals was familiar with the young Marx's interest in the alienation concept barely a few years after the texts revealing this interest had become known and available.

I recall from my own experience that by the middle 1940's, if not earlier, the term had become very much an emblem or badge of identity for people in the orbit of *Partisan Review*, some of them even occasionally jesting about the extent to which this was the case. Clearly, alienation was already understood not merely as a painful affliction but as something of an honorific condition suggesting superior aesthetic sensibility and spiritual depth, long before it acquired these overtones when popularized two decades later. There was a widely repeated tale, probably apocryphal, about a secretary at *The New Yorker* maliciously asking a secretary at *Partisan Review* if their office typewriters had keys with whole words like "alienation" on them. A short story by Delmore Schwartz about a New Year's Eve party in 1938 depicts a character unmistakably based on one of the editors of *Partisan Review* grumbling about too many strangers invited to the party: "There's enough alienation in modern life without installing it in the living room."

The *Partisan Review* intellectuals tended to use the concept primarily to describe the antagonistic relation between the creative artist or intellectual and the philistine majority. "Alienation" added a sociological and political flavor to this familiar late romantic complaint by identifying modern society with its bourgeois character, with its dominant institution of private property and the resulting "alienated labor" of proletarian wage-workers. The term indeed encapsulated neatly the two governing themes that gave *Partisan Review* its distinctiveness: its dual commitment to Marxism in politics and to modernism in the arts. Both commitments became redefined in the years following the journal's initial rupture with the Communist Party; "alienation" was increasingly used to connote primarily a literary or aesthetic sensibility rather than a socioeconomic condition (more akin to Hegel's "unhappy consciousness" than to Marx's economic grounding of the concept), a tendency that became even more pronounced after the war, when the general inhospitality to art ascribed to "bourgeois society" became more specifically identified with the commercially produced and distributed "mass culture" made possible by new communications media. By this time, the term was used with a certain ironic jocularity by the leading *Partisan Review* writers, faintly mocking both the cultural and the politically radical pretensions it suggested.

The importance of the concepts of alienation and mass culture to the New York intellectuals owed little or nothing to Lukács or the Frankfurt School or to European existentialist thinkers (except perhaps for Ortega), although obviously the convergences among them resulted from their drawing on a partially shared political and cultural heritage. The convergence with existentialism undoubtedly accounts for the fact that the ideas of its leading exponents were first introduced to an American public in the pages of *Partisan Review*. But this was after the war, at a time when "alienation" had long been a key concept typifying the journal's aesthetic-political outlook.

Anyone is free to define alienation as he or she pleases. But there is one prevailing conception of it that, divested of much of the intellectual baggage the term has inevitably accumulated over the years, accentuates elements that were central to the German philosophical tradition out of which the concept came. As Peter Berger defines it in *The Sacred Canopy*: "Alienation is the process whereby the dialectical relationship between the individual and his world is lost to consciousness. The individual 'forgets' that this world was and continues to be co-produced by him. . . . The essential difference between the socio-cultural world and the world of nature is obscured—namely, the difference that men have made the first but not the second" (1967: 85).

In another book, coauthored with Thomas Luckmann, Berger offered a definition of "reification" that is almost identical word-for-word with the definition of alienation I have quoted (1966: 89).

Lukács is the source of the conception of reification as a form of social consciousness, although he did not, as is sometimes ignorantly alleged, invent the term. It had long signified—and is still so defined in English-language dictionaries—the mental habit of treating abstract concepts as possessing a substantial or "thing-like" existence in the external world. Alfred North Whitehead labeled this practice "the fallacy of misplaced concreteness," and his vivid phrase was invoked by Talcott Parsons against the utilitarians in *The Structure of Social Action*.

Lukács's achievement was to give reification a much wider collective meaning, connoting the perception by most people most of the time, particularly social classes, of the social and political world as fixed, unalterable and external to their lived experience. Lukács, in effect, rediscovered a central aspect of the Hegelian idea of alienation and recognized that it was implicit in some of Marx's later writings, despite Lukács's own inevitable ignorance of the as yet unpublished Paris Manuscripts.

Whether one calls it alienation or reification, this conception differs from the conventional usages of American sociologists in which, as Richard Schacht remarks in *Alienation*, his thorough survey of the proliferating meanings of the concept, "alienation is conceived mostly in terms of the presence of certain attitudes and feelings. . . . Thus there is no question of alienated individuals who are not aware of their alienation" (1970: 154). Berger strenuously objects to what he calls the "psychologization" of the concept, but his own version, which, following Lukács, he explicitly links to the notion of "false consciousness," is psychological in referring to cognition even if it excludes feelings and attitudes. To be sure, it is the *absence* rather than the presence of something in a person's awareness or consciousness that is central to Berger's and Lukács's conception.

Although Berger, with alienation especially in mind, has argued that "the integration of some Marxian concepts into sociological theory [is] very important" (1966: 76), he concedes that his own "use of the concept has 'right' rather than 'left' implications" (1967: 197, n. 5). This no doubt accounts for his readiness to divest it of any affective overtones which would endow it with negative or critical implications. Berger's conservatism is evident in his insistence that alienation and reification reflect mankind's universal, even sociobiological, need for order or *nomos*, a view that correctly sees alienation and anomie as opposites rather than treating them as virtual equivalents like most sociologists. But one need not follow Berger in regarding alienation as a necessary bulwark against anomie, nor, for that matter, Lukács in seeing it as an obstacle to be overcome by a new world-transforming historical subject.

Nor should one minimize, let alone reject outright, the implication that alienation is an unpleasant, frustrating, and even painful emotional condition, even if it is impermissibly loose to equate it with any and all unpleasant, frustrating, and painful emotional conditions. Alienation as "estrangement" (*Entfremdung*), which clearly implies a sense of loss or deprivation, goes back at least to Hegel. Moreover, the notion of "self-alienation," which unmistakably suggests an undesirable subjective state, was employed by both Hegel and Marx.

Suffice it to say that alienation has always suggested *both* a cognitive and an affective relation to the world, which is indeed why it has lent itself to such facile and indiscriminate popularization.

My major purpose is to argue that the essentially cognitive definition favored by Berger stands in an apparently paradoxical relation to the more diffuse psychological and political resonances that inescapably cling to the concept. Put differently, I want to suggest that there is a contradiction between the Lukács-Berger conception of alienation as reified consciousness and the more common, equally venerable view that identifies alienation with estrangement, with a subjective feeling of loneliness and homelessness in the world.

The affinity between alienation as a failure to recognize that the social and historical world is a collective human creation and the political outlook of the left, grounded in the original ethos of the Enlightenment, is obvious enough. That "men make their own history" is at the heart of the left's worldview: men can therefore overcome the historically given, the burden of the past, and recreate the social world in the image of secular ideals validated by rational moral and political principles. It follows that the most alienated people of all are primitive men who do not sharply separate the natural from the cultural in seeing both as pervasively shaped by magical and animistic forces. Characterizations of primitive societies as changeless or "historyless," as "cold" social formations in contrast to the more incoherent and internally contradictory "hot" societies immersed in "historicity," or in an ineluctable historical consciousness, are consistent with this view. One of the clearest and least philosophically pretentious formulations of the difference is that of the anthropologist Robert Redfield, who maintains that the absence of the idea of *reform*, of deliberate attempts to alter received customs and institutions, is the crucial dividing line between primitive—he calls them "pre-civilized"—societies and civilizations (1953: 111–38).

Redfield goes on to observe that the conscious reform of their institutions is exceedingly rare even in civilized societies, noting its infrequency until "quite modern times" in both Western and Chinese history. Belief in the divine origin and legitimation of the social order obviously inhibits purposeful efforts to change it. Ludwig Feuerbach regarded religion as the prototype of alienation: the projection of human qualities onto imaginary beings who were then regarded as independent, external powers to whom man must abase himself. The overcoming of alienation required the rejection of religious beliefs and authorities in the name of a secular materialistic humanism.

The young Marx extended the idea of alienation to the state and the economy, ultimately concluding that economic alienation was the foundation of both religious and political alienation. Alienation as a form of consciousness was dissolved into the social reality of subjection to capitalism and the class domination it imposed. Anxious to repudiate the abstract and mentalistic overtones of the Hegelian and Feuerbachian conceptions, Marx, not surprisingly, virtually abandoned the term in his later works, in which the exploitation and eventual revolt of the working class became the major themes. Some sociologists who have revived the concept have echoed this in making alienation synonymous with "powerlessness," although, in contrast to Lukács and Berger, awareness of being powerless is central to their definition. It seems, inciden-

tally, quite superfluous to equate alienation with a sense of subordination, oppression, or victimization when we have so many
other less metaphysically loaded words to describe this condition.

What are the features of modern societies that are regarded as
alienating and themselves the products of alienation? One could
hardly hope to offer an exhaustive list, but the following surely
include the major candidates: the division of labor, the rule of the
bourgeoisie, capitalism, the market, private property, the big city,
bureaucracy, the centralized state, mass society, commercialized
popular culture, the impersonal norms of science and technology,
the machine, domination by "technocrats" animated by "instrumental rationality"—I don't think I have left anything important
out.

Most people indeed are often overawed by and feel estranged
from the massive "facticity" of these ubiquitous social realities.
But do they really regard them as forces that are not manmade, as
something more—or less—than human products and creations?
Might not the very opposite be the truth, namely, that it is precisely the accurate perception of their manmade nature that accounts for their power to alienate? If so, perhaps the causes of
alienation as estrangement lie not in alienation as reification, nor
in Durkheim's basically dissimilar notion of anomie, but in what
Max Weber described, and meant quite literally, in the phrase he
borrowed from Schiller, as "the disenchantment of the world."

But before exploring further this possibility, an enormously influential apparent exception to it, the paradigmatic example of
alienation itself to Marxists, must be considered. The case of the
market, more specifically of commodity production for the market, seemingly contradicts the suggestion that all of the alienating
social phenomena listed above are generally perceived as human
products. Marx's famous passage in *Capital* on "commodity fetishism," as has often been noted, echoes his youthful theorizing about
alienation, although he does not reiterate the term itself. Lukács
singled out this passage as describing the source and prime exem-
plar of reification, which in generalized form became the central
concept in the intellectual tradition of post-Lukácsian Western
Marxism, including especially the Frankfurt critical theorists.

Marx wrote that commodity production, that is, the production of objects in order to sell them, creates a situation in which the "social relation" between producers is indirect and takes the form of a relation between their material products that compete for sale on the market. "There is," he goes on to observe in a much-quoted passage, "a definite social relation between men, that assumes in their eyes, the fantastic form of a relation between things." He then alludes to the Feuerbachian theory of religion in referring to "the mist-enveloped regions of the religious world [where] the productions of the human brain appear as independent beings endowed with life." "So it is," he concludes, "in the world of commodities with the products of men's hands."

But Marx has given us no more than a highly colored description of the market where, at least in large-scale societies, the producers do not directly interact but influence each other only indirectly through the results of the exchange of their products mediated by money (and often enough by middlemen). Where is there any fantasy or mystification in this familiar circumstance? Marx, to be sure, liked neither the market nor money as the medium that made its scope and impersonality possible, expressing his socialist preference for "production by freely associated men . . . consciously regulated by them in accordance with a settled plan." No less than Durkheim or Parsons, Marx was a partisan of consensus, solidarity, and social integration over conflict, separation, and system integration (the latter connoting the mediated, indirect, and nonconsensual interdependence of men in society). He differed from them in thinking that capitalism, commodity production, money, and ultimately the division of labor itself were insuperable obstacles to the attainment of an ideal unity of mankind.

More specifically, Marx contended that the price or "exchange-value" of a commodity is perceived as an inherent property of the physical object exchanged rather than as a social meaning reflecting an actual social relation under capitalist conditions of production and exchange. But he provides no real evidence that this is so: the purported resemblances to primitive fetishism or to Feuerbach's deified projections of the human mind are at best no more than analogies. I am reminded of the old tale that children growing up in big cities—children, note, not adults—believe that milk is somehow produced by the milkman who bottles and delivers it. Marx, to be sure, ends the famous chapter with quotations from several second-rate and now forgotten economists who weirdly claimed that "value" (meaning exchange-value) was an actual property of things in contrast to their use-values which are relative to human purposes. But this is simply an instance of the reification of abstract concepts in the pre-Lukácsian or Whiteheadian sense; there is no reason to believe that the ordinary citizen, equipped only with common sense, saw things that way any more than he or she thought milk came "naturally" in bottles rather than from cows. Marx's argument reveals his own quintessential bourgeois scholasticism. A little bit of the "positivistic" survey research of American sociologists so reviled by philosophical Western Marxists might help resolve the question of the reality of commodity fetishism.

Marx's major intellectual achievement was his insistence that the principles of classical political economy had to be firmly located in their particular historical and social context, as opposed to the claims of the early economists that they were timeless natural laws comparable to, indeed reflecting and partly modeled after, Newtonian mechanics or Darwinian natural selection. The core of Marx's Marxism was his assertion of the dependence of the laws of the market on capitalist economic institutions that are historical creations capable of being transformed as a result of their own operation, which prepares the ground for eventual social revolution. The connection with the older philosophical idea of alienation lies in the rejection of the assimilation of the workings of capitalism to immutable natural forces analogous to the omnipotent deities of religion in their independence from and control over human aims and actions. Here is the rationale for the more generalized attack by critical theorists on the assumption that the sociocultural world is governed by laws of a deterministic "nature-like" character, the grounds for their ceaseless polemics against "positivism" and "objectivism" in social thought, which they manage to find almost everywhere, including in Marx himself as well as in various later versions of Marxism.

Let us recall the modern social phenomena held chiefly responsible for alienation: capitalism, bureaucracy, technology. Does anyone today really consider these to be reflections of unalterable natural laws of the same order as the motions of the planets or the evolution of new species? Just as nobody deifies them, I doubt that many people see them as anything but manmade, "socially constructed" entities. Even contemporary economists, for whom the workings of the market remain the major organizing principle or master paradigm of their discipline, no longer reify their concepts in the manner of the classical economists criticized by Marx. Modern economists regard the "market mechanism" and *homo economicus* himself as conceptual constructs or models that lend themselves to econometric manipulations permitting wide and varied inferences, but not as realistic descriptions of the world. The professional economist's "equilibrium price-auction model," as Lester Thurow names it in his recent assault upon it (Thurow 1983), certainly remains open to criticism. But such criticism is necessarily what Ernest Gellner has called "second-order" criticism addressed to the model's artificiality and remoteness from the real world, its seductive adaptability to mathematization notwithstanding, rather than criticism that indicts the builders and users of the model for naively believing that they are describing the world. Thus commodity fetishism as alienation does not apply any longer even to the abstract thought processes of economists.

Marx believed that political economy was becoming the "dominant ideology" of emerging bourgeois societies (Abercrombie et al. 1980). He was mistaken, for neither classical economics nor the social Darwinism increasingly popular during his own most active years ever fully achieved that status, not even for the bourgeoisie itself. Nor did sociology, for which Comte and even Durkheim more than a generation later had such high hopes, achieve such status, although Marxism itself became a coercively imposed dominant ideology for those non-bourgeois societies that trace their legitimation back to the October Revolution of 1917. Contemporary sociologists, however, remain curiously blind to the extent to which the leading assumptions of their discipline have entered into the popular consciousness over the past fifty years.

Raymond Aron quotes an acute observation by Marcel Mauss, Durkheim's nephew from the generation of sociologists between Aron's own and Durkheim's, to the effect that "all social phenomena are, to some degree, the work of a collective will, and

whoever says human will, says choice between different possible
options" (1984: 71). This statement suggests that the view of the
social order as arbitrary or optional presented by sociologists may
itself be a source of estrangement from the social order. Not only
does such a view disenchant the world by ridding it of humanized
gods and spirits, but it also deprives it of the aura of iron necessity and inevitability associated with the reign of natural laws.
Modern men like all men have been thrust into an external and
constraining society that is not of their own making, but they are
more acutely aware than earlier generations that this society was
made by other men rather than by God or nature. It often appears
to them, therefore, as a world of makeshift, historically accidental
social arrangements in which they feel trapped precisely because
they are so readily capable of imagining different and more attractive arrangements. The pathos of their situation is not so much
that they reify the institutions and power structures impinging
upon them, ascribing to them an existence and weight independent of human activity and choice, as that they are incapable of
reifying them in seeing them rather as purely contingent human
creations to which they are compelled to accommodate themselves. If alienation is the failure to remember the humanly produced and socially constructed nature of society, perhaps the very
overcoming of such alienation is not the solution to but rather a
cause of alienation as estrangement, homelessness, meaningless-
ness—the conception of it generally favored by existentialists and
American sociologists as well as by modernist literary intellectuals before them.

One recalls incongruities in the outlook of the youthful political and "countercultural" protest movements of the 1960's that
made alienation into a shibboleth. Marxist slogans were combined
with American Indian headbands, the chanting of mantras, and
events like the famous effort, or pretended effort, to "levitate" the
Pentagon. It often seemed as if the desired alternative to commodity fetishism was the real original fetishism of tribal cults so
looked down upon by Marx from the heights of his nineteenth-
century progressivism. Primitive peoples, far from representing
the epitome of an alienated or reified consciousness because of
their failure to see their culture and institutions as manmade and

reformable, were admired as exemplars of the lack of alienation for that very reason, for their allegedly deep feeling for the wholeness of the cosmos harmoniously embracing both nature and culture. No wonder alienation became a discredited cliché under the weight of so many contradictory meanings!

Except for the numbers of people involved and the publicity they received, little was new in the religiosity and neoprimitivism of the 1960's counterculture. Fifty years earlier, Max Weber had commented on "the need of some modern intellectuals to furnish their souls with, so to speak, guaranteed genuine antiques." "They play," he noted, "at decorating a sort of domestic chapel with small sacred images from all over the world, or they produce surrogates through all sorts of psychic experiences to which they ascribe the dignity of mystic holiness, which they peddle in the book market" (Gerth and Mills 1946: 154). What was novel about the 1960's, though by no means entirely unprecedented, was that such attitudes were expressed under the auspices of the political left and often included the invocation of Marxist phrases like "demystification" when the very opposite, the "remystification" or "re-enchantment" of a disenchanted world, appeared to be the real objective of the protesters.

Hannah Arendt is one recent thinker who understood that alienation as estrangement may for modern man result from his very awareness of living in an almost entirely manmade world rather than from the suppression of such awareness. "The modern age, with its growing world-alienation," she wrote, "has led to a situation where man, wherever he goes, encounters only himself. All the processes of the earth and the universe have revealed themselves either as man-made or as potentially man-made." Like the theorists of the Frankfurt School whose technophobia she shared, she assigned responsibility for this result to the triumphs of science and technology, which have "devoured . . . the solid objectivity of the given" (1968: 89).

As our major interpreter of totalitarianism, however, Arendt achieved a deeper understanding than the Frankfurt theorists. The leaders of totalitarian movements, she saw, had grasped that history could be "made" or "made over," that "everything is possible" and that their collective will need acknowledge no limits in objectifying its utopian absolutes after the seizure of state power. For the followers, on the other hand, the totalitarian movement was a way of overcoming their alienation by remystifying the world and endowing it once again with quasi-religious or quasi-scientific meaning and solidity. The convergence of these two tendencies gave totalitarianism its peculiarly modern yet atavistic character as neither a reversion to past forms of despotism nor, as the Frankfurt theorists thought, the culmination and inevitable end product of either monopoly capitalism or "the dialectic of Enlightenment." Arendt's archaism, what one critic has called her "Hellenic nostalgia," was a source of insights superior to those emanating from the soured and embittered futurism of the Frankfurt neo-Marxists.

Contemporary critical theorists and humanist Marxists have an obvious answer to the claim that alienation is not the result of a mystified or nature-like view of the historical world but stems rather from the unambiguous recognition that it is manmade. Their argument is that the very consciousness of the manmade, human-all-too-human nature of contemporary institutions and the routines they impose increases the sense of their oppressiveness and their dehumanizing effects so long as they are unmistakably not the creations of a unified collective will, of the "totalizations," in Sartre's phrase, of a genuine historical subject. Alienation is here identified with a powerlessness of which its victims are painfully conscious, as in the definitions favored by some non-Marxist American sociologists. The way to overcome alienation is to forge a new political will, an authentic collective praxis, aimed at dereifying what exists and reconstructing the world anew in the image of left ideals. As Neil McInnes has remarked, "The Critical Theory of Society generalizes Marx's revolutionary dialectic into the assertion that, since there is nothing in our society but our activity and its ephemeral products, it is all totally plastic and liable to instant revolution at almost any moment we wish—if only we would wish" (1972: 176).

"If only we would wish"—ah, there's the rub! We are not, after all, talking about Periclean Athens, a few thousand residents of Parisian *arrondissements*, or even the Red Belt surrounding Berlin in the 1920's, but of hundreds of millions of people of diverse origins and outlooks dependent for survival itself on a technically

complex network of goods and services that is increasingly international and intercontinental in scope. Marx had the realism to
specify a tangible historical agent in the proletariat. The proletariat failed to fulfill the mission he assigned to it, but a return
to the Young Hegelian apotheosis of humanity itself as a fictive
political actor makes even less sense today than in the early nineteenth century when there were plausible excuses for equating
world history with European and Western history.

Alienation as estrangement may be regarded as a normal rather
than a critical condition in the modern world so long as it does
not extend to all of the primary groups and "intermediate associations" that make up the fabric of everyday life in all societies,
and provided also that we use the term to refer unambiguously
to a social relation distinguishable from "self-alienation" as an
individual psychological malady. Richard Schacht and Robert C.
Tucker are scholarly anatomists of alienation who have argued for
the necessity of this distinction.[2] Alienation as a social relation
is an inevitable consequence of the disjunction between system
integration and social integration: in less technical language, of
the circumstance that we know our lives to be determined by distant, unknown, or imperfectly understood persons, organizations,
and "social forces" on a scale that utterly surpasses our limited
capacities for fellow-feeling, group and institutional identification, and personal responsibility. Redfield had in mind at least one
major aspect of this disjunction in regarding the separation of the
"technical order" from the "moral order" as a major feature of the
emergence of civilized societies from contacts between previously
isolated, small and homogeneous primitive or "folk" societies.

The dissociation of system from social integration is greatest
and most salient in modern industrial or postindustrial societies
in which it has been relentlessly increasing since at least the
sixteenth century. Alienation as reification, on the other hand,
is concentrated in primitive and archaic societies and becomes
progressively attenuated in the course of rationalization or modernization, a process that includes diffusion of the disenchanting
knowledge of ourselves provided by the human sciences and the
great modernist artists and thinkers. To a growing extent, this
disenchantment includes the awareness that alienation as home-

lessness and estrangement is, if not the human condition, at least inescapably the modern condition.

Although in other respects their views were diametrically opposed—for example, in their attitudes toward social conflict— Marx and Durkheim were alike in divinizing society, not, of course, in its existing form, but in the ideal form they hoped it would assume in the future partly as a result of the influence of their own teachings. In Durkheim the divinization is explicit: the sacred beings and objects men have worshipped in the past were in reality nothing but representations of society itself—he might just as well have said that they were "alienated" or "reified" projections of social relations had he been familiar with those terms and willing to accept their pejorative implications. He thought, to the contrary, that when we lose our reverence for the mighty and benign power that rules our lives, we fall into anomie and endanger not only our sanity but our very life itself.

To Marx, the future prospect of a fully "socialized humanity" gave meaning to history. Marxism, as Leszek Kolakowski has written, is a philosophical expression of the "self-deification of mankind" (1978: 530). For what would be the most, if not the only, sanctified object of devotion in the future that Marx notoriously described so sparsely? Clearly, it would be the collective forms of life that so many generations had labored to produce in the dark and bloody past.

Max Weber knew better. For him, as for Marx and Durkheim, the gods had been routed by the progress of knowledge, although he remained acutely sensitive to how "the ghost of dead religious beliefs . . . prowls about in our lives." But he saw in addition that "the rosy blush of the Enlightenment seems also to be irretrievably fading" (1930: 182). Over a century earlier the greatest thinker of the Enlightenment, the founder of the German idealist philosophy that gave birth to the concept of alienation, Immanuel Kant, declared that "Out of the crooked timber of humanity, no straight thing can ever be made," an observation one can readily imagine Weber having made.

CHAPTER 6

The Politics of Left and Right

Political democracy comprising regularly scheduled elections based on universal adult suffrage can be regarded as the institutionalization of the power of numbers in accordance with the normative principles of majority rule and one person-one vote. Democracy grants to every individual person regardless of what other resources he or she may possess a specifically political resource, the right to vote.[1] Democracy also gives exclusive precedence to this resource when aggregated as a collective electoral choice in the selection of a government. The one individual resource that is equally distributed in a population is, in short, accorded decisive weight. The collective resource of numbers, therefore, gives potential political ascendancy by majority vote to those segments of the population most lacking in all of the other individual and collective resources that remain unequally distributed and concentrated in the possession of a minority. Introduced into a class-divided society, democracy represents a formal, that is, legal and constitutional, equalizing tendency. The possibility that the lower classes may use the power of the ballot to win control of the state and carry out a redistribution of those resources that remain unequally distributed is inherent in mass democracy. Its introduction was therefore feared and opposed by many spokesmen for the privileged classes in the nineteenth century and even earlier, whereas extension of the franchise became a major demand of populist and socialist egalitarian movements. The battle was chiefly waged over property restrictions on the right to vote. In their later years both Marx and Engels thought that the achievement of universal suffrage eliminated the necessity of violent revolution by making the victory of the proletariat possible by legal and peaceful means.[2]

But, of course, it hasn't worked out that way in practice. In the long-established constitutional democracies there has been some movement towards greater equality in the distribution of resources other than citizenship (which includes the right to vote), but the movement has on the whole been a modest one.[3] One must ask the deliberately naive yet significant question: why don't the parties of the numerically preponderant lower classes win most of the elections and create a classless society in which the three p's of power, privilege, and prestige are more or less equally distributed? Or—to achieve the feat of quoting two American presidents in a question—why, if "God must love the poor people because he made so many of them" (Lincoln), is "conservative government in the saddle most of the time" (Wilson)?

There are two main answers. First, it is hard to mobilize large numbers of people even for so limited a purpose as casting their votes for the same candidate. And the process of mobilization takes time—decades rather than years. Second, resources other than the vote remain in the predominant possession of minorities: wealth; status; political skills based on superior information; education; range and variety of social contacts; access to means of persuasion; free time; traditional legitimacy. The upper and middle classes are at an advantage with respect to all of these resources, which enables them to exercise greater influence not only on government policy between elections but also on electoral mobilization up to the very moment of the actual voting when formal equality prevails.

The fifty to a hundred years that have witnessed the democratization of politics in most Western nations are not very long,[4] but the pattern of politics has scarcely remained the same in these nations over that period. There is in fact a discernible pattern of short-run and long-run development over time in democratic politics as the tempo of lower-class mobilization accelerates and as the upper-class parties seek new ways of trying to contain their opponents' potential majority, which is inherent in democracy based on universal suffrage—in what I have called the institutionalization of the power of numbers as a decisive collective political resource. Democratic political orders with universal suffrage and competing political parties experience a cyclical alternation of periods dominated by protest from the left and retrenchment by the right. The notion that politics conforms to such a cycle is hardly a new one: it is implicit in the most commonplace language of political journalism, which regularly uses such metaphors as "swing of the pendulum," "rising and ebbing tides," or "waxing and waning" forces.

The conception of a one-dimensional left-right continuum along which parties, movements, regimes, and ideologies can be located has often been justly criticized, yet some such conception seems indispensable and creeps back in different guises if the familiar tainted terminology is renounced.[5] The dictum that "if men define situations as real, they are real in their consequences" is especially applicable to political conflict and the alignments it produces. The idea of a left-right spectrum or of a liberal-conservative polarity is constitutive and not merely descriptive of political reality itself. To be sure, it is nearly always in the interests of democratic parties and politicians to gravitate toward the center by blurring the rigid distinctions made by ideologists and intellectuals, but even the blurring takes place with reference to recognized polar points.[6]

I shall use "left" to refer to programmatic political demands for planned or enacted social change toward a more equal distribution of economic rewards, social status, and power; or, in unpropitious times, to the defense of an existing, achieved degree of equality against advocates of increased inequality. The classic left demand is to realize for all men *"liberté, égalité, fraternité."* But the emphasis of the left in the past century has been, as noted in my definition, to an increasing degree on equality, apart from the existence and influence of Communist states that have laid claim to the heritage of the left while renouncing "bourgeois" democracy and civil liberties. Liberty and equality partially entail one another, as is recognized in Anatole France's well-known jibe that the law with majestic impartiality grants freedom to both the rich and the poor to sleep under the bridges over the Seine.[7] But they may also be at odds when the demands for certain kinds of equality require the suppression of the liberty of some individuals and groups, a fact repeatedly stressed by conservative thinkers and ideologues anxious to lay claim to at least a part of the liberal heritage or to identify freedom with "free enterprise." Since the left as a permanent political tendency came into being at the time of the French Revolution, "right" is best defined residually as resistance on any grounds whatever to further movement towards equality in the distribution of material rewards, status, and power, or as the demand for restoration of a (usually idealized) *status quo ante* in which greater inequality prevailed. Because the left, in the modern sense of support for a more egalitarian society to be created by organized political effort, did not exist before the Enlightenment, an identifiable right emerged only in response to the challenge of the left. As Mannheim wrote: "Goaded on by opposing theories, conservative mentality discovers its *ideas* only *ex post facto*" (1946: 207).

Obviously, these sparse definitions raise problems if they are applied to the rich diversity of past and present political parties and movements. Yet in emphasizing, however broadly, the *content* of political demands, they avoid the relativism of defining left and right solely in relation to attitudes towards the existing order. Thus a party of the left that is in office does not cease to be left because it conducts an election campaign with such literally conservative slogans as "Don't let them take it away" or "You never had it so good"; it remains committed to an achieved degree of equality perceived as threatened by the right. Similarly, a party or candidate of the right may often appear as innovative and "radical" when challenging an entrenched administration of the left, but the challenge still comes from the right if it defends the relatively well-off social groups and attacks enacted or proposed egalitarian reforms.

Defining left and right by the broad content of political demands also avoids the difficulties raised by classifying power-seeking groups as left or right solely according to their social bases—whether they are supported by or direct their appeals to the victims or the beneficiaries of the existing distribution of rewards and privileges. Thus Peronism in the 1940's and 1950's was not necessarily a movement of the left because its main follow-ing was among industrial workers: nor must New Left student movements of the 1960's be considered "really" right-wing be-cause their members were disproportionately drawn from upper middle-class backgrounds.[8] Nor need the structure of a party or regime affect its classification as left or right: parties of the left may be led and controlled by tiny, self-perpetuating elites, while parties of the right may be organized in a loose, decentralized, "populistic" manner. The subordination of internal democracy and liberties to the demand for greater equality is, of course, charac-teristic of communist movements.

The periodicity of left and right in democratic politics is not necessarily equivalent to the alternation of parties in power. Some-times a conservative party may be able to take advantage of a turn to the left of popular opinion in response to an economic crisis and win over part of the left's normal constituency by advocat-ing "Tory socialist" reforms. This is particularly likely to happen when a party of the left is in office and incurs blame for the crisis.[9] More commonly, the left-right cycle or dialectic may take place within a single party that has remained in office for long periods of time and that electorally overshadows its opponents. For parties of both the left and the right are usually factionalized into moder-ate and militant wings, dividing reformers from radicals and con-servatives from reactionaries. Intra-party success usually goes to those politicians capable of skilful maneuvering in the capacious center, as in the case of interparty competition. But the ideologi-cal dynamic that shapes the party's posture comes from the wings.

Nor, as the previous paragraph may seem to suggest, is it always a matter of a changed public mood turning to protest or express-ing a sense of crisis that wells up from the substratum of politics and sets the rhythm in motion. A change of parties in power can initiate rather than merely reflect the workings of the rhythm. For example, John F. Kennedy's narrow presidential victory in 1960— if indeed it was a real victory untainted by fraudulent vote counts in Texas and Chicago—began the turn to the left in the 1960's, although it is highly probable that President Eisenhower could have been reelected if it had been legally possible for him to run again. Also Nixon's close victory over a divided Democratic party and administration in 1968 intensified the backlash against the protest movements of the 1960's, which might otherwise have remained inchoate and politically unfocused. In multiparty systems where coalition governments of the same several parties remain in office for long periods, shifts in the proportions of the vote won by different coalition partners may play a similar role.

The left-right rhythm, then, is neither to be identified simply with an alternation of parties in power nor to be equated with an eruption of "deeper" social forces that penetrate and transform party politics, although both, of course, combine to play a part in it. The rhythm or cycle is essentially one of a pronounced shift in the mood and the *kinds of issues* that dominate political debate, electoral competition, and often intellectual and cultural life as well. It is not the effect of a mysterious cosmic law: a description of the rhythm, however accurate, *explains* nothing whatsoever, for the rhythm is an *explanandum* rather than an *explanans*—an effect of underlying causes rather than a causal agency itself.[10] An explanation of it must be historically bounded because party politics under conditions of mass suffrage are less than a century old in most of the stable, economically advanced constitutional democracies of the West. Yet it is at least worth observing in passing that there is some evidence of a similar periodicity in non-democratic states. Despotic rulers of absolutist monarchies have often been followed by rulers more responsive to pressures from below. Totalitarian dictatorships undertake "great leaps forward" that are followed by periods of relaxed discipline in which "a hundred flowers" are encouraged to bloom. An analyst of Stalin's rule has written of the "artificial dialectic" imposed by him on Soviet society, where rigorous demands for total ideological conformity and the use of terror to deter even the mildest dissent alternated with periods of greater permissiveness or "thaw" (Utis 1952: 197–214).

The fullest periodization of American politics into successive left and right eras—from 1765 to 1947—was presented by Arthur Schlesinger Sr. in an article first published in 1939 and later revised and expanded (1949: 77–92). Schlesinger divided American history into eleven periods of alternating "conservative" and "liberal" ascendancy, each one averaging 16.5 years with very slight deviations around the mean except in the period from the Civil War to the end of the nineteenth century. Schlesinger's attempts to explain the cycle were not very adequate, scarcely going beyond the assertion of inevitable "changes in mass psychology" resulting from boredom or disappointment with the prevailing phase of the cycle. Also, although he acknowledged the existence of a similar cycle in the Western European democracies, his explanatory remarks refer largely to alleged peculiarities of the American people, such as their preference for "empiricism" rather than "preconceived theory" and their belief in the virtues of competition. The very influence of Schlesinger's article on politicians may have helped to make his cyclical "theory" self-fulfilling in recent decades: in his autobiography (1963: 108), published shortly before his death in 1963, Schlesinger reports that Franklin D. Roosevelt's adviser, David Niles, once told him that FDR was influenced in his decision to run for reelection in 1944 by Schlesinger's calculation that liberalism would remain dominant until 1948 (not a bad forecast). Schlesinger also mentions a preelection column by James Reston in 1960 maintaining that John F. Kennedy "based his campaign on the assumption," derived from Schlesinger's theory, that a turn to the left was in the offing within a year or two (1963: 190–91). Also, Arthur Schlesinger Jr., who was active in the liberal wing of the Democratic Party in the late 1950's, revived and updated his father's thesis to argue that the 1960's were destined to be a period of reform and innovation (not a bad prediction either!). But if presidents, presidential candidates, and their advisers acted on a belief in Schlesinger's theory, then they helped make it partially self-confirming. For the decisions and actions of powerful politicians are to a considerable extent what activates the cyclical pattern rather than mere epiphenomenal effects of an underlying causal law.

The cyclical rhythm is explained neither by such a law nor by Schlesinger's observations on "mass psychology." It represents, rather, a pattern of change that is inherent in the workings of a democratic political system in a class-divided society. Political democracy based on universal adult suffrage was itself originally a demand of the left introduced into previously authoritarian and hierarchical social orders. In European nations, though not in the

United States, it was the central issue around which new working-class and socialist parties organized in the last decades of the nineteenth century. For the formal (i.e., the legal and constitutional) redistribution of power achieved by universal suffrage to lead to reforms reducing social and economic inequalities, a long period of political mobilization of the lower classes had to take place, a process that is hardly complete even today in many countries, including the United States. The higher turnout and more unified support for parties of the right by the upper and middle classes compared with working- and lower-class support for parties of the left indicates that the political mobilization of the lower classes is still by no means fully accomplished.

But left parties and movements succeed in mobilizing a large enough proportion of their potential constituency to become leading opposition parties. Sometimes they displace older parties, as in the rise of Labour at the expense of the Liberals in Britain. Sometimes they emerge as the first and largest organized mass parties confronting electoral or government coalitions of smaller parties of the right, as on the European continent. Sometimes they partially transform an older, heterogeneous, and factionalized party into a vehicle for the demands of newly mobilized lower-class groups, as in the United States. Once parties of the left have been organized, or the working class has been at least partially mobilized by older parties, some crisis such as economic depression or defeat in war, or a split in the ranks of the right, is bound to give the party that is supported by the working and lower classes the opportunity to win office, whether on their own or as part of a coalition. They are then able to carry out reforms that constitute at least their minimum program. It has often been the fate of left parties to come to power at a time of such acute crisis for the entire society that they are forced to concentrate on improvised short-run policies to restore or maintain internal peace with the result that their long-range goals of social reconstruction have to be shelved or severely modified, inspiring accusations of "class betrayal" from their more militant followers. The German Social Democrats in the first and last years of the Weimar Republic are the classic case.[11] Nevertheless, by coming to office the left party wins a kind of legitimacy in the eyes of the electorate that it previously lacked. Not only is it able to enact at least its minimum program, but it gains plausibility as an alternative to the previously dominant conservative party, which increases the probability that it will be again returned to office. Power, in effect, becomes partially self-legitimating.

But failure to resolve the crisis that brought the party to office; the passing of the crisis whether or not the government's policies are given credit for it; splits between the party's or government's radical and moderate wings once the minimum program has been passed; the temporary appeasement of the left's constituency by the limited gains—actual or symbolic—that have been won; and the retrenchment of the right all result in electoral defeat or the "co-optation" of prominent leaders before the left party has done more than institute "incremental" or "token" reforms. The party of the right then returns to office after successfully persuading a sufficient segment of the left's following that a conservative government will not wipe out the gains that have been made, that it will not "turn the clock back" on the reforms achieved by the left. Old issues bitterly contested by the parties in the past suddenly become obsolete and periods of "Butskellism" (as in Britain in the 1950's) or even Grand Coalitions between the rivals (as in West Germany in the late 1960's) become the order of the day, isolating and infuriating the more militant partisans on each side who may break away and create splinter or "ginger" groups within legislatures or "extraparliamentary opposition" movements outside. The right party, in an effort to enhance or consolidate its appeal to the constituency of the left, may adopt hybrid, apparently oxymoronic names or slogans designed to suggest that it has outgrown past hostility to left policies, such as "Tory socialism," "Progressive Conservatism,"[12] "Christian Democracy," or "moderate Republicanism."[13] The most flagrant example of such an attempt to insert an appeal to all political tendencies into the very name of the party was the National Socialist German Workers' Party, in which the first and third words were designed to attract the nationalist right and the second and fourth the proletarian left. But the Nazis can hardly be regarded either as a democratic party or as a product of the "normal" workings of electoral politics.

This recurrent sequence of events is the rhythm or dialectic of democratic politics. It falls far short of realizing either the far-reaching hopes of the advocates or the apocalyptic fears of the opponents of universal suffrage in the nineteenth century. Yet if it ensures that sooner or later reformist parties of the left will come to office, and if the return to office of conservative parties is contingent on their leaving untouched the popular reforms carried out by left administrations, then *there is an unmistakable left-ward drift inherent in the functioning over time of democratic politics*. The metaphors of pendular or tidal movements are misleading, for the overall pattern is not one of a mere repetitive oscillation between fixed points. In Schlesinger's words, "A more appropriate figure than the pendulum is the spiral, in which the alternation proceeds at successively higher levels" (1949: 84). The classical Marxist conception of the movement of history has also been described as a spiral, combining a cyclical with a secular or unilinear motion. Another apposite image would be that of a ratchet mechanism, as in an automobile jack.[14]

To counter the leftward drift rooted in the incompletely realized demographic superiority of the left, the most reliable strategy of the right is, as Seymour Martin Lipset has noted, an appeal to nationalist sentiment. Modern nationalism is itself a product of democratic ideology, born in the wake of the American and French revolutions. But this very fact has served to enhance its appeal in opposition to the class and anti-elitist appeals of the left, which has so tragically underestimated the strength of national loyalties on so many occasions in the present century. The right lays claim to the symbols of legitimacy identified with the past of the nation, indeed with its very existence in a world of competing nation-states, an existence usually achieved by wars of conquest or revolts against foreign domination that usually, though not in the case of the United States, antedated the creation of democratic institutions and the extension of the franchise. Thus parties of the right tend to wave the flag, to nominate generals who stand "above politics" as candidates for office, and to invoke the need for national unity against enemies abroad to counter the divisive appeals of the left. National leaders of the right have sometimes engaged in foreign adventurism and even embarked upon limited expansionist wars in order to overcome internal tensions generated by the domestic class struggle. War has often in this sense been "the health of the state," in Randolph Bourne's dictum. Parties of the left, on the other hand, have traditionally been isolationist in the United States, internationalist and anti-imperialist on the European continent, and Little Englanders in Britain.

One might conclude that outbreaks of war and international crises often initiate the rightist phase of the cycle. Schlesinger, however, denied this with respect to American politics, arguing that there was no "correlation between foreign wars and the mass drifts of sentiments" and that "conflicts have taken place about equally in conservative and liberal periods, sometimes coming at the start, sometimes at the end and sometimes midway" (1949: 88). The Civil War would seem to have been another matter: the longest period of conservative rule, twice as long as Schlesinger's mean figure of 16.5 years, witnessed the emergence of the Republican Party as the undisputed champion of big business and coincided with their persistent "waving the bloody shirt" at the Democrats. Moreover, the association of patriotism and militarism with the right was much more pronounced in Britain and on the European continent, both because democracy did not coincide there with the birth of the nation and because of inescapable involvement in wars and power politics in contrast to traditional American isolationism.

It can also be argued that the ideological significance of wars and international alignments for domestic division of opinion has become much greater in the present century. World War I divided the left; the Russian Revolution further divided it and enabled the right to make use of the "red scare" as a political tactic. World War II, on the other hand, was fought against nations seen as the incarnation of the values most bitterly opposed by the left and therefore did not displace its ideological ascendancy. In America at least, the cold war and Korea, fought against an enemy laying total claim to the ideological heritage of the left, delegitimated the American left, almost completely obliterating its radical wing. The unpopularity and failure of the war in Vietnam played a large, even a major, part in the revival of radical protest movements in the 1960's and greatly reduced the identification of the left with international involvements that dated back to the antifascist ambience of the 1930's. This had been particularly pronounced in America because of Roosevelt's internationalism, which was most vigorously opposed by anti–New Deal Republicans. Even the war in Vietnam was not unjustly described as a "liberals' war." More recently, both in America and elsewhere, the left has tended to resume its instinctive resistance to the salience of foreign policy and the government agencies, civil and military, that conduct it—the "natural" posture, as it were, of the left, which defines itself by the priority it gives to domestic reforms implementing greater equality. Foreign policy choices—war and peace, military spending, international alignments (what George Washington called "entangling alliances")—have more than any other issues been responsible for the factionalism to which the left is so notoriously prone.

One cannot, therefore, simply treat wars, international crises, and issues of foreign policy as irrelevant to the rhythm of democratic politics or as *dei ex machina* that occasionally impinge upon and alter it. Nationalism and foreign policy have been, if not always in the United States, the stock-in-trade of the right in electoral politics, but in the increasingly interdependent and pervasive world of nations of the later twentieth century differences over foreign policy have frequently become associated with left-right differences on domestic issues.

The identification of the right with nationalism, however, is largely confined to the older Western democracies. Nationalism of the left has been a common phenomenon of independence movements in the Third World. The elites of new, formerly colonial nations have tended to be ideologically leftist, often having acquired their outlook as students in the former metropolitan countries or in the communist world. As Lipset observes: "In a context in which a large section of the elite supports leftist ideological goals, and in which the large majority live in poverty, the chances for conservative parties representing the traditional elite to remain viable electoral alternatives to the predominant leftists are quite rare" (Lipset 1968: 164; see also 206–8). My concern has been with the politics of relatively stable democracies, and the new nations of the underdeveloped world have not, alas, produced many of these. But the legitimacy acquired by the left in these nations through identification with their foundation emphasizes the historical limitations of the association of nationalism in the West with the right, and of the greater availability of patriotic symbols to parties of the right, striving to overcome the left's potential advantage in the collective resource of numbers by appealing to the wider community of the nation.

Recognition of the leftward drift inherent in democracy is likely to disturb and alarm partisans of the right who may see themselves as winning most of the battles but losing the war. But right-wing disillusionment with democracy need not stem solely from the increasing conviction that in the long run the right is playing a losing game. The genuine commitment of some conservatives to the national community as a historical entity preserving a deep continuity with the past may give rise to distaste and contempt for the endless haggling and bickering of the politicians and their cynical pandering to the shallow and ephemeral emotions of the crowd in the constant quest for votes. The unity of the nation as "a pact between the living and the dead and those who are yet to be born," in Burke's famous words, counts for more with such conservatives than party or class victories in electoral competition. Democracy thus produces what Aron calls a Right Opposition appalled by the pettiness and baseness of its political struggles. But it also produces a Left Opposition which, outraged by the persistence of class division and social injustice, views the parliamentary "game" as a fraud perpetrated by a capitalist ruling class engaged in manipulating a shadow contest between venal political parties that never produces more than token changes in the direction of a fully classless or egalitarian society.[15] Militants of the left become disillusioned and radicalized by the glacial slowness of the leftward drift and the many counterpressures and setbacks to which it is subject. They proceed to dismiss parliaments as "talking-shops," the major parties as "Tweedledum and Tweedledee," and the "system" itself as a fraud in professing to offer opportunities for fundamental—nowadays often called "structural"—change.

When a democratic political system and the leftward drift inherent in it have been in operation for some time, the status quo does not fully correspond to the interests, values, or aspirations of either left or right: It reflects what John Rex describes as a "truce situation" resulting from a balance of power rather than the complete ascendancy of either side (1961: 127–29). If there are enough conservatives who regard themselves, like one cited by R. G. Collingwood, as "a 'brake' on the vehicle of progress," then the rhythm of democratic politics continues and the spiral pattern it traces moves to a higher level. ("He meant," Collingwood explains, "that the Conservative policy was not to stop the vehicle but to slow it down when it seemed likely to go too fast" [1942: 209–10].) The pattern of movement is also maintained if enough of those on the left persist in seeing democracy itself as a partial but crucially important fulfillment of their values and do not therefore countenance abandoning it in order to maximize other kinds of equality.

But there is no guarantee that these conditions will last. If Aron's Right and Left Opposition are products of the "normal" workings of democracy, segments of them are attracted by violent revolutionary or counterrevolutionary shortcuts: in the case of the right, to arrest and even reverse the leftward drift; in the case of the left, to accelerate and complete it. In periods of acute national crisis and distress, a "dialectic of the extremes," to use Aron's phrase, in which each side violently confronts the other, often enough in the streets, may take center stage and threaten the very survival of democratic institutions. The last years of the Weimar Republic are, of course, the classic example. At such times, *les extrèmes se touchent* and the left-right spectrum itself resembles a horseshoe rather than a semicircle or a straight-line continuum. The dialectic of the extremes represents an effort to short-circuit the "normal" pattern of alternating periods of protest and stabilization with its built-in tendency toward a glacially slow leftward drift. Democrats suspect those on both the left and the right who, out of impatience with the stately rhythm of democratic politics, wish to fracture it by making a forward "leap to socialism" or the restoration of an idealized status quo ante, and this suspicion is surely well founded. But, in a spirit of irony, democrats might well adopt as a motto for the institutions of political democracy Galileo's famous aside when forced to recant his belief in the Copernican theory: *eppur si muove* (yet it still moves).

The "democratic class struggle" and the left-right alignment it produces are not the sole content of democratic politics, although they are probably the most universal and enduring basis of conflict. Ethnic, religious, and racial divisions are central issues in the politics of a large number of democratic states, and such subcultural cleavages clearly pose a much greater threat than class politics, not only to democracy but to the survival of the existing nation-state itself.[16] The interaction between ethno-religious differences and class divisions, how they intergrade in overlapping or crosscutting ways, is a subject that requires greater attention than it has yet received. Critics of the Marxist insistence on the primacy of class have been too much inclined to present ethnicity as an alternative to class in providing a basis for group identity and conflict rather than as a difference which sometimes itself depends on and sometimes contributes to class division.[17] Obviously, in democratic politics the collective resource of numbers plays as crucial a role in the strategies of rival ethnic groups and in the outcome of their struggle as in the case of classes. The size and territorial concentration of an ethnic group may determine whether it adopts secessionist aims, seeks constitutionally guaranteed national rights within a multinational state, or strives only for limited representation. The long-term process of political mobilization that so centrally shapes the rhythm of the democratic class struggle is less relevant to ethnic politics, but there may also be a rhythmic and a long-term pattern in the electoral competition of ethnic and religious groups, a movement that intersects, is superimposed upon, or varies inversely with the left-right rhythm. But my concern here has been solely to abstract out of the welter of democratic political experience a discernible rhythm or dialectic of the latter.

If the left should ever succeed in fully and permanently mobilizing its constituency the rhythm would come to an end. The left party would win all the elections and would presumably carry out egalitarian reforms eventuating in a socialist utopia. Even in Scandinavia, however, this millennium has not yet arrived. There is also the possibility that the left's constituency of the lower classes may become more conservative.

Has the Rhythm Come To an End?

My account of the rhythm of democratic politics suggested that it reflected the cumulative effects over time of political equality in the form of universal suffrage on the social and economic inequalities that continue to prevail in democratic capitalist societies. Parties of the left propose egalitarian reforms in order to mobilize the potential majority of those who are relatively socially and economically disadvantaged. Parties of the right compete by stressing issues that are not class-linked, such as nationalism, moral values, and ethnic and religious rivalries, striving thereby to offset the advantage of the larger class constituency susceptible to the appeals of the left. Elites on the right have far greater control over all politically relevant resources except the right to vote itself, and this enables them to mobilize more fully their constituency and to conduct more intensive election campaigns. By contrast, parties of the left suffer from a "mobilization lag" because their potential majority consists of poorly informed, traditionally subservient people, more parochial in their attachments and with less free time to devote to politics. But sooner or later, often as the result of an economic or foreign policy crisis affecting the nation as a whole, a party of the left wins an election and enacts at least its minimum program. Eventually, however, the party of the right returns to office, accepting the permanence of the reforms the left has instituted. The recurrence of this sequence of events constitutes the rhythm of democratic politics and exhibits the leftward drift inherent in it.

This formulation amounts at best to what philosophers would call an "explanation sketch" of the cyclical pattern rather than a full causal account. I submit, however, that it is a good deal more illuminating than the invocation of physical or biological metaphors about tidal flows or the rhythm of heartbeats.[18] It also recognizes that conservatives have genuine popular issues favoring them in patriotic, moral, and religious sentiments; they need not merely capitalize on an alleged need for a period of tranquillity after bouts of reforming zeal directed by the left. My sketch does not, to be sure, account for the outcome of any single election, since it gives primary attention to the constants underlying the appeals of parties of the left and right to the different class constituencies most responsive to them.

The assumption that conservative eras will give way to new periods of innovation from the left presupposes the existence of a constant reservoir of potentially discontented voting groups ready to support new egalitarian reforms once the attraction of issues favoring the conservatives diminishes. But what if this reservoir shrinks in size at the end of each period of reform, each turn of the cycle? What if there is an increase in the number of people who are *relatively satisfied* with the positions they have achieved in the prevailing distribution of power, privilege, and prestige and are therefore less responsive to appeals for further egalitarian reforms, although considerable social inequality remains? In this event, one would have to conclude that the leftward drift of the rhythm of democratic politics is counterbalanced over time by a rightward tendency in which each era of left ascendancy reduces the social base remaining available for a future turn to the left. The rhythm would then slow down and even cease at a point far short of full social and economic equality—a disheartening conclusion for those who cherish this as an ideal and even more so for those reduced to permanent minority and lower-class status. The latter cannot even anticipate that their full mobilization would suffice to bring about changes leading to improvements in their condition.

Has something like this perhaps come to pass in the ages of Margaret Thatcher and Ronald Reagan and after? When I suggested this possibility after Reagan's first election victory in 1980, both Arthur Schlesinger Jr. and Seymour Martin Lipset, whose conceptions of democratic and American politics I had drawn on and welded together in the rhythm theory, took issue with me and argued that there was little reason to believe that Reagan's election amounted to a permanent change in the pattern of American politics.[19] I can only say that, despite Bill Clinton's election in 1992 with a minority of the popular vote in a three-way contest, events from the early 1980's to at least the early 1990's, notably additional Republican victories and that party's increasing turn to the right, support my analysis more strongly than theirs.

The electoral successes in the 1980's and early 1990's of parties of the right in the United States and other countries could mean that the rhythm I have described may have come to an end well before the full mobilization of the potential constituency of the left in the advanced capitalist democracies of the West. There is also evidence for the possibility suggested above of greater lower-class conservatism and greater sympathy for additional egalitarian reforms among some segments of the right's presumptive constituency. Moreover, the rhythm theory's postulation that the right would tacitly accept the reforms instituted by the left does not appear to apply to the Thatcher and Reagan administrations, at least to their rhetoric and to a lesser degree to their policies. It is even less applicable to the Congressional Republicans led by Newt Gingrich since the Democrats lost control of Congress in 1994. The first Republican-controlled Congress in half a century mounted an unmistakable legislative attack on the welfare state reforms of the New Deal of the 1930's and the Great Society of the 1960's, repealing some measures and greatly reducing in the name of budget-balancing the funding of major programs. The leftward drift of democratic politics may turn out to have been a historical phenomenon peculiar to the late nineteenth and the first two-thirds of the twentieth century rather than a cyclical spiral inherent in the politics of democracy based on universal suffrage in class-divided societies. Clearly, Western democratic societies have not ceased to be class-divided: they appear indeed to have experienced increases in economic inequality since the end of their sustained period of postwar economic growth. However, the reaction under conditions of low economic growth against the high cost imposed by the welfare state requiring relatively high rates of taxation has not been confined to Britain and the United States, although it has been most pronounced and politically successful in the latter.

The decline since 1945 in traditional class voting in the United States suggests that there has been a general long-run trend to the right underlying the two (really one and a half) cyclical shifts between left and right over the same period. True, public opinion surveys on which Lipset heavily relies show little major change over the last fifty years in the left/right or liberal/conservative class alignments on economic and welfare-state issues. Polls since the late 1960's have regularly indicated much greater working-class conservatism on "social" issues such as affirmative action, capital punishment, tolerance of homosexuality, censorship of pornography, and the like. More recent studies suggest that class voting has not ended insofar as classes and class fractions still tend to support disproportionately one of the two major parties, although there have been marked changes in the allegiances of particular classes. Blue-collar workers, the so-called "Reagan Democrats," have shifted toward the Republicans, while professionals and nonmanagerial white-collar workers have moved from the Republicans to the Democrats (Hout et al. 1995). Yet elections and surveys over the past three decades show that the working and lower-middle classes remain predominantly left of center on economic issues while the center has shifted in the long run to the left. The decline of traditional class alignments can be interpreted to mean that left/right issues have become less decisive by comparison with cultural and moral issues not as closely linked to the have/have-not division. Such issues are subordinated more readily than in the past to other issues—ethnic-racial, cultural, patriotic—on which conservatives and Republicans fare better. A change reducing the *salience* of left/right issues even if class alignments with respect to them remain much the same can be seen as a movement of the electorate to the right.

In the past left reformist initiatives have come from the activation and entry into politics of new, previously passive and under-mobilized disadvantaged groups: farmers, industrial workers, urban immigrants, blacks, women. After achieving their minimum objectives through the responsiveness of the party system, such groups, often calling themselves "movements," lose their forward momentum, sometimes as a result of arousing resistance in the form of traditionalist countermovements. The Right to Life movement, the Christian Coalition, and the antigovernment militias are recent examples of such countermovements, and it is obvious that their militancy has greatly contributed to the dominance of the right wing of the present Republican party. It is hard to discern any new groups that are substantial enough in size or sufficiently homogeneous in political outlook even potentially to be capable of sparking a turn to the left or a revival of liberalism in the near future. Of course, no one foresaw the emergence of the groups that have played such a role in the past either—history rarely fails to surprise us. But there is no reason to assume that American society will regularly produce new blocs of discontented voters mobilized to support political demands that keep alive a spirit of egalitarian protest from the left.

Many liberals and leftists have looked hopefully to the enormous population of nonvoters consisting preponderantly of minority and low-income groups who represent potential Democratic voters. A few have even conjured up visions of the mobilization of such voters by a new socialist party or a thoroughly revamped Democratic party, fulfilling at last the left's ancient dream of a restructuring of the American party system along class lines that would realize the left party's inherent demographic advantages. The assumption is that nonvoting reflects an apathy or alienation that would be dispelled if the electorate were offered the "real alternative" of a forthright egalitarian, anticapitalist program. This view is the mirror image of the old claim of right-wing Republicans in the years of Democratic ascendancy that if only the voters were given "a choice and not an echo" (the slogan of the 1964 Goldwater campaign) they would flock to the polls and reject the liberals' statist blandishments. The trouble is that there are just too many nonvoters—they make up over forty percent of the potential electorate. Surveys have long shown that nonvoters divide politically in much the same way as voters; they tend, however, to be less liberal on the average than the typical Democrat and less conservative than the typical Republican. Their varied socioeconomic composition, even if weighted toward the Democratic-voting lower classes, ensures that they include many potential Republican voters, even without taking into account the conceivably permanent shift toward the greater salience of ethnic-racial and cultural issues that are difficult or impossible to place on a left-right spectrum. A higher proportion of the potential electorate fails to vote in the United States than in other capitalist countries, and the persistence and even increase in the proportion suggests that the notion of "mobilization lag" may be a misnomer in suggesting that the lower socioeconomic groups will ever turn out in large numbers under enduring conditions of social inequality and class division.

Yet from the vantage point of the late 1990's the rhythm theory looks rather more credible than it did just over a year ago. In both the United States and Britain the unusually long periods of dominance by the more conservative of the two major parties appear to have ended. The Democrats have won two successive presidential elections despite losing control over Congress in the four-year period between them. In Britain the Labour Party under the leadership of Tony Blair ousted the Tories after eighteen years out of office. In Italy, developing into a stable democracy, the end of Communism has ended government by largely center-right coalitions and led to the decisive electoral victory of a center-left coalition including reformed Communists. The change in Italy from a proportional to a single-member majority electoral system is likely to accentuate a sharper left/right division of the electorate. The left also regained power decisively in the most recent election in France.

Increasing inequalities in the distribution of income since the end in the early 1970's of high rates of economic growth have become widely recognized and deplored in a number of nations. In the United States the labor movement under new AFL-CIO leadership has adopted a more aggressive policy both in organizing unorganized workers and in supporting Democratic candidates for political office. Insofar as women, a slight majority of the electorate, are a relatively deprived and discontented group, the widening gender gap in voting indicates the persistence of a reservoir of potential voters available for mobilization by the left party. Strong protests against efforts by conservative administrations to cut back on the welfare state and limit its entitlements have occurred in Canada and in France in addition to sparking the revival of the Democrats and of Labour in the United States and Britain.

It would be rash and premature, however, to conclude that these developments confirm the persistence of leftward drift. The relatively left parties returned to office do not advocate radical changes or even ambitious expansions of existing welfare states and have successfully identified themselves with more moderate policies

than they were perceived as having stood for in the past. Moreover, defense of existing welfare state measures is conservative
in an altogether literal sense. Indeed, right-wing Republicans led
by House Speaker Gingrich described themselves as "revolution-
aries" after their Congressional victories of 1994, which now appears to have been a serious misjudgment of the public mood.
The recent successes of parties of the moderate left does not even
contradict the view that the reservoir of discontented and deprived
voters on which the left has traditionally relied has been depleted
by past economic growth and the achievement of welfare states.
Opinion polls in the United States show twice as many people
identifying themselves as "conservative" as "liberal," although the
number of declared "moderates" is even larger. Nor has there been
any reduction in mobilization lag.

So long as two or more parties compete electorally for office,
the public after a long period of rule by one of them is disposed to
perceive the opposition party, which will have adapted its policies
to the prevailing mood, as having become an entirely credible candidate to assume the powers of government. This may be inherent
in the institution of political democracy itself, understood mini-
mally as the holding of regular elections based on universal adult
suffrage contested by two or more organized political parties. The
same underlying dynamic that worked to produce a leftward drift
will also operate to preserve and even continue a rightward drift
after right-wing parties have succeeded in instituting policies of
their own of a non- or even anti-egalitarian nature, clearly going
beyond the "mere" administration of policies previously achieved
by parties of the left. It has been said that Clinton is to Reagan-
Bush what Nixon was to Johnson-Kennedy, Nixon having continued the reforming impulses of the Great Society in such areas
as affirmative action and environmental protection just as Clinton has accepted the fiscal austerity and downsizing of the welfare
state favored by Republicans. Tony Blair won an overwhelming
victory in the 1997 British election after transforming his party
into "New Labour," winning repeal of the commitment to full
socialism in the famous Clause Four of the party's constitution
and pledging not to undo the changes in the direction of priva-
tization and limiting the power of the trade unions achieved by

Margaret Thatcher. These examples suggest that the same process of an opposition party gaining office after conditional acceptance of the reforms of the party it replaces that produced a leftward drift in the past may also operate in reverse when parties of the right have aggressively carried out changes consistent with their relatively less egalitarian outlook. This process evidently operates quite independently of the left or right alignment of the rival parties. Interruptions in recent years of decades of secure Social Democratic rule in Sweden and Austria by the strengthening and occasional electoral triumphs of right-wing coalitions may also illustrate it, though reversing the left/right identifications of the parties long in and out of office characterizing the United States, Britain, Italy, France (after a shorter period), and, at least potentially, Germany. One might conclude that the rhythm of alternation of left and right parties in winning and taking office still holds but not the previously postulated leftward drift.

In short, whether the spiral pattern traced by left/right alternation in office with its underlying roots in the class composition of the electorate can still be regarded as valid remains indeterminate, although there are stronger grounds for believing so than there were a short time ago. With acute problems of maintaining existing welfare entitlements looming in the very near future for all industrial nations when the birth cohorts of the immediate postwar decades reach the age of retirement, left/right divisions between the parties may well be intensified. This is particularly likely in the United States where the birth cohorts, the so-called "baby boomers," were largest and the conservative anti-tax and antigovernment orientation of the Republican Party became even more pronounced in the 1980's and 1990's. It is far from evident that the declines in productivity and the economic globalization that have created the trade and budget deficits responsible for increased income inequalities, loss of high-paying jobs, decline in union power, and fiscal pressure on existing welfare entitlements will be overcome in the near future. If high rates of economic growth have in the past been a solvent of class and left/right political conflicts—"a rising tide lifts all boats"—as well as rendering high taxation for redistributive welfare measures relatively painless, the end of these conditions may very well lead to an intensification of conflict. The rhythm theory might therefore hold under conditions differing markedly from those prevailing when it was formulated, conditions that conceivably could prove more threatening to the stability of constitutional democracy. It is often overlooked that full political democracy with universal suffrage for both men and women has not, even in the United States, existed for a full century.

Theories, cyclical metaphors, trend lines—none of them are infallible guides to the future. "History has many cunning passages, contrived corridors / and issues, deceives with whispering ambitions, / guides us by vanities." Perhaps the left/right distinction itself, grounded in the economics of industrial and industrializing societies now undergoing major social transformations, is becoming obsolete as a way of understanding politics and political possibility. It is based on a spatial metaphor, and space itself, let us remember, is not one-dimensional: it includes up and down, before and after, round and about, near and far.[20] Why should politics be a more simple linear realm?

CHAPTER 7

꙰

Cultural Relativism as Ideology

I want to reflect on the tangled history of the concept of "culture," which is obviously central to the current doctrine of "multiculturalism" as conceived by both its advocates and its critics. Multiculturalism is generally understood to presuppose the view long known as "cultural relativism." It might even be regarded as the conversion of cultural relativism as a theory or perspective in sociology and cultural anthropology into a political ideology containing directives for action, even if the political action is confined, as Todd Gitlin has observed, to "marching on the English department" rather than aspiring to take over the state (Gitlin 1995: 126–65). More accurately, multiculturalism as an ideology combines in a simplified blend Horace Kallen's "cultural pluralism" as a model for America with the anthropologist's cultural relativism. I shall be primarily concerned here with the latter. If one lives long enough one witnesses seemingly strange transformations and even reversals in the understanding of ideas as well as in their acceptance and ideological uses. Having learned much of my sociology from anthropologists at a time—the 1940's—when there were much closer ties and overlapping of concepts between sociology and anthropology than there have been since, I was virtually brought up on cultural relativism. Although the general intellectual public—such a public existed to a greater extent then than now—had acquired some familiarity with it, especially through the writings of Margaret Mead and Ruth Benedict, debates over cultural relativism and its wider moral and ideological significance were in the past largely confined to social scientists, a few conservative philosophers, and religious thinkers who interested themselves in the subject. The same debates are played out today on a larger and more politically and culturally embattled stage. But this is only the latest chapter in a much longer intellectual and ideological history.

The term "culture" in something approximating its later sense was originally an expression of German nationalism in opposition to the universalism of the Enlightenment that was linked to France and the international prestige of French institutions and ideas. Sir Isaiah Berlin has related this history (1992, esp. pp. 20–48, 70–90) and it has been told again with special reference to cultural relativism and multiculturalism by Alain Finkielkraut (1995). That there was no single story of human progress, no "grand metanarrative," as it is fashionably put these days, but that different peoples developed their own unique ways of life that could only arbitrarily be measured against a common standard was the gist of the idea. German culture was therefore different from French culture but not necessarily inferior despite the political and economic "backwardness" of German society. Culture was identified with *Volksgeist*, or the spirit of the people, meaning their total way of life, especially its underlying ethos or mentality. This is close to the academic anthropologist's conception of culture as embracing everything shared by a people as distinct from the Arnoldian identification of culture with the most complex, "highest" human creations in the arts and the "life of the mind." This view of plural cultures essentially different from one another and incapable of being graded according to some common measure of progress predated Darwin and the Darwinian revolution in social thought. It was, however, a short step to move from acceptance of the irreducible variety of cultures to, in Finkielkraut's words, "the theory of races that . . . *naturalized this rejection of human nature* and more generally everything else that might transcend the diversity of cultures" (1995: 79; emphasis in original). The fateful move from *Volksgeist* as a product of history to the equation of *Volk* with the zoological category of race followed and became the basis of Nazi ideology. At the rarefied level of philosophy and scholarship, the conception of cultures as unique historical creations became the governing idea of German historicism. Dilthey and Rickert were the best-known philosophers articulating this view, which influenced Max Weber.

Franz Boas brought this intellectual tradition to the United States and helped make "culture" the definitive subject matter of American cultural anthropology. His influence came at a time when the social sciences were in general revolt against the biologism of the post-Darwinian outlook that had been dominant for half a century. "Culture" was opposed to "race" as the explanation of human variety. Boas himself did much in his own research and writing to refute the belief that race had anything to do with a people's cultural achievements. The reaction against Nazi racist doctrines and practice in the 1930's and 1940's intensified the discrediting of racial explanations of human conduct. The conviction that nature rather than nurture shaped human life came to be seen as conservative or reactionary, although "progressive" thinkers such as E. A. Ross earlier in the century had partially shared such a view. The opposing view that customs and institutions were manmade products of history suggested that they could be reformed and even abolished if they ran counter to moral and political ideals, whereas it would presumably be much harder to change human heredity in any desired direction. To say that some practice was "cultural" or "culturally patterned" meant the same thing and carried the same liberal or reformist resonance as to say today that something is "socially constructed." That there was a direct temporal filiation between the culture concept and Nazi racial ideology is testimony to the strange career of ideas in history, particularly strange to those of us who were sired on the notion that the "good" and "scientific" concept of culture was the absolute contrary of the evil myth of racism.

"Cultural relativism" (or "cultural relativity," as she called it) was first used by Boas's student Ruth Benedict in her 1934 book *Patterns of Culture*, probably anthropology's all-time bestseller when reissued in 1946 as one of the first titles published in the quality paperback revolution of those years. It was understood by her and others to mean that human actions were invariably "relative to," meaning shaped or determined by, the culture in which the actors had been raised—"socialized"—since infancy. The concept assumed and in effect implied that the range of cultural variation was wide even among "primitive" peoples, as exemplified by the three different cultures Benedict described in detail in the book. Benedict's aim was primarily to demonstrate as dramatically as possible the existence of cultural variation and especially to show that it encompassed not only directly observable customs and institutions but also inner psychological dispositions expressed in a wide range of collective practices. The debate over cultural relativism, however, focused from the beginning on its alleged implication that the diverse and often contradictory values and moral standards exhibited by different cultures could not rationally, and therefore should not, themselves be morally evaluated. Since all moral standards were relative to the culture that prescribed them, any judgment of another culture's morality constituted "ethnocentrism": the "view of things in which one's own group is the center of everything, and all others are scaled and rated with reference to it. . . . Each group nourishes its own pride and vanity, boasts itself superior, exalts its own divinities, and looks with contempt on outsiders" (Sumner 1940: 27–28). I am quoting William Graham Sumner, who coined the term in 1906. It is perhaps worth recalling that he was a thoroughgoing conservative Social Darwinist who wrote essays with such titles as "The Absurd Attempt to Make the World Over" and "What the Social Classes Owe to One Another." If cultural relativism had overtones of a liberal reformist outlook when contrasted with hereditarian interpretations of human behavior, it also had deeply conservative implications in affirming the all-embracing hold that the constraints and dictates of existing cultures inevitably had over the individual human beings subject to them.

Benedict's book was published the year after Hitler came to power, although obviously most of it had been written before that fateful event. The historically accidental timing almost guaranteed that there would be intense argument over the putative normative implications of her relativism. The argument was renewed when the paperback edition was published in 1946, at the very beginning of the Cold War. I recall being reproached by a fellow student for failing to regard the Soviet Union with the tolerance I willingly extended to the Trobriand Islanders and the Zuni. I asked if he would recommend the same attitude toward Nazi Germany. That was an entirely different matter, he replied, and he remained unconvinced when I pointed out that Stalin had committed the mass murder of his own citizens on an even larger scale than Hitler. The era of Hitler and Stalin indeed cast a shadow over cultural relativism for several decades. In recent years, however, an even more far-reaching relativism that is epistemological or cognitive as well as moral has become fashionable and has spread well beyond the ranks of cultural anthropologists. Conservative thinkers have expressed alarm over the nihilism they see it as endorsing, and it has become a major theme in the continuing "culture wars." James Q. Wilson expressed shock that among his students "there was no general agreement that those guilty of the Holocaust were guilty of a moral horror" (1993: 8). In his *The Closing of the American Mind*—a "closing" he blamed primarily on cultural relativism—the late Allan Bloom complained that his students refused to condemn the Hindu practice of suttee, the burning of widows on their husbands' funeral pyres, which was suppressed by the British (1987: 26).

The original cultural relativism of Boas and his students did not advocate the eschewal of any and all moral judgment: it was directed against racism and rigidly moralistic ethnocentrism. The religious missionary was the anthropologist's major target, virtually her or his "hereditary enemy," as it were, and it was the moral judgment of *individuals* who were merely, and without having initially had any choice in the matter, conforming to their culture, acting consistently with the ways in which they had been socialized, that the anthropologist wished to rule out. The actions of individuals were thus seen as "relative" to their cultures in the sense, as I have already stated, of being shaped and determined by their previous enculturation or socialization. Such a view in no way precluded a comparative evaluation of different cultures and the conclusion that some were more humanly desirable than others. What it did preclude was condemning individual cannibals, headhunters, practitioners of human sacrifice or suttee as sinful or morally guilty. They could not help doing what they did, for they could not possibly "know any better" in the context of their culturally enclaved lives. An attitude equivalent to the injunction "love the sinner, hate the sin" is altogether compatible with this version of cultural relativism, which focuses on concrete individual humans rather than on the complex of norms, customs, and institutions that constitutes their culture. This takes care, too, of the case of the Nazis and the Stalinists: they could and did know better, having initially been socialized in a morality that regarded the killing of innocent people as sinful, immoral, and criminal. That was Hannah Arendt's point in fearfully anticipating that if totalitarianism survived to produce new generations without exposure to the norms and values of the past, the "authentic mass man" of the future "will have more in common with the meticulous, calculated correctness of Himmler than with the hysterical fanaticism of Hitler, will more resemble the stubborn dullness of Molotov than the sensual vindictive cruelty of Stalin" (1951: 319). She may have been wrong in thinking that Adolf Eichmann was such a man, manifesting the "banality of evil," in her famous phrase, but the possibility of a totalitarian future was her main concern.

As Clifford Geertz has observed, Ruth Benedict came to anthropology from a literary background and made Swiftian use of accounts of primitive cultures to hold up a critical mirror to our own culture. Geertz refers to the book's "famous—or infamous—last paragraph" in which Benedict introduced the notion of "cultural relativity," and he then alludes to "that disastrous final sentence about 'equally valid patterns of life'" (1988: 115–16). Geertz is surely right about the primacy of Benedict's satirical rather than detached scientific intent, but it seems to me that her phrase can be understood as meaning that equally genuine representations of the varieties of human nature have been produced by the contingencies of history. This would not entail that any and all patterns of culture are equally morally acceptable, with the implication that it is both ethnocentric and "unscientific" to evaluate them. The *fact* of cultural diversity is, of course, undeniable; there are, however, real debates both over the moral import of cultural diversity and over whether, or to what degree, a common human nature underlies or cuts across it. Benedict's closing chapter on psychology, essentially psychopathology, dealt with the issue of human nature. She seemed to deny that there could be any criteria of psychological normality and abnormality independent of what different cultures considered normal and abnormal. This was, inevitably, strongly disputed in psychiatric and psychoanalytic circles, which claimed scientific status for their theories.[1] At the time Benedict wrote, over sixty years ago, a much sharper line was drawn between factual or existential statements, the province of science, and culturally variable moral or normative judgments. Contemporary multiculturalists are usually epistemological as well as cultural or moral relativists, affirming "equal validity" in both a cognitive and a moral sense. Philosophers such as John Searle (1995) have challenged their cognitive relativism on logical and epistemological grounds. The debate has gone beyond the bounds of restricted academic controversy, and the issues supposedly raised by moral relativism chiefly account for this.

Why has multiculturalism as an ideology surfaced just now? The negative reaction to it of conservative polemicists hardly requires explanation, although it has become a political force and strategy in its own right, as Todd Gitlin has pointed out.[2]

1. Multiculturalism as an ideology is closely tied to what has been called identity politics. It is a reaction to the "death of socialism," to the fall of the American left (part of the title of a book by John Patrick Diggins [1992]), to the erosion of a left subculture that, as Diggins shows, has dominated intellectual and academic life since early in the century, although, of course, the decline is by no means confined to America. Multiculturalism and identity politics are fallback positions, last-ditch stands in the face of the diminished credibility of what had been major articles of left-wing belief.

Sociological studies of the South during the Jim Crow era documented that it was the "poor whites" or "rednecks" who were the most responsive to blatantly racist appeals, because, lowly as their social and economic status might be, they could at least pride themselves on being superior to African Americans. Jean-Paul Sartre advanced essentially the same interpretation of anti-Semitism: for the anti-Semite, he insisted, "the existence of the Jew is absolutely necessary: without it, to whom, then, would he be superior?" (1946: 34). Opposition to racial and ethnic bigotry is, of course, central to multiculturalism, but in basing itself on relatively permanent groups it is a mirror image of the very prejudice it opposes. Hence the frequent insistence by multiculturalists that racism is as deep-seated and virulent in America as it has ever been and that ethnocentric intolerance of cultural differences is as strong as it was when immigrants were required to take courses in Americanization. Such a view permits the retention of an adversarial outlook toward existing society that is the hallmark of what it means to be on the left. Nor is it an accident that the groups most emphasized by identity politics are those in which membership is ascribed and even biologically determined: race, gender, sexual orientation (assumed to be hereditary). One hears less about identities based on religion, education, or national origin, except in reference to peoples from "postcolonial" areas who lend credence to an anti-Western stance.

2. Multiculturalism and identity politics have the advantage of being both more and less than a politics. More because the assertion of an identity rooted in culture has emotional and expressive meaning and value independent of its political significance. If it is possible to make the personal the political, as the slogan has it, the personal is also the personal and can be retreated into and serve as a source of identity in its own right. Even if a particular identity is bound to remain a minority identity in the larger society, it is not tied to the aspiration to become a majority, to convert others and win elections, to shape public policy by capturing or influencing the state. It has a core therefore that cannot be touched by the ebb and flow of political tides. But this makes multiculturalism and identity politics less than a real political movement, which must necessarily in a democratic society be coalitional in aspiring to influence the larger society through the state, or at least to propose laws or policies that might be enacted.

3. America remains what used to be called a "mass society," in which people seek identification with groups smaller than the vast, heterogeneous total society as a protection against alienation and anomie. *Which* groups become major foci of identity formation seems to change almost by the decade, but the "quests" for community and identity are constants in American life. Race,

gender, sexual orientation, and past subjection to Western imperialism have advantages in their relative permanence, even if the "new social movements" of the 1960's gave them their assertive self-consciousness and visibility by articulating in political terms their long-standing grievances.

4. The rise of multiculturalism does not reflect an increase in the cultural diversity of American society at large, but if anything the reverse. Despite the fact that since the 1960's new immigrants have entered in larger numbers from non-European regions, they are probably more familiar with the major features of the host society than were, say, South Italian or Slavic peasants in the late nineteenth and early twentieth centuries. "Globalization" is a cultural as well as an economic tendency. The cultural differences invoked by multiculturalists are fundamentally identity markers or labels rather than ways of life or sets of values in sharp contrast to those of most native-born Americans. The very stress on supposedly irreducible cultural differences may express an uneasy awareness that they are not very great and are likely to diminish as a result of intermarriage and integration into a thoroughly urbanized and suburbanized society with pervasive mass media of communication in clear contrast to the society of a century ago. Immigrant groups are not, after all, expressing or clinging to traditional values that are profoundly at odds with the majority of Americans or likely to strike them as strange, bizarre, or threatening.

I do not think that multiculturalism and identity politics are likely to transform American society or even to endure as major ideological themes very much longer. Demographic considerations alone, such as reduced immigration and a prospective decline in the fertility of minorities, may be enough to reduce the credibility of the claim that the United States is not only already a multicultural society but is likely to become even more of one.[3] What has been called "civic" as distinct from "ethnic" nationalism[4] has, of course, always been especially characteristic of the United States and that will not change.

II

INTELLECTUALS AND MIDDLE CLASSES

CHAPTER 8

The New Class: Does It Exist?

I want to argue three propositions about the social phenomenon called the "new class": (1) it may be a class, but it is not new; (2) it may be new, but it is not a class; (3) it may be both new and a class, but its appearance on the scene explains little about the political and cultural changes that modern societies are undergoing.

Put so bluntly, these propositions are reminiscent of the Jewish joke Freud told to illustrate the psychic mechanism of rationalization. Asked by a neighbor to return a borrowed pot, the borrower replied, "First, it was badly cracked when you lent it to me; second, I already returned it whole to you weeks ago; third, I never actually borrowed it from you." I have avoided such blatant self-contradiction only by conditionally accepting one claim while rejecting the next. There remains the question of what the social phenomenon called "new class" is, even if it is neither new, a class, nor of major explanatory importance. I shall try to answer this question indirectly in the course of criticizing the three claims made for the phenomenon. To be sure, we might be dealing with a mere figment of the imagination of some social analysts or an expression of their total "false consciousness," but even unicorns and mermaids were presumably distorted impressions of some real experience.

What has been called a "new class" does correspond to a real social phenomenon. It is, first, an interpretation of the manifest increase in the number of people pursuing certain occupations, some of them old, a few even ancient, access to which depends on educational credentials. In the past few decades, the ranks of doctors, lawyers, professors, public and private administrators, accountants, journalists (including those using the nonprint media), applied scientists and technicians, social workers, nurses, psychotherapists, artists, and entertainers have all swelled considerably. The expansion of these occupations and the link between most of them and higher education has been a recognized trend for a long time. But until fairly recently it was regarded as part of the overall growth of what has been variously called "the new middle classes," "new intermediate groups," the "salariat," and "white-collar" or "black-coated" workers. Since the beginning of the twentieth century, the increase of this stratum has been seen as a challenge to traditional Marxist views of the class structure under capitalism and its future course of development, as in the debate over revisionism in the German Social Democratic party before the First World War and the later writings of neo- or post-Marxist German sociologists in the 1920's.

C. Wright Mills reopened the question with reference to the United States in the early 1950's. In *White Collar*, he devoted separate chapters to managers, the old professions, and intellectuals, locating these groups at the top of a "new middle class" that did not "make up one single compact stratum" but formed "a new pyramid within the old pyramid of society at large rather than a horizontal layer." Mills, in short, did not separate out those occupations requiring higher education or earning a relatively high income as a new class, but continued along the Marxist lines of regarding them as a segment of the larger intermediate stratum between the dominant propertied classes and wage-earning manual workers. A few years later, however, responding to the beginnings of the New Left, Mills rejected the "labor metaphysic" of "Victorian Marxism" and proclaimed "the intellectuals" (although he had contemptuously titled the chapter on them in *White Collar* "Brains, Inc.") as the new "historic agency of change" in the West.

Mills was a post-Marxist. Therefore he did not denominate the intellectuals as a class, just as he chose for well-considered reasons to call the dominant groups in American society a "power elite" rather than a "ruling class." Yet his view of intellectuals elevated them into more weighty and politically autonomous actors than the once fashionable view of them as "alienated" pure spirits eternally criticizing from the sidelines. He made them seem more weighty and autonomous even than the Leninist or Gramscian conception of intellectuals as bearers of doctrinal truth seeking attachment to a larger plebeian class that under their guidance would be capable of becoming a force for revolutionary change. This, of course, was the source of Mills's appeal to the early New Left, which then as later was primarily a student movement. Since the New Left failed to last very long, Mills's intellectuals were transmogrified or, as it were, "Marxified" into a new class, both by former New Leftists anxious to find a more solid social base for a radical politics than the student movement and by the neoconservatives who were seeking to identify a collective agent responsible for all the changes they deplored in contemporary politics and culture.

In its recent incarnation the very term "new class" was borrowed from political dissidents in the Communist world, notably from Milovan Djilas's courageous 1957 book with that title. Although I shall concentrate on the democratic capitalist societies, those groups described as a new class in both the capitalist and the Communist worlds do have common features. Moreover, the earliest versions of a new class theory were put forward before the division into two worlds, that is, before the October Revolution in Russia.

The New Class: Is It New?

Many of the occupations of the new class have a long history antedating the rise of capitalism. Several of them—doctors, lawyers, journalists, some kinds of teachers, municipal officials— have always been regarded as representative members of the bourgeoisie, which never consisted solely of merchants, tradesmen, and manufacturers. The overthrow of the *ancien régime* freed the learned or mentally skilled occupations from dependence on the church, the monarchy, and aristocratic patrons, enabling them to sell their services in a wider and more anonymous market paralleling the new commercial and entrepreneurial freedoms won by the owners of productive resources. The interests of the two groups converged in abolishing exclusionary privileges, territorial monopolies, and rigid social hierarchies unrelated to function.

The social transformations since the sixteenth century have involved not only the triumph of capitalism but also the process that Reinhard Bendix has called "intellectual mobilization," or "the growth of a reading public and of an educated secular elite dependent on learned occupations" (1978: 266). The expansion of learning and intellectual freedom was not a mere by-product of the expansion of trade and production, except in the obvious sense that the economy sets limits to the scope of activities not directly related to the satisfaction of basic material needs. It has never made sense to treat the learned occupations as mere adjuncts to a ruling capitalist class. The so-called new class has been with us for a long time, and it has sustained complex relations of interdependence with capitalists, or with private owners of the means of production in the strict sense.

What about the political and cultural attitudes of the new class, which account even more than the growth of its occupations for the recent attention it has received? Have not these attitudes become increasingly hostile toward business and the bourgeois ethos? A little historical perspective goes a long way, even if presented in autobiographical form.

I am myself a fourth- or fifth-generation member of the new class (though perhaps downwardly mobile within it). My paternal grandfather, who was an academic historian, became interested in his old age in his genealogical roots. In a privately printed "Chronicle of a Family," he noted that the Wrongs have never displayed much aptitude for making money, although their ranks have included doctors, lawyers, professors, clergymen, and civil servants—a veritable roster of old "new class" occupations. My maternal grandfather was also a professor (of classics) and he too descended from a long line of people in the same occupations, though with a much greater preponderance of Anglican country clergymen—literally members of "the Establishment."

I might have said that my grandfather remarked "sadly" on his family's lack of business acumen—his own father went bankrupt twice, once as farmer and once as small-town storekeeper, and my grandfather lost a lot of money in the 1929 crash. However, he made the observation with an unmistakable note of satisfaction. And therein lies the major relevance of this saga to my subject. A contempt for money-grubbing, a distaste for capitalists, or people in "trade," as persons of crass and limited vision, a commitment to what were seen as the higher things of life, a belief in service, whether to God, to learning, to the state, or to an exalted profession—all these values were characteristic of the noncapitalist segment of the bourgeoisie to which my forebears belonged. So it had been well back in the early nineteenth century, if not earlier.

My immediate ancestors were Anglo-Canadians, only recently removed from England. Perhaps they reflected the blend of aristocratic and bourgeois culture for which England is noted. But what of the United States, that most purely capitalist country of all, notoriously lacking any prebourgeois past? I was brought up, in fact, to think of most Americans as rich and vulgar. Yet much the same outlook prevailed among the learned professions in New England and the Northeast in general; this "genteel tradition" provided one basis for the Progressive movement early in the century. There were, moreover, close ties between the Anglo-Canadian intelligentsia and that of the northeastern United States. Dean Acheson, for example, a friend of my family who was always described as "aristocratic" in bearing, was of Anglo-Canadian origin through both parents. Since his father was Episcopal bishop of Connecticut, he was also born a member of the disestablished American counterpart of the original Establishment.

This old "new class" spawned its own opposition. The *locus classicus* was Nietzsche's attack on the "educated philistines." Nietzsche, like Dean Acheson and my maternal grandfather, was the son of a Protestant minister; my paternal grandfather was himself a minister before becoming a professor of history. The Protestant ethic, whatever they may have made of it, was a living reality to all of them. Rejection of its narrow, repressive, and quintessentially "bourgeois individualist" aspects was central to the avant-garde culture of modernism, and it often found diverse forms of political expression. In the 1960's, strands of the antibourgeois "adversary culture" were taken up by young people and then commercially exploited. They also assumed left-wing political accents, although as recently as in the 1930's many of the same themes had been central to reactionary movements.

It was, however, a transitory moment and recent interpreters scarcely agree on its significance. For Christopher Lasch, the resultant "culture of narcissism" reflects a decadent capitalism whose main agents are the therapeutic professions. For Daniel Bell, the popularized antibourgeois culture of modernism threatens the rationality and discipline required by the economy. For the neo-conservatives, the rejection of traditional bourgeois values is part of a political attack that a new class has launched on capitalism.

Certainly, the highbrow culture of modernism and the pop counterculture of the 1960's are antithetical to the traditional bourgeois values of both businessmen and the old "new class" of the learned professions. But, lacking any inherent tie to an anticapitalist political mass movement, the values of this culture are also open to commercial exploitation in vulgarized form and are readily assimilable as personal culture, or even lifestyle, by the educated. Capitalism may still require rationality and work discipline but, Lasch and Bell notwithstanding, I see no reason why someone cannot work hard all day at the office or laboratory and seek hedonistic gratification in the evening. Human beings are capable of prodigious feats of compartmentalization, and economic change has increasingly separated the spheres of work and leisure.

Bourgeois values themselves just as much as antibourgeois values can be turned against capitalism or neocapitalism, as Lasch's example demonstrates. Fernand Braudel and Ernest Gellner have both remarked that the most significant thing about capitalism is that nobody invented it. It is a condition rather than a theory, a condition whose survival does not depend on the ideological indoctrination of the population living under it. Like the flush toilet—which was, to be sure, invented—capitalism may be accepted as a utility needing to be tinkered with, or as an unfortunate necessity for which no palatable alternative is available. Recent Marxists have greatly exaggerated the degree to which the supposed "ideological hegemony" of the bourgeoisie perpetuates capitalism. A matter-of-fact, often grudging acceptance of capitalism based on its manifest success in raising standards of living, the work imperatives of everyday life, and fears of revolutionary disruption have been more potent conservative forces than any ideological belief in the ultimate rightness of the system.

Yet surveys in the 1970's revealed an unmistakable departure from the old, post–New Deal correlations between class and what are regarded as "liberal" or "conservative" views on various issues.[1] The change was greatest when measured by educational level, and educational differences held within broad occupational categories —professional, managerial, white-collar, blue-collar. Not surprisingly, they were most marked with respect to "social issues," the more educated holding more favorable attitudes on divorce, abortion, formerly tabooed forms of sexual behavior, and equality between the sexes. But educational differences were also present on more directly political and economic issues, with the well-educated favoring less economic growth, more government spending on urban problems, environmental protection, and education itself; they also favored busing and affirmative action to achieve racial integration, and less defense spending. On foreign policy, the more educated, in sharp contrast to the past, were more isolationist, showing a greater inclination to oppose American commitments abroad and to doubt that "communism" threatened the United States. Apart from personal impressions, these survey data provided the main basis for the claim that a new class had emerged with a distinctive, antitraditional outlook of its own.

The evidence was scarcely overwhelming. For one thing, the differences were not very great except on the moral or "lifestyle" issues and, to a lesser extent, on environmentalism and economic growth. Most of the surveys were taken in the middle and late 1970's, before subsequent sharp declines in employment and economic growth and at a time when the "Vietnam syndrome," obviously more prevalent among the educated, still governed attitudes toward foreign policy. Inevitably, many of the issues these surveys touched upon are less salient today. One doubts whether the educated and relatively affluent remain as indifferent to concerns of

economic growth and the standard of living in general. Some of
the imputations to the new class of coherent and shared political
and economic interests already sound dated.

The parochially American ideological preoccupations of the
neoconservatives are revealed by their failure to look beyond the
borders of the United States when they employ the new class concept. Not only do they never mention its namesake and possible
counterpart in the Communist world; they do not even look com-
paratively at other capitalist countries. If "postindustrial" capitalism has really produced a formidable new class with political aims
that express its interests, then, like the old bourgeoisie and the old
working class, it is presumably not confined to a single country.

Yet one need look no further than Britain to wonder about the
alleged political unity of the new class. Witness the split in the
Labour party that produced the Social Democratic party. Labour
loyalists have argued, and the evidence seems to bear them out,
that the SDP is primarily a middle-class party appealing to the
very occupational and professional groups that American neoconservatives have called new class. The SDP is clearly not a party
of the business community committed to unrestricted free enterprise, but its leaders quit the Labour party because they opposed
the growing power of its Marxist-inclined left wing. The SDP fa-
vors a mixed economy giving far greater scope to private capital
and market forces than does the Labour left. But the Labour left
too is hardly proletarian in composition and support. Its activists
have variously been described as "polytechnic Marxists" and even
as a "bourgeois lumpen-intelligentsia"; the left's strongest union
support comes from public-sector and white-collar unions.[2] The
followers of both Roy Jenkins and Tony Benn therefore represent
the new class, though perhaps different segments of it. The interests and political outlook of this class are evidently more diverse
and ambiguous than the American neoconservatives suggest. Indeed, the neoconservatives oversimplify the relation between politics and imputed class interests as greatly as doctrinaire Marxists.

Still, the increase in the numbers of the educated and the
occupations requiring educational credentials has undoubtedly
weakened the past identification of many in these groups with
the business community and the Republican party. There are

even structural preconditions for the changes reflected in the new lifestyle differences, although hedonistic self-fulfillment and tolerance of sexual variety are continuous with the values of sexual therapists and reformers, bohemian countercultures, and the one-time literary avant-garde dating back at least to the late nineteenth century and the Edwardian era. The bureaucratization of capitalism severs the link between productive property and family stability that took the form of permanent marriage and fixed rules of descent and inheritance.[3] The erosion of puritanism and Victorian morality fits in well with the way credentialism has replaced both accumulation and hereditary transmission of private property as the basis of class position.

Is It a Class?

Have credentials and the declining importance of private property produced a genuine new class rather than a congeries of diverse interest groups?

New class theorists have always moved in the ambience of Marxism. Indeed, the proletariat was the original new class assigned the mission of realizing a new social order by expropriating private owners of the means of production. Anarchist opponents of Marxism in the late nineteenth century argued that Marxism itself was the creation of bourgeois intellectuals masking their own aspirations to collective power by claiming to represent the proletariat. Recent versions of new class theory have resuscitated this idea; they modify it in seeing "intellectuals" not as marginal or deviant persons of bourgeois origin but as an occupationally rooted intelligentsia brought into being by the technical and organizational imperatives of industrial society.

Somewhat earlier, such groups as engineers, technicians, and salaried managers were put forward in place of the proletariat as the new class destined to supplant the bourgeoisie and reorganize society. Berle and Means's famous study and Burnham's sweeping claims in *The Managerial Revolution* precipitated an interminable debate over the significance of the separation of ownership from management under corporate enterprise. But the precise relationship between the new "new class" of professional and scientific intelligentsia and the old "new class" of managers remains some-what obscure. Burnham himself has pungently remarked: "Who hires and fires whom? How many men can Norman Mailer or Walter Cronkite set in motion when he picks up the telephone compared to Harold Geneen or to What's-His-Name at the top of IBM? Come now" (quoted in Bazelon 1979: 447).

Burnham turned conservative well before the emergence of the "neo" variety, and he certainly no longer regards managers as a rising anticapitalist class already in power in the Soviet Union, with people like Harold Geneen representing its vanguard in the United States. Today neoconservative new class theorists lump owners and managers together as the embattled old capitalist class under challenge by a "new class" of the intelligentsia. On the other hand, writers who have taken a more approving view of the latter fail to distinguish sharply between managers and the professional/scientific intelligentsia, though separating both from old-style owners. B. Bruce-Briggs (1979a: 16–17) has done a val-iant job of identifying three distinct groups in the upper reaches of American society that figure in these discussions: a "traditional bourgeoisie" of rentiers, business owners, and "free" professionals; salaried managers and engineers in the profit sector; and "intellec-tuals" who are salaried professionals in the nonprofit sector. The latter "new class" is, of course, the bête noire of the neoconserva-tives.

The problem remains as to whether there are real class bound-aries separating these groups. Alvin Gouldner (1979) differentiates the "intellectuals as a New Class" from the old "monied" or "prop-ertied" classes, which they are destined to supplant in the West, and also from the Communist party ruling elite in the East. Gould-ner agrees that there is a major trend under capitalism toward the replacement of owners by managers, and he includes the latter as part of the new class. He cites Frank Parkin, who has argued that conflict between the professional/scientific intelligentsia and the political elite in Communist countries is much more acute than that between their equivalents in the "late-capitalist" West (1982: 574–87).

One groans at the thought of all the ink expended on tedious and eternal disputation over definitional distinctions between "class," "stratum," and "elite." It is worth noting, however, that

Parkin writes of conflicts between elites rather than classes. Andrew Hacker, who with Gouldner has made by far the most sensible case for the importance of the trend toward managerialism under capitalism, bluntly affirms that "Mills's term, 'elite,' is clearly preferable to 'class,' since it refers to individuals only for as long as they remain the occupants of particular institutional positions." He adds: "The very conception of a 'ruling class' militates against understanding capitalism today" (1979: 161).

It scarcely makes sense to draw, with the neoconservatives, a class line between those employed by the public or nonprofit sector and those working in the private or profit sector when so many members even of the old professions—for instance, law[4]—move back and forth between the two sectors. The public/private distinction, however, "brings the state back in" (in Theda Skocpol's phrase) with a vengeance and the state was, of course, always there when the new class concept was applied to Communist societies. The state is currently a fashionable subject among academic social theorists, some of whom write as if its very existence had only recently been revealed. This is especially true of Marxists eager to grant at least a "relative autonomy" to the state as they abandon the economic reductionism of traditional Marxism. Some Marxists have even written of a "state bourgeoisie" in both Communist and capitalist societies, an oxymoron that surely confuses more than it illuminates. Neoconservatives, on the other hand, have attributed dark "statist" aspirations to the educated but propertyless members of the new class whom they see as their political adversaries.

What all of these discoveries of new classes possessing or bidding for state power seem to have in common is recognition that collective power can be won and held by means other than ownership or control of private productive resources: it can be won by special knowledge or skill acquired through education, by office in public and private bureaucracies, and by leadership of popular political movements, parties, and even currents of opinion.

Does It Matter?

Perhaps classes, whether old or new, are no longer the chief collective actors of contemporary history, though they may have been in the past. Such a claim involves empirical and theoretical issues that transcend the question of whether or not there is a new class. I shall touch briefly on them in closing, drawing on the contributions to the 1979 Bruce-Briggs symposium by both Andrew Hacker and Daniel Bell. Hacker and Bell are alone among the contributors in forthrightly rejecting the new class concept. In addition, Hacker and Bell are, not by coincidence, among the few contributors who cannot be classified as neoconservatives. Nor are they Old Believers, whether of the left or the right, convinced that the traditional division between owners and workers remains the fulcrum of the class structure of capitalism.

Hacker begins by sharply distinguishing between the old and new versions of a new class: the managers, on the one hand, and the professional/scientific intelligentsia on the other, two groups "with almost no overlap in membership." He repeats an argument he has developed before to the effect that the aggregate of What's-Their-Names at the top of IBM, General Motors, Exxon, et al. do not constitute a class.[5] Their tenure at the top is too brief and comes too late in life, not before their late fifties or sixties and after what Mills once called "the long bureaucratic crawl" upward; their origins are modestly middle-class, and their education usually was not acquired at private schools or the more distinguished universities. Although they acquire stock in the companies they work for, they do not build up their portfolios until they are near the top and their holdings are relatively modest, far from placing them in the super-rich category.

Power, Hacker contends, resides not in a class of owners and managers, nor in one of partially owning managers, but in the corporate organizations themselves. The collectivity that wields power is the organizational structure itself in which the managers hold high positions, not a ruling class that uses and controls this structure in the service of its interests. This seems to me a much more authentically institutional, or "structural" (to use that much-abused word), view than the notion of a propertied ruling class held together by family ties and a common upper-class subculture. For those who need the authority of Karl Marx to legitimate it, Hacker notes its consistency with the discussion of the joint-stock company in the third volume of *Capital*, the discussion that

Bell once called Marx's "schema two" for capitalist development as distinct from his better-known forecast of increasing polarization of owning and nonowning classes.[6]

Individual corporate organizations are not, of course, autonomous actors. Their directorates interlock with those of other corporations and of banks and financial institutions. Critics of the original managerial revolution thesis were clearly right to insist that corporations remain capitalist profit-seeking enterprises whether they are controlled by owners or by managers, quite apart from the very considerable problems of definition and empirical measurement in determining which is which. Hacker, Maurice Zeitlin (1982: 205–7), and others have also noted that there are no marked differences in economic behavior between corporations classified as owner-controlled and those seen as management-controlled. Certainly, there are heirs of the original founding owners of the major corporations who continue to draw large incomes from them, although their money, like invested trade-union pension funds, is usually managed by professional trustees. Let us apply to them what I like to call the Saint-Simon "drop dead" test.[7] Suppose that all members of the 25,000 families in the United States owning (in 1974) over $1 million worth of paper assets, mostly in the form of stock,[8] were suddenly to expire, stricken with a mysterious fatal disease or perhaps liquidated in an unbelievably efficient Red Brigades action. Would their removal in itself change "the system," bring about a fundamental "structural" transformation of American society? I think not.

In short, the relative or absolute autonomy of corporations vis-à-vis a dominant propertied class—their relation to the state raises questions of a different order—does not mean that we live in a postcapitalist society. We do live, however, in a postbourgeois society in two senses: (1) There is no longer a ruling class of private owners of the means of production; (2) the old bourgeois culture of asceticism, the work ethic, deferred gratification, and repressive familial and sexual morality has dissolved.

As for the second "new class," Hacker dismisses it as no more than a collection of new service occupations entered by means of educational credentials whose practical value he questions in sardonic remarks and anecdotes.

Bell provides a more detailed analysis of the irreducible hetero-geneity of this alleged new class, although his earlier writings had been widely, if incorrectly, understood as supporting what he now calls a "muddled concept." Bell identifies six distinct groups: intel-lectuals, mainly scientists and scholars; creators and critics of cul-ture; transmitters of knowledge and culture; news and entertain-ment workers—usually designated as "the media"; appliers and transmitters of knowledge organized in the old and new profes-sions, and managers and bureaucrats, or the old version of the new class (1979: 182–83). These groups not only differ, but each group is internally differentiated.

More important, all six groups are distributed unevenly among five of what Bell calls situses, defined as "vertically organized locations of *interest-bound* activities": economic and business enterprises, government, universities and research organizations, "social complexes" (hospitals, schools, community organizations), and the military. The interests and allegiances of members of the new class are therefore fragmented by occupation or profes-sion and by the situs where they are employed, not to speak of the particular organizations they work for, which was true also, of course, of the old bourgeoisie. Thus there is little basis for a common interest leading to the emergence of a shared "class con-sciousness" expressed politically. Bell concludes that "the idea of a 'new class' . . . cannot be located in social-structural terms; it must be found in cultural attitudes."

Alvin Gouldner, on the other hand, adduces precisely a com-mon culture, which he calls the "Culture of Critical Discourse," to support his conception of intellectuals, both East and West, as a true new class. Evoking Marxist echoes, he even suggests that it is a "universal class" supplanting the proletariat, albeit a "flawed" one. Since I am on record as admiring Gouldner's lengthy final book, I trust that I may be forgiven for saying that his penultimate short one on the new class was not one of his happier efforts.[9] Yet even Gouldner describes there classes as "cache areas in which political organizations mobilize, recruit and conscript support and in whose name they legitimate their struggle. Classes as such are never united in struggle against others" (1979: 31). Classes, in other words, are always partly ideological constructs, although there are good grounds for thinking that this is even more the case today than in the past. Both Hacker and Bell accentuate in different ways the primacy of organizations over classes. If I may quote another older authority, completely free of any conservative taint, Hans Gerth and C. Wright Mills wrote years ago: "The bureaucratization of modern government, of corporate business life, the spread of totalitarian, one-party states may be more dynamic than all the riots, mobs, and crowds of the last fifty years put together from all over Western civilization" (1953: 417).

Future social analysts could do worse than to inscribe on their banners: "The history of presently existing society is the history of organizational struggles."

※

CHAPTER 9

Knowledge and Power: Intellectuals, Universities, and the Class Structure

By "knowledge" I mean credentialed knowledge certified according to established rules and procedures of an institution, specifically, the modern university. By "power," I mean social and political power in society at large accruing to those who have been properly certified as possessors of knowledge. I am not primarily concerned with the kind of power that may be intrinsic to the very possession of knowledge as in the Baconian maxim "knowledge is power,"[1] although the *belief* that certified knowledge is itself a source of power may be important in legitimating the status of those who possess it.

In the last two centuries there has been a general movement from ownership of land to ownership of capital to ownership of educational credentials—what some have called "cultural capital"—as the dominant route to the most powerful institutional positions. This trend towards "credentialism," or the "diploma disease," has of late come in for considerable critical attention. Much of the attention has been centered on the competitive advantages possessed by the children of those who have accumulated impressive cultural capital, thus negating, at least in a de facto sense, the universalism and equality of opportunity supposed to prevail in the competitive system of educational certification. It is here that the issues raised by quotas, affirmative action, and equality of results going beyond "mere" equality of opportunity have aroused fierce controversy, particularly though not exclusively with reference to universities and schools.

I shall comment briefly on these issues at a later point. I want first to mention two different senses in which a social hierarchy based on educational credentialism is at least formally more egalitarian than a hierarchy based on property in land or capital. First, cultural capital acquired as a result of education cannot be transmitted *directly* to one's children like land, money, control of a privately owned business enterprise, or positions filled by rules of hereditary succession. Parental encouragement and continuous intimate exposure in the bosom of the family to educated discourse and values can, as we know full well, give unquestionable advantages to children starting out on their own educational careers. More tangibly, superior schooling can be purchased by the more affluent. It may even be the case, as Pierre Bourdieu and Randall Collins have argued, that educational credentialism allows for no more upward social mobility than earlier modes of intergenerational transmission of high position through the family. But high-status parents cannot guarantee that their offspring will succeed them by clearing all the necessary hurdles involved in completing the requisite courses of study, nor can they prevent outsiders who may be "upstarts" of humble or even despised origins from gaining access to higher positions as a result of successful competitive effort. (Of course, this was—and is—also true of keeping intact inherited fortunes and maintaining successful family economic enterprises, although in these cases anxieties over the "reproduction" of social position take a different form and are usually slower to manifest themselves.) A formal meritocracy based on credentialism is, as Frank Parkin has noted, "a system designed to produce a class formation biased more in the direction of sponsorship and the careful selection of successors than of hereditary transmission" (1979: 63).

The second egalitarian tendency represented by credentialism is even more ambiguous. Perhaps a society based on educational credentialism should be considered more egalitarian than preindustrial social orders in which only a small minority of the population was even literate. Presumably, the mental gulf between an illiterate peasant, speaking perhaps a strictly local dialect or vernacular language, and an aristocrat, churchman, or bourgeois was greater than that between the holder of an advanced degree today and someone who has received only the minimum schooling required in contemporary advanced industrial countries. It does not follow, however, that differences within the limits of universal literacy, a common language, and minimal educational requirements may not in the future become wider. This possibility is a major theme of negative utopian, or dystopian, literature from Orwell's *Nineteen Eighty-Four* to Michael Young's brilliant sociological satire *The Rise of the Meritocracy*. And here, of course, we confront the problem of what is meant by, and how exactly we measure, the steepness of the social hierarchy or the degree of inequality in power (and status).

Independently of Young's particular argument, which was closely related to debates over educational policy in the British Labour Party in the 1950's, the term "meritocracy" acquired negative overtones in the United States in the late 1960's and the 1970's. The American context was that of the civil rights movement and the efforts it stimulated to overcome the long-standing deprivations suffered by blacks in American society. "Meritocracy" was linked to the absence of "equality of results" or "outcomes," which came to be contrasted with "equality of opportunity." An equality of opportunity that was purely formal in banning discrimination against individuals on irrelevant "collectivist" grounds[2] — such as the traditional "race, color, or creed" to which "gender" was shortly added — did little to redress the actual inequalities experienced by groups that had suffered such discrimination in the past.

The idea that the achievement of formal equality of opportunity in education and employment was not enough to overcome racial inequality was initially broached by Daniel Patrick Moynihan, Nathan Glazer, and Daniel Bell.[3] The very phrase "equality of results" appears to have been first used by Glazer in the early 1960's. Ironically, all three men became critics of some of the social policies later adopted in the name of achieving greater equality of results. Glazer published a tightly argued book against affirmative action in the form of statistical requirements imposed on educational institutions and employers for the racial composition of their students or employees (1975). All these men were labeled "neoconservatives" in the late 1970's, although today none of them can plausibly be so classified, all three having taken steps to dissociate themselves from recent manifestations of that political tendency.

Apart from the complex issues raised by some of the policies designed to go beyond the limits of formal equality of opportunity, the original, highly specific meaning of equality of results quickly became blurred in the ideological polemics of liberals, conservatives, and radicals. If after the elimination of racial or ethnic discrimination in the initial selection of candidates for jobs or education, it still remains the case that blacks and other groups once victimized by discrimination continue to be clustered at the bottom of the hierarchy of positions or the distribution of rewards (including educational grades), then clearly the elimination of discrimination in selection or access has done little to mitigate the subordinate position of the groups that suffered it in the past. The demand for equality of results, and policies ranging from Head Start programs for preschool children to rules of so-called reverse discrimination, aimed at the elimination of the persisting bunching at the bottom of racially or ethnically defined groups. This is what the term equality of results originally meant, suggesting a policy goal the attainment of which would indisputably attest to the final overcoming of the handicaps burdening minorities victimized by past discrimination. Whatever the merits or demerits of the policies proposed or adopted to try to realize this goal, this is all, it must be stressed, that the phrase itself ever meant.

Equality of results was not, therefore, a synonym for equality of condition, that is, for the elimination of *all* inequalities among individuals as well as groups. Long before the 1960's, equality of condition was regularly contrasted with equality of opportunity. Both terms referred primarily to individuals, not to groups or social categories. Clearly, equality of opportunity logically implies the persistence of some forms of inequality among individuals, for the opportunities that are equalized are precisely opportunities to compete for unequal rewards or scarce values that are not available in equal proportions to everyone. Equality of condition, however, has always meant exactly what it says: the absence of any and all inequalities, or a distribution in which everyone receives an equal share, or at least a share satisfying his or her possibly different needs in conformity with the old socialist slogan "from each according to his quality, to each according to his needs."

Equality of results, originally pertaining only to racial or ethnic *groups*, and equality of condition, implying across-the-board equality of individuals and groups, were blurred together and equated both by conservatives opposed to egalitarian social policies and by some left-liberal activists favoring more far-reaching policies. Thus the specificities and limits of the original debate over affirmative action were quickly elevated or reduced to the level of familiar ideological rhetoric about equality versus individual opportunity of the kind that has traditionally dominated debate between conservatives and liberals.

Since the student revolt of the 1960's, the university has been the main locus of radically egalitarian political outlooks. The incongruities and ironies this suggests have not escaped notice. My friend the late Irving Howe once remarked on the presence of "guerrillas with tenure" in the ranks of the New Left of two decades ago. Parkin has noted the prominence in the 1970's of a "professorial Marxism" in Western universities and commented that the "new breed of Marxists" are as eager to storm the Winter Palace as the older kind "provided that satisfactory arrangements could be made for sabbatical leave" (1979: x).

Howe and Parkin succumbed to the temptation to be funny, but conservative and neoconservative writers have made a great deal more of the real or apparent contradictions between the left-wing views of contemporary intellectuals and the sinecured jobs in the academy held by most of them, guaranteeing them a secure income and an assured audience while whetting their appetites for greater power in the larger society. So at least runs the negative version of the theory of the new class. Despite the fact that it is favored by conservative defenders of capitalism, the theory is unmistakably of Marxist provenance: the ideology of the academic intellectuals makes universalist claims in calling for more equality, but in fact expresses the particular collective interests of a sectional group that can only be realized at the expense of the interests of other groups, especially the unlettered and uncredentialed. For none other than the academic intellectuals themselves will lead political movements striving for greater equality, will fill high offices should such movements win governmental power, and will administer the programs and policies implementing the movement's egalitarian ideals. This is a classic illustration of the Marxist theory of ideology here turned against those most likely to be sympathetic to Marxism. And, of course, liberal-left writers pejoratively labeled new class by such Marxising conservatives have not failed to point out that their critics and adversaries are indisputably intellectuals themselves, most of them with berths in the academy, that their ideas—to put it mildly—won a respectful hearing from the Reagan and Bush administrations, and that the corporate leaders they eulogize are not without material resources and have not been averse to bestowing them upon their intellectual defenders in the form of foundation support for individual writers and publicists, new conservative policy journals, and conferences held in luxurious settings at home and abroad. By now we have had ample polemics back and forth, left and right, on this topic, and the law of diminishing returns with regard to further enlightenment has doubtless been reached.

The idea that knowledgeable persons certified as such by their educational credentials form a class bidding for social and political power has become widely accepted by analysts of diverse political persuasions who are animated by more serious intellectual purposes than scoring points off their ideological enemies. This idea has a long history in the modern era; it was at least adumbrated by such pre-Marxist thinkers as Saint-Simon and Comte despite the Marxist resonance of the very conception of classes as collective political and historical actors. Since then "new class" theories have seemed to pop up in every generation, many of them stressing knowledge or certified expertise as a source or mode of access to power, privilege, and prestige—the three p's of social stratification or institutionalized social inequality. Perhaps the continual excited discoveries of emerging new classes that do not owe their position to private ownership of the means of production, like the bourgeoisie, or to the possession of nothing but labor power, like the proletariat, merely attests to the hold that Marxist categories have had over our minds, even the minds of those who are not Marxists in any doctrinal sense. For there have always been non-propertied bases for social and economic power: military prowess and holiness or access to supernatural forces in preindustrial societies; administrative office, ideological rectitude, and political popularity, as well as knowledge, in modern societies.

The possessors of scientific, technical, and professional knowledge—the "intellectuals," or the "intelligentsia"—have been only one of a number of candidates for new class status. Others include bureaucrats, managers, and party officials in one-party totalitarian states. Recently, to be sure, educational credentials have been required to an increasing extent for at least initial entry into the hierarchical ranks of bureaucratic officialdom, both public and private. The much-publicized pursuit of MBAs and the expansion of schools of management and public administration even in countries other than the United States are evidence of this. Educational credentialism has thus been extended to positions in organizations formerly governed by strictly internal rules for promotion within their distinctive hierarchies. This is also true, as several critics have pointed out, of the military.

Such a development obviously enhances the importance of the university as the credentialing agency for a growing number of occupations and entry-level jobs in large organizations. However, the actual role played by knowledge fundamentally differs among the various groups proposed as new classes or components of a single new educated class whose position is based on knowledge acquired through formal education. Veblen and Burnham long ago imputed increasing collective power to scientists, engineers, and technicians in view of their growing functional indispensability in industry. Scientific experts exemplify Bacon's "knowledge is power" in the most direct and literal way. Moreover, of all the occupations included in the composition of variously defined new classes, pure and applied scientists are the only authentically new ones that do not antedate the modern era, as doctors, lawyers, administrators, professors, publicists, state officials, and party politicians most definitely do.

But the non-scientific professionals and "humanist" intellectuals who have been featured most prominently in recent discussions and polemics about putative new classes do not (with the arguable exception of lawyers) possess knowledge that is functionally indispensable to the economy. Indeed, as B. Bruce-Briggs remarks, "academic dissidence is concentrated in the subjects that are least necessary to the workings of the industrial/capitalist system" (1979b: 196). Such knowledge is not seen as a source of power in its own right, but as providing the content of a common culture or language, a shared set of values, endowing its possessors with social cohesion often grounded in an oppositional attitude towards the conventional, conformist, or "philistine" values of the majority of the population. So much is implied by Trilling's phrase "the adversary culture," which has loomed large in recent debates over the intellectuals as a new class.

Finally, there is the MBA phenomenon: the spread of educational credentialism to beginning jobs and in some cases promotional prospects in public and private organizations where in the past purely internal criteria of selection or evaluations of on-the-job performance prevailed. The new credentialism, as Charles Perrow has pointed out (1972: 56–58), helps erode the venerable distinction between line and staff positions within bureaucracies. Although what is learned in schools of business and management no doubt contributes something to administrative know-how and competence, it is obvious that managerial authority was exercised more or less effectively before academic degrees became a requirement for or entitlement to it. The professions might be regarded as the reverse case in that, as Eliot Freidson has observed (1968: 34), professional authority explicitly derived from certified knowledge has tended to assume many of the features of the authority of office in an organizational hierarchy.

Can one really regard a *galère* of computer scientists, engineers, professors of the social sciences and humanities, schoolteachers, bohemian artists, junior corporation executives with freshly minted MBAs, and army officers who must nowadays earn advanced degrees in economics or international relations to rise above the rank of major as constituting a coherent class? It seems equally far-fetched to label them all "intellectuals" simply because they have all been exposed to some higher education as a condition for acquiring or holding their jobs. Statements such as "the university is the Trojan horse through which the intellectuals seek to bring ever wider sections of the economy and society under their control" (Konrad and Szelényi 1979: 26) are scarcely credible. The authors of this statement, George Konrad and Ivan Szelényi, attribute common material interests rather than shared values to "the intellectuals" and have been deservedly criticized for making such an assumption (by Cohen 1983: 499–504). One might claim with greater plausibility that the university, an institution or organizational situs rather than a class,[4] has a material interest in promoting a credentialism that requires candidates for an ever-increasing number of occupations to pass through its doors.

In any case, the idea that intellectuals are a class or the creators of an ideology that has been taken up by a new class of cultural capitalists or propertyless but credentialed jobholders must be rejected. The concepts of "intellectual" and "intelligentsia" need further examination in order to identify the glamour—and the pathos—that make them so evocative today while indicating at the same time their historically time-bound nature.

If intellectuals are simply defined as the bearers of specialized knowledge or the transmitters of esoteric traditional lore in prescribed institutional roles, they have clearly existed in all moderately complex societies. They may also be defined more specifically as a universal social psychological type: as personalities driven by an intense ambition "to convert as wide a range of experience as possible into conscious thought" (Malraux 1941: 396), or as "persons with an unusual sensitivity to the sacred, an uncommon reflectiveness about the nature of the universe, and the rules which govern their society" (Shils 1982: 179), or as "those who exhibit in their activities a pronounced concern with the core values of their society" (Coser 1965: viii), to mention a few useful characterizations. Clearly, such persons may be found in any society or historical era. But the term "intellectuals" itself was first coined in the plural form less than a century ago to refer to some French writers and thinkers who had issued a manifesto in support of Alfred Dreyfus.[5] And it was in the wake of the Dreyfus case that the term was first used honorifically in the United States by William James, in 1898 in *The Nation*. The term "intelligentsia," which is itself a collective noun, originated about forty years earlier in Russia to describe a generation of educated gentry that had become critical of czarist backwardness and authoritarianism.

Both historical contexts suggest that intellectuals tend to be protesters against or dissenters from powerful established groups or institutions, which they oppose as dishonest and oppressive. But it would be a mistake to regard intellectuals as virtually by definition on the political left, a "herd of independent minds," in Harold Rosenberg's marvelous derisory phrase, to whom alone certain universal, counterfactual moral and political truths have been vouchsafed. The identification of intellectuals with the left has become conventional in recent decades because the defeat of the Nazis and fascists discredited the political right and shifted the ideological spectrum leftward, at least verbally. Such an identification is especially common in the United States because until recently there have been few right-wing or conservative intellectuals in its history. Russell Jacoby, for instance, in his influential *The Last Intellectuals* (1987), tends to treat the idea of a conservative intellectual as a self-evident contradiction in terms, and he has been rightly criticized by reviewers for having done so. Perhaps tacit recognition of the dissident, adversarial posture of the first as well as of Jacoby's "last" intellectuals explains why contemporary self-styled "conservative" publicists like to picture themselves as intrepid battlers against an entrenched academic and media establishment despite the support they receive from wealthy foundations and their close identification with and influence in the Republican party.

But in both nineteenth-century Russia and early-twentieth-century France the appearance and high visibility of dissenting intellectuals quickly produced adversaries to oppose them with counter-ideologies in the form of systematic statements of belief and principle that went far beyond routine ritualistic legitimations of existing institutions. If left-wing intellectuals came first, in short, it did not take long for right-wing intellectuals to appear, often recruited from those who had become disillusioned with the other camp. Nowadays it is frequently forgotten that as recently as just before the Second World War many of the most prominent and admired Western intellectuals, particularly among the literati, were reactionaries and even fascist sympathizers, although they were usually as fiercely antagonistic to existing society as their opposite numbers on the left. "The Waste Land" was hardly a lyrical celebration of the status quo!

As the reference to T. S. Eliot suggests, cultural and artistic innovation, or at least a positive attitude toward such innovation, is also central to what William Phillips once called "the intellectuals' tradition." Ezra Pound's injunction "make it new" was the hallmark of avant-garde aesthetics. If Marx and Freud have been what someone—Susan Sontag, I think—once called "the two great tutelary deities of the Western intelligentsia," or the "Smith brothers of modern thought," in Jack Beatty's jocular designation, intellectuals have also been defined by their enthusiastic support for the full range of modern movements in literature, music, painting, the plastic arts, and architecture.

These brief and banal observations nevertheless make it plain that intellectuals cannot be equated with the incumbents of institutional positions involving symbolic activities or the transmission of ideas and values. In fact, the incumbents of such positions have often enough been the major targets and adversaries of representative modern intellectuals from exhibitors in the *Salon des Refusés* to mockers of pedantic, dry-as-dust professors, epithets that are less common than they used to be since so many who might once have bandied them about have become professors themselves. Intellectuals, accordingly, have at least since the coinage of the term been perceived and have perceived themselves as maintaining a certain distance from any institutional attachments and a certain coolness toward those who seem too securely attached.

Jacoby has drawn a sharp contrast between the "public intellectuals" of the past, whom he pictures as addressing a wide audience of concerned citizens on major public issues, and contemporary academics who, preoccupied with tenure, promotion, and professional standing, speak and write only for their colleagues in specialized disciplines within the university. Jacoby's *The Last Intellectuals* (1987) is essentially a long lament over the disappearance of the former breed, largely, as he sees it, owing to the academicization of American cultural and intellectual life. He manages to dredge up just about everything that has ever been said against the American university from Veblen early in the century to the present day. Jacoby's label "public intellectual" has become generally popular and is often used as an encomium bestowed on anyone who appears on "serious" TV panel shows or writes for

nonspecialist periodicals. It is, however, a thoroughly misleading label. Jacoby's "last intellectuals" were essentially the group
commonly identified as the "New York intellectuals," with the
addition of a few prominent unconnected radicals and mavericks.
The passing of the New York intellectuals without their being replaced by any true descendants is by now generally recognized;
Irving Howe's account of them (1968), which initially gave them
their name, was essentially a requiem. Their range and influence
has been exaggerated in retrospect, for they were a small and isolated circle who largely wrote for each other in low-circulation
magazines of eternally precarious financial status. Their intended
audience, namely themselves, was for the most part no larger than
that of contemporary academics who write for their colleagues in
specialized disciplinary journals. That the New York intellectuals wrote better, more lucidly, wittily, and less pretentiously in a
jargon-free prose, as Jacoby correctly reports, cannot therefore be
explained by their occasional aspirations, mostly unfulfilled, to
reach a wider audience, although the retreat into the university of
the generation following them may indeed account for the scho-
lastic ponderousness and proclaimed scientificality of the latter's
prose.

Jacoby may well be right to doubt whether academics should
virtually by definition be classified as intellectuals, whether "public" or "private," rather than regarded simply as jobholders or, to
give them a more exalted label, as professionals, some of whom—
like some schoolteachers, doctors, lawyers, or journalists—may
qualify as intellectuals while others do not. This is not to say
that intellectuals are no more than an aggregate of independently
formed like-minded persons, nor that they are an entirely self-
selected group like some cults and sects. The initial use of the
term as a noun in the plural form and its later use as synonymous with "intelligentsia" are significant. Lewis Coser correctly
captures the social but noninstitutionalized nature of the habitat
of "men of ideas" when he identifies "eight institutional settings
for intellectual activities: the salon; the coffeehouse; the scientific
society; the monthly or quarterly review; the literary market and
the world of publishing; the political sect; and, finally, Bohemia
and the little magazine" (1965: 4). Daniel Bell remarks of the kind

of collectivity typically formed by intellectuals that "by some odd linguistic quirk I do not understand, almost all the words one wants to use to describe this begin with the letter *c*: coterie, clique, circle, cenacle, club, college, chapel, curia, and so on" (1980: 125). The fragile, often ephemeral nature of these settings and social formations is obvious.

Things have changed as we move towards the end of the twentieth century and the academicization of just about everything. The doctrines of Marx and Freud have been thoroughly absorbed into the academy. Freud's have been medicalized rather than academicized, especially in America and contrary to his own hopes and wishes. Since the 1960's the pervasive academicization of Marxism signifies not its strength as a political movement but rather its decline and domestication, the university having long been the graveyard of dead or dying religious and political faiths. (There were Jacobites at Oxford well into the nineteenth century.)

As for the avant-garde in the arts, it has become a cliché to note its conversion into an establishment and to speak of the present as a "postmodernist" period. The great modernist artists have become standard fare in university teaching and the objects of scholarly industries rather than models for emulation by creative aspirants or the cult heroes of invisible colleges of admirers. Not all that surprising a development perhaps, for no one in the past expected Renaissances or Periclean Ages to last forever. The late nineteenth and early twentieth century now takes its place as one of the great creative periods in history that come along every few hundred years or so.

The academic absorption and encapsulation of both political radicalism and aesthetic modernism has resulted in their dissociation from one another. Despite the sentimental populism of the Communists and the enthusiasm for popular culture and antagonism to highbrow elitism of the 1960's New Left, the twentieth-century intellectual has characteristically combined political dissent with a taste for complexity and innovation in the arts. By now time and change have almost completely sundered what once went together; it is hard to realize today how much it used to be almost taken for granted that there was a profound and intrinsic affinity between leftist political sentiments and aesthetic avant-gardism. Marxism and literary modernism are typically regarded as having been the defining interests of the New York intellectuals as well as of their predecessors earlier in the century, whom John Patrick Diggins (1992) calls "the Lyrical Left," and whose most prominent latter-day representative was Edmund Wilson. The mournful query *"où sont les Wilsons d'antan?"* is posed by Jacoby as well as many others.[6]

Victor Brombert has written that the idea of the intellectual "remains bound up with the notion of a social, political and moral crisis. Better still: it implies *the notion of a permanent state of crisis"* (Brombert 1983: 107; original italics).[7] Brombert asserts only that there may be a "notion" of permanent crisis, not that crisis itself as an actual condition might be permanent. Does it make sense to think of crisis as a permanent state? Not in its original medical usage, from which the term has been metaphorically extended to refer to immaterial mental and social states of being. The conception of a permanent political and cultural crisis is as illogical as that of a perpetual Renaissance in the arts. Intellectuals who indulge in such rhetoric are, I daresay, guilty of "false consciousness."

More probably, they are still living in the shadow of the first half of the twentieth century, which, as we have seen, witnessed the birth of intellectuals as a self-conscious, loosely integrated, largely self-selected collectivity. The first fifty years of this century, more specifically, the period from 1914 to, say, 1950, were years of apocalypse to a degree virtually unmatched in the historical record. They continue to dominate our language and imagination, which is still chiefly the imagination of disaster. It is rarely noticed, and even felt to be a bit improper to suggest, that since 1950 stability, continuity, and at most recurrent minor cycles of change have generally prevailed rather than the economic breakdowns, wars, revolutions, and rise of passionate new ideological movements sweeping all before them that so unforgettably marked the early part of the century. The collapse of Communism in 1989–91 ended the near-stasis of the post-1950 world and unleashed considerable social, political, and economic change, much of it of a disturbing and unpleasant nature. Perhaps it will be the occasion for the appearance of new kinds of intellectuals outside the university striving to formulate solutions to unprecedented problems; more probably, the absorption of intellectual life by the academy and the economic and ecological changes cited by Jacoby that have destroyed bohemian shelters for independent intellectuals eliminate this possibility.

We tend to think of the last half of the previous century, the late Victorian Age, as a period of unparalleled peace and relative comfort, the high tide of bourgeois civilization, which was abruptly shattered by the guns of August. Yet as we approach the end of the present century, the last fifty years have been comparably placid and, one ventures to suggest, rather more culturally stagnant. This applies, to be sure, only to the advanced nations of the West, not to the Middle East, China, Southeast Asia, or Africa, where upheavals and catastrophes of considerable magnitude have continued to occur. One recalls Sir Edward Grey saying prophetically on the eve of the First World War, "The lamps are going out all over Europe," a remark that I feel was first quoted to me when I was in my cradle. Our vastly expanded global awareness today inhibits our awareness of the unprecedented stability achieved by democratic industrial-capitalist societies.

If intellectuals are products of social crisis and their ranks are thinning today because crisis is relatively absent in the late twentieth century, what, then, accounts for the widespread belief that they are becoming numerous and powerful enough to amount to an ascendant new class? The answer lies partly in nothing more than conceptual confusion. Intellectuals traffic in ideas and symbols and there has indeed been a vast expansion in the number of occupations that deal primarily with ideas and symbols, from what used to be called the learned professions to new high-technology fields; in addition, new educational credentials are required in old positions of power and pelf. The perception of "intellectuals" as "on the road to class power" is particularly understandable in the case of the otherwise valuable book of that title by Konrad and Szelényi, for they were writing from Eastern Europe "before the fall," where not only was educational credentialism especially rampant but Communist regimes claiming to represent an ideology once ardently supported by many Western intellectuals had restructured the social order.

The exaggerated claims made for intellectuals in the Western democracies represent a halo effect, a desire to bask in the aura of the great dead gods of dissent and modernism by the growing numbers of people engaged in humdrum, routinized occupational pursuits that include some deployment of ideas and symbols and require higher educational credentials (including most university teaching). The assaults by neoconservatives on the alleged new class of intellectuals reflect the familiar need of intellectuals to see themselves as children of light pitted against dark forces and stifling conformity, in this case the alleged domination of the academic world and the media by post-1960's leftist ideology. It seems unlikely that this particular line can retain plausibility for much longer; if I may repeat an earlier remark of my own (1981: 102), neoconservatism as a recognizable beast seems to be disappearing, the "neo" fading last of all like the smile on the face of the Cheshire cat. The presence, however, of a conservative outlook among men and women of learning, taste, and talent is not an aberration reflecting the venality of a few intellectuals who have been "turncoats" or "sellouts," but represents what has usually been the norm in human societies. When Trilling wrote in 1950 that "in the United States at this time liberalism is not only the dominant but even the sole intellectual tradition . . . for it is the plain fact that nowadays there are no conservative or reactionary ideas in general circulation" (1950: lx), he was describing a situation that is unlikely to recur even in the United States, let alone elsewhere. And this is so for more substantial reasons than the inevitable fading of memories of the real or imagined association of the political right with fascism.

Conservative men and women of ideas will, of course, continue to find critics and adversaries, many if not most of them located in the university, advocating reform and change in our institutions. But the conception of "intellectuals" or "the intellectual community" as speaking out on most issues with a single voice, let alone forming a coherent class, even one with purely self-serving political aims, is likely to pass from the scene. Intellectuals were the product of the greatness and grandeur of nineteenth-century bourgeois civilization, an antibody to it, certainly, yet nevertheless bound to it as its distinctive creation. I have a distaste for "neo-"

and "post-" prefixes—I once wrote that there were enough posts in modern social thought to make a picket fence—but our civilization can accurately be described as "postbourgeois," though the extent to which this represents an unqualified advance remains open to argument. A more far-reaching possibility is that classes themselves as major collective historical actors may have been peculiar to the bourgeois-capitalist era, which would make the constant search for new classes itself an anachronistic irrelevancy.

✥

CHAPTER 10

The Influence of Sociological Ideas
on American Culture

My aim in this chapter is to identify broadly concepts and notions originating in academic sociology that have entered the awareness, or at least the vocabulary, of Americans during the past half century. Surprisingly few discussions, let alone empirical investigations, exist of the influence of sociological thought on the beliefs and attitudes of Americans. On the other hand, the reverse relationship, that is, the influence of American culture and society on American sociology, has been examined to a fare-thee-well, the sociology of knowledge having become a recognized perspective and even an established subfield.

The relevance of sociological researches to public policy has, of course, been widely acknowledged. Sociologists have collected data bearing on social policies and have sometimes played a role in formulating and even executing policy in various areas. Criminology and demography are two major subfields, antedating the birth of sociology itself as an academic discipline, that were always tied to the activities of governments. The impact of sociology as a "policy science" on American society is not, however, my concern in the present chapter. I am interested in the less direct, often highly nuanced, influence of themes and ideas, including mere catchwords and popular labels, that have diffused from academic sociologists to some segments of the American public.

Sociology Within the University

The first and most direct influence of sociology and sociological ideas has inevitably been on its own students and on
colleagues and students in neighboring disciplines within the university. When I encountered sociology for the first time as an
undergraduate in the 1940's, the field was still infused with a missionary spirit. My teachers continually emphasized its newness,
conveying the definite impression that it had come into being
only yesterday, challenging the older disciplines in the university,
especially the other social sciences. These were often pictured
as ancient bodies of lore hopelessly addicted to antiquated conceptual formulas utterly incapable of grasping the dynamic realities of the twentieth century. Not surprisingly, the hostility to
sociology of representatives of the older social sciences and the
humanities gave added plausibility to this view of sociology as
gadfly, maverick, and intrepid intellectual pioneer, assaulting the
complacencies and gentilities of the established academic order.
Several professors of history tried to dissuade me from majoring as
an undergraduate in so newfangled and disreputable a pseudodiscipline, deigning to bestow such attention on a lowly sophomore
only because it so happened that my grandfather had founded the
university's history department and my father had also briefly
taught history there. Both of *them*, needless to say, also regarded
sociology as a presumptuous upstart of little or no value.

It was quite some time before I realized that all of the social sciences and most of the humanities were not much more than half a
century old as clearly demarcated subjects of instruction and fields
of research. Sociology was at most only a decade or two younger
than the others. If it pretended to a youthfulness to which it was
not truly entitled, most of the other academic disciplines fell back
on traditionalist legitimations that also lacked solid foundation in
reality.

Sociology's sense of mission and insistence on its youthfulness
had roots in the global intellectual reach of the early-nineteenth-
century philosophers of history. Auguste Comte, the name-giver
of the field, was but one of the thinkers whom Frank Manuel has
called "the prophets of Paris," and Paris was but one of the locales

where social and historical prophecy flourished in the high noon of the modern era. The institutionalization of sociology as an academic discipline diluted and restricted the prophetic role assigned to it by Comte. The fledgling sociologist of fifty or so years ago was usually admonished that he or she should aspire to no more than the status of humble laborer in the great unfinished temple of science, content to lay the small brick of a modest piece of completed empirical research on the slowly rising walls of an edifice whose ultimate completion lay far in the future.

Such diffidence failed to mollify practitioners of the other human disciplines, who continued to take a skeptical view of the totalistic ambitions of the collective enterprise no matter how self-effacing a posture was assumed by its individual servants. Even the more modest quest of latter-day sociologists for limited "middle-range" generalizations as opposed to sweeping sociohistorical laws seemed to downgrade the patient accumulation of knowledge about highly particularized persons and events that characterized the humanities. The inclination of sociology to present itself as what C. Wright Mills called "the methodological speciality" also appeared to devalue the scholarly labors of those who were more interested in their subject matter than in the methods they used to examine it. Nor did the subordination of topic to method quite eliminate the apparent boundlessness of the area— human social life in all of its manifestations—that sociology aspired to conquer as the Comtean "queen of the sciences," the *scientia scientorum*. The critics of sociology from the other disciplines with their more clearly defined and delimited fields of inquiry were not, therefore, altogether wrong in detecting remnants of the grandiose programmatic project of the nineteenth-century fathers in the more modest "value-free" union of theory and research that became the goal of their mid-twentieth-century successors.

Debunker of Popular Beliefs

The identification of sociology with science building on the model of the natural sciences was primarily relevant to interdisciplinary relations within the university. In confronting nonaca-

demic publics, sociology has often presented itself as the relent-
less critic of popular belief, the debunker of hoary folklore and
social myth, the exposer of alleged common sense as common
prejudice and even nonsense. This particular rationale for the existence of sociology has proved more durable than the goal of creating a science, which has come under widespread attack within
sociology itself since the 1960's with the result that "positivism"
has acquired inescapably pejorative overtones. Some years ago no
less a figure than Robert K. Merton (1961) advanced this "scourge
of popular fallacies" justification for sociology in the *New York
Times Magazine* in attempting to rebut the conventionally "hu-
manistic" antisociological strictures of Russell Kirk.[1] Introductory
textbooks frequently if not habitually present as the main task of
sociology the scrutiny of popular opinions and attitudes, which
are invariably declared to be unsupported by sociological data and
deformed by ideological biases endemic to the American or the
bourgeois or liberal or capitalist way of life.

One sometimes receives the impression that the authors of
introductory textbooks see themselves as addressing an allegedly
typical American who is frozen in the attitudinal and ideological
postures of the late 1930's or the early 1940's, the era when major
publishing houses began to produce their own comprehensive
lines of textbooks covering all subjects taught at the college level.
The typical American of the texts naively believes in windy "July
Fourth oratory" denying any class differences in the United States;
he is full of nostalgia for the small-town life depicted in Norman Rockwell's legendary *Saturday Evening Post* covers though
himself a resident of a big city; he is convinced that a woman's
place is in the home, and that homosexuality and premarital and
extramarital sexual intercourse are morally wrong; despite formal
denials he remains incurably "racist" and antiforeign in his attitude toward those who are not middle-class white Anglo-Saxon
Protestants like himself. Textbook writers quite often to this day
cite the Lynds' famous chapter "The Middletown Spirit" from
Middletown in Transition, published in 1937, as an accurate description of *prevailing* American "values" or "culture," although
elsewhere they are apt to emphasize the tremendous changes they
see America as having undergone in the past half century, particu-

larly when contemplating a president like Ronald Reagan, who unapologetically embodied the older attitudes. Reagan, come to think of it, actually took courses in sociology in the 1930's at a small-town college in the Midwest.

The assumption that Americans are forever committed to a set of beliefs that run counter to sociological knowledge certainly suggests that the teaching and diffusion of sociology must be a peculiarly futile enterprise. Millions and millions of students have taken introductory courses and have been assigned textbooks and books of readings. Many of the people who report the news and current affairs in both the print and the nonprint media are, though they usually were not fifty years ago, college graduates who have been exposed to and quite often even majored in sociology. A fair number of professional politicians and officials in the executive branch of the federal government have studied sociology more fully, and more recently, than Ronald Reagan.

The Interaction of Topic and Resource

Textbook authors are perhaps a special case. Yet in the past most sociologists were inclined, at least implicitly, to regard sociology as providing a completely autonomous and independent point of view quite distinct from that of the human subjects it studied. The latter were seen as contaminated and, therefore, atypical if they had encountered and been influenced by sociology in college courses. Back in the 1950's, a researcher on class structure in the new suburbs wondered cautiously whether "the awareness of class differences might in some part be due to the social science courses these suburbanites took during their undergraduate days." "May it not be," he went on to ask, "the voice of sociology feeding back on itself through the voice of a corrupted respondent?" (Dobriner 1963: 37). Today, after the antipositivist revolts inside sociology in the 1960's, we are less disposed to insist on, or even to regard as desirable, a total insulation of "topic" from "resource," to use the language of ethnomethodology. Few sociologists would nowadays deny or deplore the inescapable and ubiquitous interaction between sociology and a wider public whose views on many matters have been increasingly shaped by the transmission of sociological ideas through media ranging from formal education to television.

The impact of sociological perspectives on the very opinions and behavior of the human beings that constitute the subject matter of sociology as a discipline has been recognized as a crucial epistemological difference between the human sciences and the natural sciences. Far from being no more than intriguing oddities, Merton's "self-fulfilling" and "suicidal" prophecies reflect possibilities inherent in the relationship between social science and its object domain. Only a hermetic insulation of social scientists from their lay subjects—at least *after* the former have gathered their "data" from the latter—might eliminate the infection of the subjects by the findings and conclusions about themselves presented in diverse public forums by social scientists.[2] Such insulation savors of authoritarian rule by an elite of protected experts. The repudiation of this possibility, which seemed implicit in such phrases as "social engineering" that were popular a few decades ago, has contributed to the prevalent skepticism about science building or "positivist" models for sociology.

The Sociology of Sociology

The opposite extreme from the conception of a totally independent sociology is to treat sociology as nothing but a particular reflection of the social realities it pretends to study from a delusive vantage point of Olympian detachment. Two decades ago, at the peak of the revolts against the "establishment" then allegedly dominating sociology, there sometimes seemed to be more sociologists of sociology than students of the social world outside the academy that was the field's ostensible subject matter. Facile, crudely reductive readings of sociology as a mere reflection of the times, often of the ideological coloration of whatever political party happens to be in office, are legion. Only slightly more subtle interpretations have imputed ineradicable national or class or ethnic or secularized religious biases to various sociological standpoints. In regarding sociology as possessing its own partly autonomous intellectual tradition, one need not reject altogether such influences. One can accept what has been called the "weak program" in the sociology of knowledge while disavowing the "strong program" as reductionist. I am, in any case, prepared to make the assumption that familiarity with the leading ideas of sociology amounts to more than merely the adoption of a new language in which to couch a preexisting awareness of contemporary life.

Neither the view that sociology partly shapes, nor the opposed view that it merely reflects, the beliefs and attitudes of the society in which it is practiced sustains the spirit of missionary enthusiasm that pervaded the field in my youth. If sociologists merely rationalize the ideological tenets and cultural presuppositions of their own society or some subgroup within it, they were never the prophets they evidently took themselves to be. If, on the other hand, they have succeeded to some degree in converting their audience, then their message no longer comes across as a new dispensation, although it may have done so in the past. Charles Page has observed: "Among outsiders in recent decades much of sociology's rhetoric and bits and pieces of its substance have become 'common knowledge,' thereby diminishing its status as a popular field that nevertheless requires special study" (Page 1985: 6). The sociological researcher who assumes that he or she is exploring a pristine social world untainted by previous exposure to the thoughtways of academic sociology may find him- or herself in the undignified posture of a dog chasing its own tail.

How can one identify the source of an idea common to both academic sociologists and a larger public? Given that both groups are reacting to the same external reality, they may have independently come to perceive it in much the same way: great minds and small—or at least sociologically untutored—minds may think alike. Whatever the original source of the idea, the fact that it is shared by experts and their subjects or clients may reinforce its authority in the eyes of both. Such convergences of outlook may be more frequent than unilateral influence in either direction. A "sociological idea," in short, need not be the exclusive property or creation of academic sociologists, although my interest here is in ideas that are at least widely held and disseminated by them.

Catchwords and Clichés

At the most obvious and direct level, a few terms of unmistakable academic sociological provenance have passed into popular parlance, or at least into the common argot of journalists. "Charisma" and "charismatic" are the most visible—painfully so, one is constrained to add in election years—and have been so promiscuously used that they are now freely applied to just about any politician able to hold an audience's attention for longer than several minutes. There is a woman's dress shop in Brooklyn named Charisma, which advertises on local television. A few years ago a boutique named Gemeinschaft existed on the Upper West Side of Manhattan. The term "lifestyle" is even more ubiquitous than "charisma" and also derives from Max Weber. In his Sunday *New York Times* column "On Language," William Safire traced "lifestyle" to the psychoanalyst Alfred Adler, in whose theory of personality it played a prominent part. I am fairly sure he is mistaken that this was its source.[3] Adlerian psychotherapy was never very popular in America. "Lifestyle" is of more recent origin: the term spread like wildfire at the height of the student protest movements of the late 1960's. As is well known, sociology students played a leading role in these movements. They were familiar with Max Weber on the "style of life" of status groups and often extolled their own "alternative lifestyles" as a revolutionary break with the past while damning the materialistic, "consumerist," suburban, or bourgeois "lifestyles" of their hopelessly unredeemed parents and teachers. However, in treating "lifestyle" as a psychological notion, Safire correctly gauges a movement away from its original sociological, that is, collective, connotation when people speak of "my" lifestyle as a personal possession like "my" toothbrush, pet goldfish, or soft brown eyes. True, it is also still used as a synonym for a shared set of beliefs and habits, a "culture," or, closer to the original Weberian usage, a "subculture." But the blurring of the line between the individual and the collective is itself a very American tendency.

Sociology as Social Criticism and Worldview

I shall now make a leap from these simple examples of sociological terms that have become banalities through overuse to a much more uncertain realm of vague and inchoate sociological "ideas" affecting the outlook of Americans, bypassing altogether Page's more restricted "bits and pieces of [sociology's] substance" that have shaped public definitions of social problems. I want to discuss three such ideas or themes: (1) the loss of community and the wish to recover it; (2) society made us, so we should not be blamed; (3) the social construction of reality, or we made society and can remake it into something different.

1. The claim that the greater size, territorial scope, and internal differentiation of modern society have robbed individuals of close, lifelong, protective group memberships is almost coterminous with the birth of sociology itself. It was, of course, asserted earlier in broad terms, most saliently by Rousseau. The classical sociological version of the emergence of modernity is the transition from *Gemeinschaft* to *Gesellschaft*, with emphasis on the dissolution of community and the alienation of the individual as the painful outcome of the process. "Alienation" and "anomie," counterconcepts to "community" specifying just what has been lost as a result of its decline, have become only slightly less popular outside the ranks of sociologists than "charisma" and "lifestyle." Here if anywhere is the central or root idea with which sociological thought confronts the modern world. Consider the following roster of familiar phrases: "the quest for community," "the eclipse of community," "the need for roots," "the alienation of modern man," "the lonely crowd," "the pursuit of loneliness," "escape from freedom," "the homeless mind," "the world we have lost." All of these were titles of books by social scientists published in the past forty or fifty years, some of which reached a large, nonacademic reading public.

The "search for community" has become virtually the standard sociological explanation for just about any new social phenomenon. It plays the same all-purpose explanatory role for American sociologists that the ever-impending final crisis of capitalism has long played for Marxists. It was invoked to account for the

populism and class solidarity of the 1930's, the appeal of totalitarian ideologies to the atomized "mass man" of the 1940's, the
baby boom and the great migration to the suburbs of the 1950's,
the discontents of "alienated" student protesters in the 1960's, the
proliferation of new religious cults in the 1970's, and the rise of
a New Right committed to Christian fundamentalism and traditional family values in the 1980's. It is hard not to greet with a certain skepticism the recent insistence by a number of prominent
social scientists that today, in the wake of the so-called Me Decade, Americans are yet again experiencing a yearning for community; a sense that their present social bonds are "superficial, transitory and ultimately unsatisfying"; a "hunger for deeper social
relationships," greater "spontaneity," and more "expressive" rather
than "instrumental" ties to others; and "tremendous nostalgia . . .
for the idealized 'small town.' "[4]

  We have heard all this many times before and there may be less
to it than meets the ear. A former president of our Association,
Herbert Gans, suggests in his book *Middle American Individualism* that recent authors of what he calls the "communal critique"
of American life have placed "a heavy load of cultural and political expectations on community and on actual communities which
neither can bear" (Gans 1988: 113). Nor does Gans miss the note
of moral censoriousness underlying the critique. The people inter-
viewed by social researchers are unlikely to have had no inkling
of it. They can, in any case, hardly be expected to declare that all
their ambitions have been realized and that their lives are without moral blemishes or spiritual deficiencies. Casting about for an
appropriate, fairly toothless critical gambit, they may very well
come up with what might be called, in the mode of George Bush,
"the community thing." The wish for more community may, accordingly, have no greater significance than the ritualistic expression of a hope for more love, peace, and altruism in the world; indeed, complaints about the lack of community may, not to put too
fine a point upon it, amount to just such a pious hope expressed
less sentimentally in what is taken to be the more acceptable "objective" language of academic social science.

  2. Social determinism and its limits have always been a major
theme in sociological thought from the belief of the nineteenth-

century fathers in "iron," naturelike laws governing society and history to contemporary theoretical debates over the relative importance of "agency" and "structure." The contention that "social conditions," or "social forces," or the imperatives of the "social system" or capitalism or whatever, powerfully shape the lives we lead comes as close as anything does to having been the essence of the sociological outlook from its beginnings. Clearly, it lends itself to a wide range of morally exculpatory uses by individuals. The mocking song of the delinquent youths in *West Side Story* claiming to be victims of poverty and "broken homes" is only the most obvious of such uses.

Yet one of the standard beliefs attributed to Americans by introductory sociology textbooks is their readiness to assume individual moral responsibility for the circumstances of their lives, praising or blaming themselves alone as the case may be. This attitude is often interpreted as a secularized echo of the Protestant ethic, or as congruent with the economic individualism allegedly buttressing a capitalistic market economy. It is also sometimes treated as the antisociological illusion par excellence that sociology aspires to correct. "Individualism" is identified with a belief that human beings are fully formed by biological or psychological influences that operate independently of, or at most underlie, variations in culture and social structure. Treating such a view as the dominant popular one allows sociologists to swing into their ancient rain dance intended to exorcise biological and genetic factors as well as undue stress on differences in individual personality, whatever their origin.

"Individualism" is often regarded as a characteristically American ideology. If so, it surely illustrates the apparent futility of the sociological enterprise to which I previously referred, for a larger public has been exposed to sociology for a longer time in the United States than in any other Western country. Since the 1930's, the stock example of the imputed tendency of Americans to blame themselves as individuals for social conditions clearly beyond their control has been unemployment of a cyclical or structural nature (in the economist's language). I remember C. Wright Mills expatiating on this example in class when elaborating his well-known distinction between personal troubles and public issues, or milieu and structure. But there is obviously a great deal of evidence that Americans, as their voting behavior since at least the New Deal demonstrates, regard the economy as a supraindividual system that can be managed more or less effectively by the government. Americans are certainly "individualists" in Herbert Gans's sense of wishing to "obtain personal control over the general environment so as to minimize threat and unwanted surprise, and in order to lay the groundwork for self-development" (1988: 2). But this need not entail any insistence on the primacy of biological or individual psychological determinants, nor even ignorance of the distinction between micro and macro levels of social reality, or the collapsing of the latter into the former. It does imply, however, a preference by "middle Americans" for what Gans calls their "micro society" of informal personal and family relations as opposed to the "macro society" of large-scale formal organizations and impersonal market forces and, it should be added, social and political mass movements.

3. This sociological theme appears to be the direct opposite of the preceding one. Although there is no reason why the public mind, or, for that matter, sociologists themselves, might not entertain contrary ideas at the same time, the "we" implicitly refers to different groups in each case. The "society made us" dictum is applied primarily to lower-class victims of poverty, racial discrimination, or negative labeling for deviant behavior. Exemplifying what Paul Hollander (1973) has called "selective determinism," it lends itself to easy conversion into the left-wing taboo against "blaming the victim." On the other hand, the voluntarism as opposed to determinism implicit in the "social construction of reality" formulation refers to humanity at large as a collective actor. It insists on the fact that society and history are the products of human actions rather than effects of divine ordinance, invariant social laws, or a historical fatality working silently "behind men's backs." When beliefs and practices are described as "socially constructed," the meaning is much the same as that intended in calling them "culturally patterned," as was more commonly done not so long ago.

There is a difference: "Social construction" suggests that institutions are the products not, certainly, of any unitary collective will or plan guiding action like the blueprint for a building, but at least of intersecting, frequently clashing wills or plans. The clear implication is that the existing order, any existing order, despite its seeming solidity, or—as the phenomenologists like to say—massive "facticity," is nothing but a human artifact, a thrown-together contraption, an exercise in *bricolage* quite unworthy of sanctification and lacking the impersonal inevitability of natural law. Applied to the future, however, the phrase communicates the promise that what has been constructed can be altered and improved, a wing added here, a barrier broken down there, the foundations strengthened and broadened. Or the whole building can be demolished and replaced with something more satisfactory. There is an echo here of Marx's contrast between prehistory and history. The popularity of the "social construction" image is largely accounted for by the possibility it projects of far-reaching planned social change, which gives it special appeal to sociologists of a left-liberal persuasion, that is, to the vast majority of sociologists. Ironically, the two authors most responsible for the popularity of the concept, Peter Berger and Thomas Luckmann (1966), are fairly conservative fellows not at all disposed to regard what has been socially constructed as ephemeral and insubstantial, ready to be instantly razed for rebuilding.

The phrase, with its particular resonances, is largely limited to sociologists. The "social construction of reality" has certainly not become a household cliché like "charisma" or "lifestyle" or even formulations of the other two sociological ideas I have discussed. Yet awareness of the purely manmade and largely provisional nature of the social order has, I think, entered popular consciousness, and the diffusion of sociology deserves some credit or blame for this. It perhaps represents sociology's major contribution to the "relativist" outlook complained of by conservative thinkers such as Allan Bloom.

"To our customs and beliefs, the very ones we hold sacred," Raymond Aron (1984: 76) has written, "sociology ruthlessly attaches the adjective 'arbitrary.'" This goes to the heart of the matter. The arbitrariness, the humanly invented and makeshift character of our routines and institutional practices, is the most general and also the most pervasive impression transmitted by sociology to a wider public. Modern men and women are conscious of having been thrust into a world they never made, but unlike most men and women of the past they know it was made by other people not so very different from themselves rather than by God, natural law, or deep-seated covert historical forces. Sociology is, therefore, an agent of disenchantment.

But if the notion of "social construction" seems to delegitimate the present order by regarding it as the contingent outcome of a series of historical accidents that might easily have produced something different, it also throws into question confidence in progressive social change. If it accentuates the vulnerability and precariousness of the status quo, it also casts doubt on the grounding in social reality of efforts to reform or transform that status quo. If social constructionism lends support to the convictions that "things don't have to be the way they are" and that it is possible purposefully to "make the world over" in the image of our most cherished ideals, it also robs the left of any assurance that its project is rooted in immanent currents of change reflecting powerful underlying social forces.

Social constructionism amounts to final and total abandonment of the nineteenth-century belief in laws governing society and history comparable to the laws of nature discovered by the physical sciences. Marxism, only occasionally convergent with "bourgeois" sociology in the past, represented the most elaborate version of the claim that history was subject at least to "tendential laws" that could be looked to for political guidance. But since at least the 1960's, the most fashionable readings of Marxism, especially by American sociologists in sympathy with it, have been voluntaristic rather than deterministic and entirely congruent with social constructionism. The political lesson of social constructionism would seem to be that "where there's a will, there's a way," understood, of course, in collective rather than individual terms. But this constitutes a reversion to utopianism. Moreover, optimism of the will, in Gramsci's phrase, is likely to flag in periods of stability such as the present.

Sociology, therefore, provides no comfort for radicalism any more than for necessitarian arguments of a conservative character. In this sense, it may have contributed both to what has been called the "end of ideology" and to "legitimation crisis." Indeed, it perhaps suggests that ultimately these are twins, different aspects of the same thing, rather than the opposites they are usually represented as being.

CHAPTER 11

Professional Jargon: Is Sociology
the Culprit?

Over forty years ago Lionel Trilling wrote: "A specter haunts
our culture—it is that people will eventually be unable to say,
'They fell in love and married' . . . but will as a matter of
course say, 'Their libidinal impulses being reciprocal, they acti-
vated their individual erotic drives and integrated them within
the same frame of reference.'" Today the same spook still haunts
us, although the fear is rather that people will say, "They accom-
modated to their conflictual lifestyles and maintained a viable ongoing relationship." Trilling's example of what he called the "language of non-thought" was largely drawn from the terminology of
psychoanalysis; my updated version uses the jargon of sociology—
even "lifestyles," now a tiresomely popular cliché term, comes
from the greatest of sociologists, Max Weber.

A few years before Trilling, George Orwell wrote his famous
essay "Politics and the English Language," included in innumer-
able anthologies for freshman English composition courses and
rightly a canonical text for all word watchers and purifiers of language. Orwell begins by reproducing five "representative samples"
of bad English prose circa 1946; the only one by an American
is full of phrases like "institutional approval," "institutional pattern," "the social bond." Later in the essay, Orwell brilliantly trans-
lates the "the race is not to the swift, nor the battle to the strong"
passage from *Ecclesiastes* into lifeless, abstract modern English

—a feat that critics of contemporary language have ever since repeatedly but less successfully tried to imitate with other examples of classical prose. Many readers today would instantly describe Orwell's American sample and his parody of the Bible as "sociologese" attributable to the baneful influence of academic sociology. But Orwell knew nothing of sociology, which scarcely existed in England at the time he wrote, and the author of his American specimen (though Orwell forebore to name him) was none other than Paul Goodman, that man of wide-ranging creative and intellectual interests who liked to describe himself by the old-fashioned name "man of letters."

There's no denying that most sociologists write very badly, but so do most psychoanalysts, psychologists, and educationists (itself an offensive word), not to speak of most administrators both public and private. If Trilling parodied the mindless use of psychoanalytic language, he was also an outspoken admirer of Freud and believer in the essential truth of what psychoanalysis has to tell us about the human condition. By contrast, the condemnation of sociological prose has usually involved an outright condemnation of sociology itself. Undoubtedly, pretentious and portentous writing has since the 1940's drawn heavily on sociological language. Yet since sociology is hardly the sole or even the main offender, one must inquire as to why it is so often seen as the outstanding culprit in addition to facing the primary question as to why sociologists do indeed tend to write badly.

Sociology has drawn the lightning mainly because of its claims to intellectual imperialism ever since Auguste Comte coined the word (itself an illegitimate coupling of a Latin prefix and a Greek suffix), declared it the "queen of the sciences," and saw sociologists as the future high priests of a new religion of humanity based on positive science.

Later sociologists have deprecated Comte's vast ambitions, but something of the breadth of his original claims has still remained implicit in their insistence that they bring to the understanding of human life in society new techniques and instruments of scientific investigation designed to replace the "mere" insights and bookish learning of traditional scholars. The guardians of our literary culture have eagerly pounced upon the failure of sociologists to deliver on their promises and discharged upon them their antipathy towards science itself. (A weakness of C. P. Snow's "two cultures" thesis was his failure to consider the in-between, no-man's-land position of the social sciences.) Sociologists have counterattacked that the humanists are just defending their academic turf against vigorous, invading newcomers. Humanists reply that sociologists try to borrow from the prestige of the natural sciences by aping their technical language to conceal the emptiness and banality of what they have to say, which at worst amounts only to calling a spade a manually operated digging implement, at best to gauche reiterations of folk wisdom, at its very best to no more than labored restatements of what Shakespeare or Dr. Johnson or Dostoyevsky or the chairman of the Harvard (or NYU) English Department have said before with elegance and economy.

This debate is by now an old and tired one, itself a species of sociological reductionism overpreoccupied with whose academic bull is being gored. In recent years, the scientific pretensions of sociology have been widely assailed within sociology itself by writers who have newly discovered various European antipositivist intellectual traditions such as phenomenology, existentialism, English analytical philosophy, and Hegelian or "humanist" Marxism. Contemporary philosophers and historians of science—most notably, Thomas Kuhn—who have argued that natural science itself is not "scientific" in the old sense have also powerfully reshaped the self-definitions of sociologists. One wishes one could report that the abandonment of claims to scientific status and the consequent need to strive for an arcane, pseudo-technical vocabulary has led to better, more lucid and graceful prose. But, alas, such is not the case: if anything, sociologists critical of the effort to model sociology on the natural sciences write in an even more abstract, prolix, and syntactically bizarre style than those they criticize.

Here is a horrible example, admittedly from a letter to the organizer of a conference rather than from a published work:

Most of what passes under the title of ethnomethodology merely assumes the constraint of interrelation between actor and idea, solipsistically reducing things to idea, and in no fashion explicates the external or dialectical constraint between the reciprocally delimitative predicate membership of things such as actors, ideas and language adequately depictive of their relation.

My specimen echoes professional philosophical discourse, especially that deriving from German idealism. Except when it violates (as it does here) rules of syntax, there is nothing objectionable in itself about this way of writing: its abstractness and ponderous epistemological self-consciousness are inseparable from the intense straining for universality, for a language that transcends the particular and the commonplace by breaking through its own limits, that characterizes the great critical philosophers. Moreover, most of them, including Kant and Hegel, were capable of writing vividly and eloquently on concrete matters, as were such "difficult" social thinkers as Marx and Weber. My example, however, is by an American and I fear that one would be only too justified in doubting whether someone who writes such English is capable of expressing himself with clarity on anything much more abstract and complicated than a note to the milkman. (One also hears complaints, incidentally, that the language of Racine and Descartes has been corrupted by the immense prestige of German thought in France since the Liberation.)

The late Talcott Parsons has often been assigned major responsibility for the awfulness of sociological prose. Parsons studied in Germany, introduced a number of leading German social thinkers to an English-speaking academic audience, and for forty years it was habitually said that his books read like translations from the German. He certainly wrote clumsily and opaquely, but he was genuinely trying to raise the theoretical consciousness of Anglo-American sociologists by enumerating systematically the most general common features he thought underlay all social— and, indeed, all human—experience. One may question—as many, including myself, did—the huge significance Parsons attributed to this enterprise, but it undeniably required a formidably abstract level of thinking and writing. Neologisms, especially in the form of hyphenated nouns ("role-expectation" and "pattern-variable" were two Parsonian favorites), were scarcely avoidable—

there are, after all, occasions when it is useful and appropriate to classify a spade as a manually operated digging implement. Yet when Parsons wrote, as he often did, on specific delimited topics such as the American family or the medical profession, his prose was heavy and undistinguished but in no way notably abstruse or impenetrable. Radicals were wont to accuse Parsonian theory of ideological obscurantism, charging that its convoluted prose was designed to support without seeming to do so that old whore, the "status quo." If so, one can only wonder what contemporary academic Marxists are concealing, for most of them write just as obscurely and Germanically.

Recent sociologists have exhibited an ugly linguistic habit which Parsons was only rarely guilty of practicing: the ready conversion of common words into different parts of speech, usually of nouns into verbs, adjectives, or adverbs. My example above, for instance, includes such non-words as "delimitative," "depictive," and "solipsistically." Several that have unfortunately passed into fairly general use among sociologists are "conflictual," "processual," "liberative," "politicality," "critique" used as a verb, and—from the Marxist camp—"commoditize" and "hegemonize."

Slovenly monsters like these defy all justification by the need to maintain a high level of abstraction or to coin neologisms that avoid the misleading associations of ordinary words. They are symptoms of plain educated (trained?) semi-literacy.

Sociologists write badly in the end for the same reasons that other intellectual and administrative specialists write badly: they lack any other language in which to express themselves on subjects that cannot easily be dealt with at the level of clichés worn threadbare by the constant chatter of the media. I have the impression that many young scholars who at first quickly adopt academic jargon eventually grow out of it as they mature intellectually. The trouble is that the jargon is picked up by the media and diffused to the half-educated who lack opportunities for continuous self-cultivation. The result, as Trilling saw it, is that more and more people become unable to express themselves except in the stilted language of academic or bureaucratic abstraction even when discussing the most vital everyday matters. Trilling's specter lurks in the vast expanding middle ground between the patter of the disc jockey or sportscaster and the specialized discourse of the academy. The task of reclaiming that ground for a common speech that is supple without being vulgar or banal is a herculean one.

CHAPTER 12

The New York Intellectuals
and McCarthyism

Few historical judgments appear so unassailable as the almost universal condemnation of the harassment inflicted on Americans accused of Communist sympathies over forty years ago. The period has been named after the politician who became most closely linked to the harassment, Senator Joseph McCarthy of Wisconsin. McCarthyism, though named after a particular person, is often used as a vague epithet or label utterly lacking in historical specificity. Politicians invoke it to counter attacks they consider unfair; some journalists and scholars equate it with any sharp criticism of domestic Communists; others broaden it to include denunciations of leftists or "nonconformists" in general. Even the most militant right-wing politicians and publicists, whose like-minded predecessors in the early 1950's would probably have enlisted in the ranks of McCarthy's supporters, are apt to complain of "left-wing McCarthyism" when accused of misdeeds by liberal critics or when protesting what they see as restrictions on the civil liberties of "conservatives."

As a historically meaningful concept, McCarthyism should be restricted to the political and legal harassment of real or alleged, past or present Communists and Communist sympathizers that took place on a national scale from 1947 through 1954. This period includes three years preceding the emergence of Senator McCarthy as the personification of the movement or tendency; the censure of Senator McCarthy by the U.S. Senate in the last month of 1954, however, provides a useful cutoff point, although the anti-Communist campaign retained a decelerating political momentum for a year or so afterward.

Three historical circumstances combined to produce McCarthyism: the cold war; the fact that the Second World War had ended only a few years before; and the Republican party's loss of its fifth straight presidential election, one that it had been confident of winning. Since the first of these, the cold war, was by far the most important, arguably not only a necessary but a fully sufficient condition for McCarthyism, I shall postpone discussing it until after a brief review of the two other causes or preconditions.

Up to a point a legitimate parallel can be drawn between McCarthyism and the Red Scare after the First World War. The earlier episode was, though shorter-lived, more extreme, violent, and diffuse, being directed against radicals of all stripes chiefly out of fear of domestic insurgence inspired by the Russian Revolution. Its main difference from McCarthyism is that McCarthyism was essentially directed against suspected partisans of an unfriendly foreign power in a new and threatening international situation. Indeed, a more appropriate comparison than with the Red Scare of the 1920's would perhaps be with the earlier wartime hostility toward all things German and toward pacifists and antiwar socialists. The Red Scare and McCarthyism were alike in that they occurred right after major wars that had aroused intense patriotic emotions but had remained geographically distant and resulted in relatively few American casualties. The upsurge of patriotic sentiment found an outlet in assailing domestic deviants and dissenters in the one case and suspected traitors in the other. One tends to forget today how large veterans' organizations loomed as political actors well into the 1950's; the American Legion was primarily responsible for the blacklist in the entertainment industry that was so salient a manifestation of McCarthyism.

A mood of desperation overcame the Republicans after their unexpected loss of the 1948 election, as has been generally recognized. The party's presidential selection process had been dominated for over a decade by its Eastern wing, moderate on domestic issues and internationalist in foreign policy, and the election defeat in and of itself increased the power of the bitterly anti–New Deal, formerly isolationist wing of the party, to which McCarthy and his supporters belonged. The shock of defeat even induced so respectable a figure as Senator Taft to proffer his famous advice to Senator McCarthy that if one accusation of disloyalty against a government employee proved unwarranted, he should keep on trying with others. I doubt that anyone would wish to argue that McCarthyism would have become a significant political force, or even be remembered today, if the Dewey-Warren ticket had been elected in 1948.

The eight years of McCarthyism coincided with the beginnings of the cold war and its period of greatest intensity. This not only made possible the conflation of external and internal threats that was the essence of McCarthyism, but continues today to lead to confusion of causes and effects on the part of some historians. McCarthyism was a political strategy for converting an alarming and complex problem of foreign policy into a bogus domestic issue: the infiltration of Communists into American government and society. Such a reduction was obviously attractive to former isolationists who were suspicious even of American foreign commitments justified by opposition to an enemy some of them hated more than they had hated Germany, Italy, or Japan. Treason at home, not the rise of powerful states overseas, was identified as the real problem, to be solved by criminal prosecutions, new laws against so-called subversion, and negative publicity to isolate persons and groups of doubtful loyalty rather than by military alliances, costly defense expenditures and foreign aid programs, and participation in international organizations.

McCarthyism reached its maximum strength when the United States became involved in a full though undeclared war with a lesser Communist state in Asia and for a time even with China, the largest and second most powerful Communist state of all. Hostility toward Communist sympathizers was also intensified by a spy scare following the discovery of several independent Soviet espionage networks involving scientists and highly placed civil servants. The entire eight years of McCarthyism were marked by widespread apprehension, often amounting to virtual expectation, that a third world war with the Soviet Union was imminent. In so ambiguous a situation, with the country neither clearly at peace nor officially at war, whether or not sympathizers with the enemy should be allowed to retain their customary peacetime civil liberties was bound to become an issue. It would have been surprising if it had not. I remember liberals with low tolerance for ambiguity wishing for a formal declaration of war against North Korea to clarify the legal situation. (Like demands were made fifteen years later during the similarly undeclared war in Vietnam.)

McCarthyism should be considered in relation to the condition of civil liberties during the Second World War. Active partisans of Germany, Italy, and Japan were deported or imprisoned; the mass internment of Japanese Americans on the West Coast simply on account of their ancestry is now seen as a monstrous injustice. The Smith Act was passed in 1940 and was soon invoked against the Minneapolis Trotskyists and assorted native fascists with the strong approval of the Communist Party. After the war, the Communists were themselves prosecuted under the same law.

During the 22 months of the Stalin-Hitler pact, the House Committee on Un-American Activities, chaired by Martin Dies, provided a preview of the behavior of congressional committees under McCarthyism in its inquisitions of Communists and fellow travelers. Ellen Schrecker, in her study of McCarthyism and higher education (1986), shows the continuity between the personnel and procedures of the New York State Rapp-Coudert Committee of 1940 and the celebrated investigative committees of Congress a decade later. A more important similarity is that in both periods the Soviet Union was perceived as hostile to the United States, in 1939–41 as the ally of Nazi Germany, with which it had divided a conquered Poland whose invasion by Germany had initiated the Second World War.

Historical interpretation sometimes requires counterfactual speculation in accordance with what Max Weber called the "method of objective possibility." Imagine a reversal of the dates of the German attack on Russia and Pearl Harbor. Or, since it is hardly credible that Hitler might have chosen to invade the Soviet Union in December, suppose that the invasion had occurred a full year later than it did. We would then have experienced in the United States, I venture to suggest, most of the manifestations of what was later called McCarthyism in the six months separating American entrance into the war and Hitler's betrayal of his Soviet ally. Doubtless we would have been spared the noisome demagoguery of congressional inquisitors like McCarthy, but the Communist Party would probably have been outlawed and its leaders imprisoned, as happened in Canada in 1939 in the very first months of the war. Communist and fellow-traveling journalists, trade unionists, professors, and entertainers would probably have come under attack by patriotic groups.

Despite what many of its opponents proclaimed at the time, and what is still widely maintained today, McCarthyism was *not* aimed at radicals, liberals, New Dealers, socialists, trade unionists, atheists, dissenters, or nonconformists as such. People in these categories came under attack only if they could be charged with past or present Communist associations or sympathies. Many were vulnerable to such charges and were attacked and often unjustly vilified, but there were also many people with left-wing or unpopular views who were left alone, never having had any Communist affiliations, although conservatives were often unable to resist the temptation to claim an affinity between even quite moderate liberal beliefs and Communist ideology.

I am sensitive, however, to one exception to this, because I complained in person about it to the then attorney general of the United States, Herbert Brownell. In 1955 or 1956 I was a panel member on a Canadian Broadcasting Corporation television program interviewing Brownell on the occasion of a visit he paid to Toronto. When we were drinking coffee after the show, I said to him that, regardless of whether or not the much-publicized attorney general's list of subversive organizations was a good idea— I had criticized it in the television interview—several Trotskyist organizations did not belong on the list because Trotskyists had been among the earliest and best-informed enemies of the present Soviet regime. Brownell quickly agreed with me and assured me that they were scheduled to be removed shortly from the list, which, in fact, came to pass. At one point, I recall, Brownell demurred mildly, remarking that the Trotskyists did, after all, advocate the "violent overthrow of the government." This nicely recalls the legal ambiguities of the situation, for he was clearly referring to the Smith Act, which proscribed the advocacy, not the commission, of acts of armed rebellion in peacetime. I believe I told him that at least one of the listed organizations, the Shacht-manite Independent Socialist League, no longer favored even in principle violent revolution.

Why are the New York intellectuals so often mentioned in connection with McCarthyism, often with the suggestion that they were complicit with it or at the very least did not oppose it vigorously? Why not the Southern Agrarians or the San Francisco Beats or the Algonquin wits? The answer is obvious: the New York intellectuals were anti-Communists, or anti-Stalinists as they preferred to call themselves, long before the cold war. Their anti-Stalinism was, moreover, the essential bond uniting them despite their otherwise highly diverse cultural and intellectual interests. Before 1945 and even as late as 1948 anti-Stalinism had a different meaning than it acquired at the height of the cold war. It involved the discovery of shocking and painful truths the proclamation of which brought no advantages to the bearers of such bad news but placed them in ferocious opposition to powerful groups in their own milieu, that is, to an important segment of the New York Jewish community and to the political world of Popular Front liberalism in the era of the Depression and the war against fascism. The anti-Stalinism of the New York intellectuals was animated by a primary concern for truth and moral principle which invariably made it a special irritant to Communists, fellow travelers, and anti-anti-Communists. The ignorant, self-serving, and mendacious anti-Communism of demagogues like Martin Dies and Joseph McCarthy, on the other hand, discredited itself among those with a grain of political sophistication. The old anti-Stalinist left again and again proved to be right not only about the Soviet Union but also about the brutal tyranny of a succession of later Communist states, most notably China, Cuba, Vietnam, and Cambodia, in which "the left" invested for a time hopes that proved to be illusory.

Cultural historians and retrospective commentators have shown an anachronistic tendency to assume that the New York intellectuals already in the late 1940's and early 1950's occupied the position of cultural authority and political weight they later attained. Thus it has been charged that they failed to "take a stand" against McCarthyism, which had the effect of aiding and abetting it at the very least. The charge is false, but even if it were true, the views of the New York intellectuals at that time were quite unknown to the general public or to relevant political elites. They were still an isolated—"alienated," they might have said—coterie of obscure, occupationally insecure artists and writers.

One historian has actually gone so far as to argue that "McCarthyism was an extension, however distorted, of the liberals' own militant anti-Communism" (Pells 1984: 77, 97–100). By "liberals" he means both the politicians and policymakers of the Truman administration and the "anti-Stalinist intellectuals," who, he claims, made common cause against Communism. This is triply wrong. The anti-Communism of supporters of the Red Scare in the 1920's and of the Dies and Rapp-Coudert committees in the 1930's owed little or nothing to liberals of any variety, and McCarthyism clearly owed much to this right-wing populist brand of anti-Communism. As for Washington policymakers collaborating with the New York intellectuals to oppose Communism, I happened to know personally Dean Acheson and George Kennan, the two major architects of the policy of "containing" the Soviet Union as well as the two top officials who could most accurately be characterized as "intellectuals." I am quite sure that neither of them had ever heard of Sidney Hook, Lionel Trilling, or *Partisan Review*, at least before the 1950's. During the year 1951–52, when I worked for him as a research assistant in Princeton, Kennan did join the American Committee on Cultural Freedom, the creation of which in early 1951 first brought the New York intellectuals to the attention of both Washington elites and a wider public. The ACCF was an unambiguous product of the cold war, specifically organized to counter pro-Soviet intellectual and cultural journals and associations in Europe and America.

Some of us were not inclined at the time to break into applause when reading Sidney Hook on the Smith Act, the Fifth Amendment, and academic freedom, or Irving Kristol on civil liberties, but it is a real ordeal to have had to endure ever since repeated rehashes of what they said. Their opinions are rehashed not in

order to affirm them, but rather to hold their authors up to oblo-
quy for the lengths to which they went in doubting that American
Communists were routinely entitled to civil liberties as much as
anyone else. And these lengths are invariably exaggerated. Hook's
defense of the Smith Act was a highly qualified one, and he did
not, as is often charged, advocate firing Communist teachers; he
merely stated that the academic authorities rather than the government should investigate them to decide their fitness to teach
according to quasi-judicial procedures—certainly a questionable
view, as I thought then and still think, but hardly the recommen-
dation of a purge. Far from justifying Senator McCarthy, Kristol
was contemptuous of him, although he was also less than chari-
table to his victims and critics. Max Eastman and James Burnham
were probably the only bona fide New York intellectuals who were
pro-McCarthy, and they resigned from the ACCF after it took a
number of actions against McCarthyism.

Hook and Kristol were highly visible as officers of the ACCF,
but their unwillingness to defend consistently the rights of Communists and their refusal to regard McCarthyism as the major
domestic threat to cultural freedom were not shared by many,
probably not by most, of the New York intellectuals. In addition
to those like Irving Howe, Paul Goodman, and Harold Rosenberg who actively criticized the ACCF from the outside, there
was vigorous opposition to Hook and Kristol, and to the positions
with which they were identified, from within the organization, an
opposition that was led by Dwight Macdonald, Mary McCarthy,
Philip Rahv, and Arthur Schlesinger Jr. The journal *Dissent*, one
of several journals created in and reflecting the New York intellectual milieu, was founded by Irving Howe and Lewis Coser in
1954 in considerable part for the purpose of dissenting from the
views of other New York intellectuals who, while opposed to Senator McCarthy as an irresponsible demagogue, were not inclined
to take him very seriously or to defend without qualification the
civil liberties of Communists. (I was the author of a full-length
article in *Dissent* on McCarthyism in 1954, the year the journal
was founded, which was also the year that McCarthy was finally
discredited as a result of the famous Army-McCarthy congressional hearings.) One cannot therefore attribute to the New York

intellectuals a single position on McCarthyism beyond refuting the slander that many of them actually supported it.

Still, this having been said, it needs to be noted that some New York intellectuals were painfully slow to grasp that they were no longer an isolated minority armed only with the weapons of truth and morality now that mass patriotic sentiment and even the state's powers of coercion had been thrown into the balance on the anti-Communist side. They continued to castigate domestic Communists, and even liberals who were still "naive" on the subject of Communism, for several years after the confrontation with the Soviet Union in Europe and Asia had won virtually the whole country over to the cause of anti-Communism.

New York intellectuals were sometimes guilty of blurring the distinction between foreign policy and domestic politics that was the sine qua non of McCarthyism. Acutely sensitive, unlike the McCarthyites, to the enhanced worldwide power of the Soviet Union, they insisted that Communism was a much greater threat to freedom and democracy than McCarthyism. This was indisputably true and was indeed persistently ignored by those labeled "anti-anti-Communists" at this time. Anti-McCarthyism was often a mask for opposition to American foreign policy, for a new, or surviving, isolationism of the left, or for neutralism in the cold war. In the United States, however, except for the limited problem of espionage and sabotage—vastly exaggerated, to be sure, by the McCarthyites—Communism was an insignificant and rapidly declining force after 1948.

McCarthyism itself went into rapid decline after 1954. The fears and obsessions of the early 1950's were dispelled very suddenly by a surprising sequence of events all of which occurred within less than four years. Stalin died, the war in Korea ended in a stalemate, McCarthy was censured by the Senate, the "spirit of Geneva"—the first interlude of what was even then called "détente"—brought about a thaw in U.S.-Soviet relations, Khrushchev's speech denouncing Stalin caused a crisis in world Communism, and the Hungarian Revolution both deepened the crisis and exposed as fantasy right-wing Republican slogans about "rollback" in Central Europe. Court decisions that struck down the major inroads on civil liberties made by McCarthyism were probably as much an effect as a cause of the altered atmosphere.

The abruptness with which McCarthyism ended makes it all the easier to accuse in retrospect various respectable and even liberal authorities, such as university administrations and faculties, of having been excessively timid or opportunistic in accommodating themselves to it. Undeniably, many institutional leaders, including university administrators, bent with the prevailing political winds against their own principles and better judgment in the belief that they were protecting their institutions from a gale of patriotic anger that could only grow stronger as war with the Soviet Union drew closer. Yet the passing of McCarthyism happened so suddenly that we are able today to look back on it as a bizarre, hysterical period of mindless malice and madness.

If McCarthyism was, as I believe, *primarily*—not exclusively, but primarily—the result of world political events that took place beyond the borders of the United States, and if its demise was also largely the result of changes in world politics, it nevertheless seems to have had a self-immunizing effect on American domestic politics. Happily, there has been nothing remotely like it since, neither during the war in Vietnam nor in the course of the militantly anti-Soviet and right-wing Reagan administration. While it is gross hyperbole to write about it, as some do, as if it were a veritable fascist era in American life, there is a point, nevertheless, in keeping cautionary memories of it alive.

※

CHAPTER 13

David Riesman:
'The Lonely Crowd' Revisited

David Riesman's *The Lonely Crowd* (1950) is inseparably linked —in name and image both—to the 1950's. The title evokes at once such themes as the spread of large organizations manned by a grey-suited "new middle class," delusive attempts to escape their reach in pseudo-pastoral suburban retreats, the flush of a new and un-expected prosperity inducing a frenzied accumulation of material goods, and an underlying malaise that expressed itself in compulsive conformity in tastes, habits, and opinions, including political opinions. This era, with these strikingly salient associated images, stands out so sharply because it was actually of rather short duration, although I often encounter younger people who equate "the fifties" with a dreary, interminably long succession of "bad old days" (rather the way my generation thought of the Victorian Age or even the nineteenth century) from which we were all "liberated" in the blessed "sixties."

In reality, *The Lonely Crowd* was published in 1950 and was written in 1948–49 when Riesman, joined by Nathan Glazer, was on leave at Yale from the University of Chicago, where Reuel Denney was a colleague. Interviews, intended to illustrate rather than confirm the book's major ideas, were conducted in 1948, and 21 of them provided the basis for a separate volume, *Faces in the Crowd*, published in 1952. The tone of both books reflects, therefore, what Riesman himself later called the "innocent optimism" of the immediate postwar years rather than the rising tide of inchoate spiritual discontents of half a decade or more later.[1] Most of the conditions with which *The Lonely Crowd* is so readily linked—affluence, rising mass consumption, suburbia, alienation, and the like—postdate it, although Riesman's pioneering insights, including those in later essays, contributed considerably to the identification and interpretation of these phenomena. The social science perspectives shaping *The Lonely Crowd* are also more representative of the 1930's and 1940's than of the 1950's.

The Lonely Crowd, subtitled *A Study of the Changing American Character Type*, argued that an older "inner-directed" American character type was being supplanted in central and even dominant segments of American society by an "other-directed" type shaped by and adapted to recent cultural and technological trends. The inner-directed character is guided by standards internalized in early childhood, by generalized values and ideals rather than by the specific detailed rules and rituals that governed an earlier "tradition-directed" character that Riesman only briefly discussed as a pre-modern forerunner of his two major types. Riesman used the metaphor of a built-in psychological gyroscope to describe what orients the inner-directed character, keeping it on a steady course in life. The new other-directed character is more sensitive to the immediate social setting than to the echoes in his or her head of parental injunctions long ago. The other-directed person is both more attuned to and more tolerant of the feelings, wishes, and expectations of other people encountered in the diverse situations of daily life. Riesman used the metaphor of a radar screen scanning the surrounding environment to describe the other-directed person, who adapts his or her responses to signals from the existing social situation.

Since character is formed primarily in childhood, shifts in the major agencies socializing children, and in the values and exemplary models held up to them, are reviewed as the proximate causes of the change in character. A good part of the book is taken up with this review. To sum up this review briefly: the nuclear family is seen as having lost ground as the prime agency of socialization to nursery and primary schools, to schools of all kinds in later childhood and adolescence, to mass media beamed directly into the home, and most of all, to the peer group of the child's age-mates, increasingly encountered at an ever earlier age in the organized settings of play groups, schools, and summer camps.

But these changes were at least in part the effects of more distant and impersonal social forces—large-scale "structural trends," as those more addicted than Riesman to sociological jargon would call them both in 1950 and today. The rise of big bureaucracies employing an increasing proportion of the labor force in white-collar jobs, technical advances bringing about a shift from the production of material goods to the provision of services, the concentration of the population in urban and metropolitan areas spreading beyond established city boundaries—these are the major trends Riesman associated with the rise of the other-directed character and other-directed values in various areas of our culture including politics, the mass media, children's books, and consumption habits.

Indisputably, the book's most original and controversial idea was the notion of other-direction and its spread. Much of the book's imaginative force came from its relating of changes at the level of everyday life—in personal and family relations, school and work routines, and leisure pursuits—to the larger, more vast economic and demographic transformations of advanced capitalism— the linkage between "micro-" and "macro-levels" of social reality, in today's preferred sociological lingo. Riesman amply exhibited what his contemporary, onetime associate, and my own teacher C. Wright Mills called "the sociological imagination," the capacity "to grasp history and biography and the relations between the two in society" (1959: 6).

Mills thought that the aspiration to achieve such a unified grasp was disappearing among his contemporaries, who limited themselves to the narrower atemporal concerns and routinized research methods of mainstream social science. He exempted a few, including Riesman, from his indictment (139, 171). Many writers have since cherished the aspiration, but few have matched Riesman's success in realizing it. Perhaps Riesman's most distinctive trait was his extraordinary psychological sensitivity, his penetrating insights into the immediate conjunction of transitory cultural images and psychic vulnerabilities grounded in the specifics of contemporary socialization experiences. Riesman's up-to-theminute sense of the zeitgeist, comparable to that of a writer like J. D. Salinger (who was at the same time drawing fictional portraits of the very kinds of people Riesman characterized as other-directed), discomfited some critics—including myself in a 1956 *Commentary* article (Wrong 1956: 337–38; also Hardwick 1954)— and may have contributed to the later tendency to treat the book as a period piece from the 1950's.

Except for rendering other-directed as "outer-directed" and misspelling Riesman's name by transposing the "i" and the "e," the most common misreading of *The Lonely Crowd* has always been to see it as a straightforward tract against other-direction in the vein of what came to be called "social criticism," a label that was invented to accommodate a genre of which *The Lonely Crowd* was just about the first specimen. The perceived counterpart of the attack on other-direction was a lament for the decline of the firm moral commitments and unyielding idealism of the inner-directed character type. Riesman declared this a misapprehension in his 1961 preface to a new abridged edition of the book (1969: xxvii), noting that it rested on an unjustified equation of inner-direction with "autonomy," the latter belonging with "adjustment" and "anomie" to an additional threefold psychological typology presented in *The Lonely Crowd*, a more universal or transhistorical one than the three historically specific forms of direction. Riesman also noted that he had defined both inner- and other-direction as "modes of conformity," so other-direction alone should not be identified with the "conformity" or "conformism" that became widely and vigorously pilloried in the 1950's. Both types could produce extreme, rigid, and irrational variants: narrow-minded, condemnatory puritanism displaying "curdled indignation" as a political style in the case of inner-direction; frantically anxious fashion-mongering and political "inside-dopesterism" in the case of other-direction.

Riesman's insistence that other-direction had its virtues—tolerance, flexibility, personal warmth—and inner-direction its defects may have been well taken. But he ruefully noted, and I can confirm from memory myself, that virtually nobody proudly or even unassumingly declared himself or herself to be other-directed, whereas people were only too ready to "confess," often with an air of false modesty, that they were, alas, incurably inner-directed. As Riesman observed in the 1961 preface: "The great majority of readers in the last ten years have decided that it was better to be an inner-directed cowboy than an other-directed advertising man, for they were not on the whole being faced with the problems of the cowboy, but rather those of the advertising man. Everybody from the free enterpriser to the socialist has come out against conformity" (1969: xxix–xxx).

As the last statement suggests, liberals as much as conservatives, those on the "left" as well as those on the "right," agreed in denouncing other-direction, even though Riesman's portrait plainly suggests that the other-directed person is much more likely to be a political liberal than a conservative. Why liberal and left-wing intellectuals should have so unanimously deplored other-direction is far from obvious from the vantage point of the present. "The other-directed person prefers love to glory," in Riesman's words, as well as cooperation to competition; his or her outlook is clearly more group centered than individualistic, while tolerant of deviance and cultural variation—all traits and values commonly associated with the left rather than with the right. More recently, "caring" and "compassion," extolled to the point of becoming clichés by liberals, are unmistakably more consonant with Riesman's other-directed orientation than with inner-direction.

The case of Ronald Reagan suggests additional ambiguities. Reagan's proclaimed verities echoed old-fashioned American values, and his small-town midwestern and Protestant upbringing locates his origins in a quintessential inner-directed milieu. Yet his entire prepolitical career was in radio, the movies, and television—a more other-directed locus is scarcely imaginable. Indeed, in the opening chapter of *Faces in the Crowd* Riesman selected an interview with a Hollywood scriptwriter to introduce and exemplify the very concept of other-direction (1952: 22–25). In his political career, Reagan's stage presence, superb timing, and empathy with the sentiments of his audience—all other-directed interpersonal skills par excellence—earned him the reputation of "The Great Communicator" and have been seen as the very foundations of his political appeal.

Riesman would doubtless classify Reagan as an instance of

an other-directed style with inner-directed content, and he has also recognized the existence of the reverse type—such as a high-minded socialist with a passionate commitment to the ideal of communal living. There is rarely if ever a one-to-one correspondence between any typology and the complexity of reality. It is to Riesman's credit that he acknowledged the prevalence of blends and compounds of his basic types. But his admirably nuanced awareness of possible discrepancies between explicitly affirmed values and the manner or underlying psychological tone with which they are held points to fundamental, unresolved problems in his work. The existence of different levels of character, and the precise location of the line of division between culture and character itself, are issues that cannot in the end be evaded (Wrong 1956: 332–35; Gutman and Wrong 1961: 302–7).

In any case, other-direction quickly became identified with the imputed mindless conformity and gullibility of "mass man," with hypocritical—if unconscious—pretensions to sincerity and intimacy in even the most casual of personal relations, with a chameleonlike adaptability to any company one was presently keeping, suggesting an inner emptiness and lack of true convictions. Woody Allen's movie of some years ago, *Zelig*, caricatured a totally and indiscriminately other-directed man. Allen himself, as well as Saul Bellow, Irving Howe, Susan Sontag, psychoanalyst Bruno Bettelheim, and historian John Morton Blum (who make brief mock-serious appearances as talking heads in the movie), undoubtedly remembered the ubiquitous anathematizations of conformity in the 1950's to which Riesman's diagnosis of the changing American character was so readily assimilated. Allan Bloom in his surprise bestseller *The Closing of the American Mind* perceives a link between *Zelig* and other-direction (1987: 144–46). He proceeds, however, to a new and bizarre distortion of *The Lonely Crowd* that deserves comment in view of the attention his book has received.

The Closing of the American Mind is a long and passionate denunciation of contemporary education since the 1960's, bewailing the increasing neglect of the timeless wisdom enshrined in the great books of the Western past, especially the Greek heritage. Bloom's major target is the value relativism of modern thought, extending, as he sees it, even to tolerance for totalitarian political regimes; he lays the blame primarily on German philosophy, especially on left-wing versions of the ideas of Nietzsche and Heidegger. An important early channel for the diffusion and popularization of their views was, we are repeatedly told, *The Lonely Crowd*, whose author had been profoundly influenced by the refugee psychoanalyst Erich Fromm. Bloom, reversing the temporal succession of Riesman's two main types, construes inner-direction as the new enlightened tendency celebrated by Riesman and other trendy intellectuals engaged in Americanizing the potent brew of Nietzsche and German existentialism. Other-direction represents the "bourgeois" norm despised by all men of thought and virtue, and previously denigrated by, in addition to Nietzsche and Heidegger, such German intellectual giants as Marx, Freud, Weber, and Hannah Arendt.

This is ludicrous, to say the least. Bloom perpetuates the error of earlier writers in interpreting *The Lonely Crowd* as unconditionally favoring inner-direction over other-direction. But he goes far beyond this in regarding inner-direction as equivalent to an extreme individualistic antinomianism, to, in effect, a Nietzschean transcendence of good and evil, vulgarized as the "do your own thing" ethic—or anti-ethic—of the culture of the 1960's, to Bloom the source of all that is most reprehensible in American life. Erich Fromm was indeed a major influence on Riesman, who acknowledged his debt to Fromm for the concept of social character in both the original preface and the opening chapter of *The Lonely Crowd* (1950: vi, 5). But the concept is of Freudian derivation; Fromm was in no sense a follower of Nietzsche or Heidegger. Bloom must have confused him with Herbert Marcuse. Fromm and Marcuse were associates of the Frankfurt School in Germany during the Weimar period, and Marcuse had previously been a student of Heidegger. However, of all the Frankfurt figures Fromm was the most strongly attached to his Jewish origins and the least likely to respond, therefore, to the proto-Nazi aura surrounding Heidegger and the memory of Nietzsche in the 1930's. Twenty years later Marcuse attacked Fromm's neo-Freudianism for its alleged conformist orientation, an attack that was included in his *Eros and Civilization* (1955: 238–74), one of the canonical books of the

1960's counterculture. Bloom has indulged in a thoroughly questionable and irresponsible flight of ideas, surprising on the part of a student of Leo Strauss, for whom the close reading of original texts was the very first principle of sound philosophical scholarship. Perhaps left Nietzscheanism is sufficiently insidious to have turned Allan Bloom into a deconstructionist *malgré lui*!

The phrase "the lonely crowd" is an oxymoron full of implication. It looks as if it might have been intended as a vivid image of "mass society," perhaps the most general label used by sociologists to characterize the United States in the early postwar years. Yet Riesman was free of both the apocalyptic political forebodings and the cultural despair so pronounced in the theory of mass society, nor did he share in the slightest the crisis mentality promoted by conventional Marxists. Riesman once told me that he had originally thought of de Crèvecoeur's famous question in *Letters from an American Farmer* "What is this American, this new man?" as a possible title for the book.

Indeed, despite the reputation of *The Lonely Crowd* for having revealed the alienating conditions of American life against which the countercultural and New Left movements of the 1960's rebelled, Riesman was actually a mild and early participant in what C. Wright Mills derisively called "the American Celebration" of the 1950's. He explicitly rejected the Old Left vision of an America dominated by rapacious capitalists and jingoistic politicians in which workers were exploited and minorities victimized. This did not prevent liberal and radical readers from construing other-direction as at most a new variant of the shallow materialism, narrow herd mentality, and glad-handing commercial spirit familiarly attributed to America by its intellectual critics. Yet one can find, as I once did, clear-cut documentary evidence in Riesman's few articles written before *The Lonely Crowd* that his idea of other-direction originated in criticism of the "anti-elitism" (as it would be called today) and sentimental egalitarianism of well-educated and high-minded liberal academics (Gutman and Wrong 1961: 307–9). Other-direction, in short, was partly the product of self-consciously avant-garde academic intellectuals, not just an updated version of traditional bourgeois attitudes.

Riesman also questioned the long-standing conviction of intel-

lectuals that most middle-class Americans were hopeless philistines blind to cultural excellence or spiritual distinction. While
not concealing his distaste for many aspects of other-direction, he
was more hopeful about the nation's political and cultural prospects in part because of, not in spite of, other-direction, which
included such traits as psychological openness and flexibility.
Riesman and Glazer commented a decade later, "Our ambiva-
lence reflected not only lack of moral clarity but genuine doubt
about contradictory trends in American life" (Riesman 1969: xlv).
This tentativeness did not, however, spare Riesman from acidu-
lous criticism by political radicals like Mills (1956: 243–44) and
literary highbrows like Elizabeth Hardwick (1954) when his moderately sanguine attitude toward America became more evident in
his later writings of the 1950's. I recall one critic quipping that his
work was a case of "the bland leading the bland."

One is not surprised to discover that Riesman was the first person to apply the label "postindustrial" to the United States (Bell
1973: 37, n. 45). It is possible to see him today not just as a chroni-
cler and interpreter of the novelties and anxieties of forty years
ago, but as a prophet who grasped the permanent significance of
a number of developments in American society that we now take
for granted but that were just becoming visible in the late 1940's.
Negatively, he doubted that another depression was imminent or
that there was a dangerous "fascist potential" in American life. On
several fairly concrete matters, one can say of *The Lonely Crowd*
what Riesman himself once said of Tocqueville's *Democracy in
America*: it rings even more true today than when it was written.
For example, Riesman grasped the rising influence of the mass
media, even on the socialization of children, at a time when television had not yet established itself as the dominant and most pervasive medium. Already in the 1940's, Riesman anticipated what
Philip Rieff later called the "triumph of the therapeutic," the dis-
placement of traditional moral judgments by psychological assessments requiring the appropriate ministrations of psychotherapy.
Riesman was right about the decline in the authority of the
nuclear family, by now obvious with only 15 percent of the American population living in intact traditional family units. Initially,
however, his linkage of other-direction to low birth rates and in-

cipient population decline looked to be a glaring mistake, for *The Lonely Crowd* was published at a time when the baby boom was already well underway. A decade later, Riesman did point out that the "option for children" on the part of the postwar middle class rather than for more luxuries or conspicuous consumption was consistent with the trend toward other-direction, notwithstanding his previous uncritical faith in the mistaken population forecasts of the demographers (1969: xlii). He has turned out to have been right about low fertility too in the long run, if not in the short run.

In a more recent retrospective comment, Riesman observed that "*The Lonely Crowd* manifested a special concern for the situation of women," but he concedes that he was thoroughly surprised by "the intensity of the new feminist mobilizations that occurred in the 1960's" (1987: 6). In general, the movements of the late 1960's and the tumult they caused were in no way foreseen by Riesman, or, for that matter, by other social analysts. The stress on community and overcoming "alienation," the insistence on striving to unify the personal and the political, were in some ways reminiscent of Riesman's discussion of other-direction, but the angry moralism most definitely was not, nor was the revival of left-wing slogans and beliefs that had survived only in sectarian seclusion for a good many years. Christopher Lasch, one of the very few writers to continue the kind of psychocultural analysis of which *The Lonely Crowd* was a distinguished example, may well be right in arguing that Riesman, Fromm, and other analysts in the 1950's "exaggerated the degree to which aggressive impulses can be socialized" and "saw man as entirely a product of socialization, not a creature of instinct whose partially repressed or sublimated drives always threaten to break out in all their original ferocity" (1978: 64).

I want to make one final claim for *The Lonely Crowd*. Riesman was, I believe, one of the very first social observers to perceive that what Lionel Trilling later called "the adversary culture" of the intellectuals had already by the 1940's fundamentally and probably irreversibly influenced the general culture of the middle classes. He saw with utter clarity that capitalists could no longer grind the faces of the poor with unclouded consciences, that unabashed know-nothingism with respect to the arts and modern thought was no longer an option, that the age of windy moralizing and repression of feeling and sexuality in the family was over. (Riesman contended in *The Lonely Crowd* that sex was "the last frontier," but that frontier has been rather thoroughly overrun and colonized since the 1960's!) No revolutionary transformation had occurred, nor was one likely in the future, but the persistent drip-drop of interminable criticism emanating from artists, intellectuals, scholars, and the new breed of applied social scientists, including psychotherapists, had changed the world. We are now fenced in by all those posts: postindustrial, postbourgeois, postmodern, post-Freudian, post-Marxist, postsocialist, and even postnationalist. Perhaps there has been something of a regression in awareness of these changes in recent decades as a result of the histrionic revolts of the late 1960's and the equally histrionic reaction to them of Reaganism. We are getting back on track, however, and Riesman saw the track almost fifty years ago.

CHAPTER 14

Daniel Bell: A Specialist
in Generalizations

In 1960 Daniel Bell drew a contrast between the intellectual and the scholar. "The intellectual begins with *his* experience, *his* individual perceptions of the world, *his* privileges and deprivations, and judges the world by these sensibilities." The scholar, on the other hand, "has a bounded field of knowledge, a tradition, and seeks to find his place in it. . . . [He] is less involved with his 'self.'" Bell put forward this distinction in the epilogue to his first collection of essays, *The End of Ideology*, the only place in that book where he actually used the phrase. I almost wrote "offending phrase," for the "end of ideology" became the tag epitomizing all that the radical intellectuals of the 1960's most fiercely set themselves against. Since Bell imputed to intellectuals a special affinity for political ideology, his comparison was widely taken to be an invidious one favoring the objective scholar over the self-preoccupied intellectual. Some years later, when Bell began to write about applied science and technological change, he was stigmatized as an apologist for the "technocrat" rather than the scholar and weirdly seen as the partisan of a social scientific positivism on which he had always cast a skeptical eye consistent with his origins in the literary and political New York intelligentsia of the 1930's and 1940's.

These reactions were completely wide of the mark: even in the 1960 epilogue Bell's definition of the intellectual was obviously in part a self-description and not an apologetic one. In a rare autobiographical aside in *The Winding Passage* (1980), he tells us that as a graduate student in 1938 he shocked a visiting British professor by confidently declaring himself to be a "specialist in generalizations," a characterization he reaffirms half seriously forty years later. Irving Howe, who certainly ought to know one when he sees one, praises Bell as "a true intellectual" on the jacket of the book. In one essay, Bell returns to the problem of defining the intellectual as a type and complicates and qualifies his earlier dichotomy in a characteristically learned yet incisive survey of the etymological and cultural history of the term in Russia, France, and America since it came into use less than a century ago. This essay closes with a remembrance of the world of the New York Jewish intellectuals that sired him, melancholy in tone because Bell is well aware of the dissolution since the 1960's of that extraordinary community, knowing, as another former "insider" has put it, that "death is now gathering us into a generation." Acknowledging the enormous expansion in the numbers of scientific and professional experts of all sorts, Bell insists that they possess "little vitality" because "in the nature of their activities, they cannot seek the larger moral and prophetic perspectives which intellectuals in the past have striven for" (1980: 135).

According to the Greek aphorism revived by Isaiah Berlin, Bell is quintessentially a fox who "knows many things" rather than a hedgehog who "knows one big thing." The metaphor has been a bit overworked, but Bell's foxiness is perhaps his most salient trait. An uncharitable soul might accuse him of writing his two major books to prove that *he* at least could bridge the divide between C. P. Snow's "two cultures," displaying his familiarity with physical science in *The Coming of Post-Industrial Society* and with art and literature in *The Cultural Contradictions of Capitalism*. Yet the knowledge exhibited in both books is nearly always brought to bear upon his—and our—present political and cultural concerns, the mark of the intellectual according to Bell's own definition. Indeed, Bell is often vulnerable to the charge that, far from maintaining an excessive scholarly or scientific detachment, he overreacts to and reads too much into what turns out to have been a passing historical moment. As Peter Steinfels has put it, Bell "is repeatedly caught announcing that last week's cold snap is the approaching Ice Age."

Perhaps because oversimplified and pejorative versions of the "end of ideology" and "post-industrial society" became so firmly linked to his name, Bell chose a fairly innocuous title for *The Winding Passage*. (I must remember to call my own next essay collection "The Cunning Corridor," which not only echoes T. S. Eliot but conveys a whiff of sexual *double entendre*.) The seventeen essays in the collection include a number that repeat or expand upon the themes of Bell's two major books, several discussions of Jewish identity, and treatments of such disparate subjects as national character, the utopianism of Charles Fourier, Veblen's late technocratic writings, and criticisms of C. Wright Mills and Michael Harrington, both of whom had singled out Bell himself for polemical assault. The review of Harrington is a typically versatile "one-upping" performance, chiding him for ignoring much of the current technical debate on Marxist economics while making confident pronouncements on the subject.

The Winding Passage also contains two absolutely first-rate pieces of social analysis, one on the so-called "new class" and the other on ethnicity. I read both of them in their original places of publication and they are even more impressive on rereading. The fluency and accessibility of Bell's prose often result in his being patronized as an "intellectual journalist" by more ponderous academic writers, a label that entirely misses his originality and grasp of the concrete. The new class essay is subtitled "a muddled concept," indicating Bell's refusal to join the neoconservative writers with whom he is often associated in blaming everything they most dislike in contemporary politics and culture on this supposedly new historical phenomenon (see Chapter 8). Sometimes they seem to mean by it little more than the sort of people they meet at Manhattan and Georgetown cocktail parties; on other occasions, the new class is defined to include just about all college graduates, or at least those employed in the "public sector." Bell identifies six distinct groups—from top civil servants to moviemakers—that have been included under the rubric and underlines their irreducible heterogeneity. But he does more than this to demolish the concept. All of the groups in question, he notes, are distributed among different large organizations or institutional "situses"—government bureaucracies, business enterprises, universities, hospitals, etc.—which accounts for their manifest lack of social cohesion and community of interest, essential attributes of classes as collective political actors. "The idea of a 'new class,'" he concludes, "cannot be located in social-structural terms; it must be found in cultural attitudes. It is a mentality, not a class" (1980: 161).

Those who are persuaded of the existence of a new class—and there are some on the left as well as the more publicized neoconservatives—quite rightly reject the older models of capitalist or bourgeois society that no longer correspond to a changed reality. But the implications of Bell's criticism of the concept, although he does not fully spell them out, suggest that organizations and interorganizational relations have supplanted classes and class conflicts as the major agencies of social change in the advanced societies. Differences in culture and lifestyle continue, of course, to be strongly associated with social class—although this too, Bell suggests, may be diminishing—but classes are no longer the most significant political actors, as were the aristocracy, the bourgeoisie, and even the proletariat (though never living up to Marxist expectations) in the past.

The persistence of ethnic loyalties is often invoked, especially by anti-Marxists, to counter claims made for actual or potential class consciousness. To writers like Andrew Greeley and Michael Novak, the recent resurgence of ethnicity is evidence of the strength of "primordial" identities rooted in kinship and community ties in contrast to economic interests shaped by position in the division of labor. Bell sees this as at most a secondary consideration: the "new ethnicity" also reflects an instrumental as well as an affective or expressive interest, at least since the civil rights movement made it advantageous for racial and ethnic minorities to seek political redress for their grievances. Moreover, antiimperialism or "third worldism" appeals, often in racial and religious terms, to the West's "external proletariat" and has become, with the decline of nationalism and revolutionary socialism in the West, the most vital and passionately asserted ideology throughout the world today. Even ethnic groups in the older nations of the West have stirred from their long political slumber and begun to define themselves as victims of "internal colonialism." Yet as Bell cautions in a "coda" to his original essay, the forces attenuating ethnic attachments—such as high intermarriage rates—are still at work and the changes in the international order and in the politics and social structure of the advanced societies that have revived ethnic assertiveness may very well prove to be transitory.

The discussions of both the new class and ethnicity fit loosely into Bell's general conception of modern society, which has also served him as a framework for his theses about postindustrialism and the cultural contradictions of capitalism. He reiterates this "theory" in a long essay opening *The Winding Passage*: instead of constituting a unitary system cohering around a central institutional principle, modern society contains three disjunctive realms, each governed by its own "axial principle." The techno-economic realm is subject to the logic of efficiency; the dominant consideration for the polity is equality of representation and participation; the culture, especially since the 1960's, gives pride of place to demands for unrestricted hedonistic self-fulfillment. These three principles are not different refractions of some single underlying structure such as the mode of production in the Marxist canon or the value-consensus given primacy by Talcott Parsons's version of functionalism. The realms, in fact, are increasingly at cross-purposes, which is the source of many of our social problems and of our pervasive mood of crisis and disaffection.

Bell is right to reject the model of contemporary society as a tightly integrated system or "totality." Yet his alternative model amounts to no more than a rough sketch. Theory, I daresay, at least the kind that prides itself on deductive and analytical "rigor," is for hedgehogs. Bell's refusal to write at a high level of abstraction is no defect, but his most ambitious formulations remain little more than static points of reference in his thought and fail to grow in density and suggestive richness as a result of his movement between them and the topics they are meant to illuminate. His profuse examples and illustrations are often intriguing in themselves, but they never lose a disjointed ad hoc quality. He seems unwilling or unable to sustain the theoretical "moment" of inquiry. One can often quote him against himself. Indeed, he himself frequently responds to critics by pointing to statements in his text that acknowledge what they accuse him of overlooking. An example from his earlier work is his claim, justified in a literal sense, that he had diagnosed in advance the persisting hunger for ideology among young intellectuals that exploded in the 1960's. This and other comparable qualifications of his major arguments do credit to his sense of reality and lack of dogmatism, but he scarcely seems to realize how damaging they are to his original generalizations.

Bell's major example of the disjunction of realms is the contradiction between the disciplined rationality on which the economy depends and the cultural legitimation of unbounded sensual gratification. The latter he sees as the final triumph over the repressive bourgeois outlook that for more than a century was the major target of the "adversary culture" of avant-garde art and thought. The quoted phrase is, of course, Lionel Trilling's, as is the view, also adopted by Bell, that the counterculture of the 1960's represented "modernism in the streets," with the acting out of impulses and fantasies replacing their sublimation through artistic creation. This perspective is obviously very much that of a New York intellectual for whom the *Partisan Review* of the 1940's was a de facto graduate school. Bell's survey in *The Cultural Contradictions of Capitalism*, extended in several essays in *The Winding Passage*, of the links between the visions of the great modernist writers and thinkers and the "pornotopian" culture that has recently achieved mass popularity reads as if he were documenting Saul Bellow's observation that "the dreams of nineteenth-century poets polluted the psychic atmosphere of the great boroughs and suburbs of New York" (1970: 33).

Bell is also truly an intellectual out of the 1940's in his uneasiness over the connection between instinctual liberation and attraction to violence. He has not forgotten that between the wars many of the most famous avant-garde writers were drawn to fascism, which fed on currents of black romanticism, the thrill of the demonic, and the *frisson* of contact with the tabooed realms of cruelty and death. Such currents were unmistakably present in the modish cultural creations of the 1960's despite their left-wing ambience, as evidenced in Godard's movies *La Chinoise* and *Weekend*, of which Bell remarks that "a corrupt romanticism was covering some dreadful drive to murder" (1976: 142–43). C. Wright Mills's complaint that by the "end of ideology" Bell meant only his own disillusionment with socialism was at most only part of the truth: the phrase was also meant to cover the discrediting of fascism after its defeat in World War II (and later of McCarthyism as well), something that scarcely needed emphasis in 1960 but which deserves notice today with the reappearance under left-wing auspices of a sensibility once associated with fascism. I actually recall none other than Mills assuring me in 1948 that the Chandler-Bogart movie *The Big Sleep* revealed a trend toward the "legitimation of violence" and was therefore the portent of a nascent American fascism. Mills died in 1962, but what would he have made of *Bonnie and Clyde*?

Bell's views on culture are interesting and often persuasive to one who attended the same de facto academy (and, for that matter, the same de jure one in Columbia). But his angle of vision is a highly special and partial one and it is impossible not to think that he overestimates the broad social impact of modernism in general and its nihilist strain in particular. Without doing too much violence to their attitudes, one can describe most of the great modernist writers as antibourgeois, but many of them were far from being defenders of instinct against the claims of reason and morality. What of Kafka, Eliot, Mann, to name only three of the greatest? More recently, Norman O. Brown, whom Bell discusses as a "postmodernist" in *The Winding Passage*, is indubitably an extreme irrationalist, but Bell to me seems to over-stress the dark side of Brown's vision, perhaps only because twenty years ago I myself fell under the spell of that strange and potent book, *Life Against Death*.

The question of causal responsibility is more important. The trends that disturb Bell are obviously identical with what Christopher Lasch has called the "culture of narcissism" (see Chapter 15). One recalls that Bell and Lasch were both invited to Camp David to confer with President Carter at the time of his publicized withdrawal in the spring of 1979 to reflect on the nation's problems. For Lasch, however, the mindless hedonism of the culture has been fostered by the therapeutic professions rather than resulting, as for Bell, from the mass diffusion of adulterated versions of the values of the old avant-garde. Lasch's message might be rendered as "let's get the shrinks off our backs." He regards the "helping professions," ultimately, as agents of corporate capitalism engaged in undermining the independence of the individual, which is not very convincing unless one clings to the Marxist conviction that everything in our society is necessarily a manifestation of capitalism and serves its alleged needs.

Bell, on the other hand, has been criticized for blaming modernism rather than the capitalist mass consumption economy that commercializes all desires, however perverse and subversive of traditional restraints. Although he had occasionally noted this in his earlier book, he now lays much greater stress on it, asserting that "although the new legitimations derive from what had once been an adversary culture, the engine of modern capitalism has taken over these cultural styles and translated them into marketable commodities." The culture proposed, as it were, but the market disposed. He concludes that "in the end, this is the cultural contradiction of capitalism: having lost its original justifications, capitalism has taken over the legitimations of an antibourgeois culture to maintain the continuity of its own economic institutions" (1980: 163–64).

But the contradiction, then, is *within* capitalism (though not the one the Marxists harp on) rather than *between* capitalism and the culture, as the theory of disjunctive realms would have it. Moreover, it was foreseen by Weber and Sombart early in the century before modernism had even become fully visible as a distinctive tendency. Weber's famous reference to "specialists without vision, sensualists without heart" was an anticipation of the erosion, especially in the United States, of the bourgeois Protestant ethic under conditions in which "victorious capitalism, since it rests on mechanical foundations, needs the support of the spirit of religious asceticism no longer." Whether the mechanical foundations are industrial or postindustrial in Bell's sense is not really a crucial consideration. Indeed "postindustrial" seems nugatory, for the visionaries of industrialism as far back as Saint-Simon foresaw that increasingly it would substitute trained mental skills for physical labor as machines approached automatic operation ever more closely.

Weber did not suggest that the purblind specialist and the philistine sensualist could not live together, nor even that they might not peacefully coexist within the breast of the same individual. Bell contends that "the business corporation wants an individual to work hard, pursue a career, accept delayed gratification . . . and yet, in its products and in advertisements, the corporation promotes pleasure, instant joy, relaxing and letting go. One is to be 'straight' by day and a 'swinger' by night" (1976: 71–72). The opportunism and triviality may inspire disgust, but is this necessarily a contradiction threatening us with an ominous social instability? Cannot someone work hard all day at the office and attend an orgy in the evening without any sense of incongruity? More than a few people have done that. Then there is Japan, a most successful capitalist country where asceticism never prevailed. (Someone has said that "but not in Japan" is the only verified sociohistorical law.) The end of puritanism and our "liberation" from bourgeois repression have produced disappointing results far from the exalted hopes and expectations of both the artistic visionaries and the more prosaic therapists and sexual reformers, as well as producing tawdry and dehumanizing effects of their own. Bell and Lasch are right to point this out. If they frequently strike a note of *Gestern war es doch besser*, this hardly makes them potential recruits to the Reverend Falwell's Moral Majority. Yet both of them express a sense of crisis that often seems excessive.

Weber's pessimism about the future was based on his fears that a materially affluent bureaucratic society would prove to be an "iron cage," stagnating in a state of "mechanized petrifaction" devoid of the "highest spiritual and cultural values." After two world wars, Auschwitz, and Stalinism, Bell's forebodings are more catastrophic: he is closer to Bellow's Mr. Sammler who, "having seen the world collapse once . . . , entertained the possibility it might collapse twice" (1970: 33). Bell does not, however, always sufficiently separate his fears of collapse from his negative judgments of the quality of contemporary culture.

In the past Bell occasionally has suggested that we need a revival of religion to revitalize modern life. The closing essay in *The Winding Passage*, entitled "The Return of the Sacred?" explores this theme much more deeply than before with all of Bell's customary erudition. Bell has been accused of favoring religion as a social cement, as a bulwark against anomie, even as a support for the status quo, although he never has been properly classified either as a specialized professional sociologist or as a neoconservative. (He is, as we have seen, a generalist intellectual of the old school and politically a skeptical social democrat.) While he often has stressed the socially restraining and unifying bonds of religion, he moves beyond such sociological reductionism in the present essay, locating the role of "civil religion" within a much larger frame.

Religion, in his view, need not involve supernatural belief; it is a mythic and ritualized response to "the existential predicaments which are the *ricorsi* of human culture." Bell would certainly agree that nostalgia for religion is a far cry from the real thing: "Religions, unlike technologies or social policies," he remarks, "cannot be manufactured or designed." I lack the space to do justice to the richness of his discussion and shall confine myself to quoting one of his final observations:

> When there are few rituals to mark the turns in the wheel of life, if all events become the same with no ceremony to mark the distinctions—when one marries in ordinary dress, or receives a degree without a robe, or buries one's dead without the tearing of cloth—then life becomes grey on grey, and none of the splashiness of the phosphorescent pop art can hide that greyness when the morning breaks. (1980: 353)

Bell may here be (as Berlin said of Tolstoy) a fox trying to imitate a hedgehog, but I worry about the sensibility—or should it be the soul?—of a reader who remains unmoved by such a statement.

CHAPTER 15

Christopher Lasch:
Is Progress a Delusion?

Christopher Lasch's earliest books were about radical intellectuals in late-nineteenth- and twentieth-century America and the movements of the left they supported. Lasch was critical of these movements and their intellectual allies for failing to maintain a consistent and realistic opposition to capitalism, identifying himself with the assault on "corporate liberalism" of the then-ascendant New Left. It did not take Lasch long, however, to discern in the New Left itself all the faults of its predecessors writ large. Without abandoning his earlier criticisms of "cold-war liberals" and "technocrats," he assimilated the New Left to the broadly elitist and self-serving assumptions shared, in his view, by all progressivist intellectuals. The books that established Lasch's reputation as a social critic, *Haven in a Heartless World*, *The Culture of Narcissism*, and *The Minimal Self*, drew on Freud and the culture and personality tradition in sociology and anthropology to buttress rejection of the anxious hedonism of contemporary American life.

Lasch's Freudianism is a major strength of his cultural criticism, providing it with a foundation that makes it more than a cantankerous catalog of complaints. In *Haven in a Heartless World* (1977) he describes how, in order to get rid of Freud's pessimism and alleged "biologism," the neo-Freudians of the culturalist school of the 1930's and 1940's and Talcott Parsons and his followers in the 1950's adulterated Freud by eliminating his insistence on the importance of the unconscious, the primacy of infant experience, and the inevitability of repression and intrapsychic conflict as constants in the universal resistance offered by human nature to the most ambitious efforts to "socialize" it. Lasch's case has been made before, but not with such close attention to the literature of family sociology and the practice of the therapeutic professions making use of it. I am grateful to Lasch for noting that my own widely accepted criticism of the oversocialized conception of man in modern sociology was frequently misunderstood by rebels against "establishment sociology" as a celebration of individual creativity and autonomy, whereas its actual intention was to assert a deeper determinism rooted in the stressful interaction of biology and culture as understood by Freud that undercut the smoothness and regularity of the processes of acculturation and socialization.

The main thematic chapter of *The Culture of Narcissism* (1978) examines the psychoanalytic clinical evidence showing the increasing frequency of a narcissistic personality type very different from the older kind of neurotic identified by Freud and his early followers. Drawing on the theories of Melanie Klein and Otto Sternberg, Lasch argues that the new type does not suffer from specific hysterical symptoms arising out of sexual repression but from more general "character disorders" consisting of a lack of purpose in life, confused identity, and inability to form permanent satisfying relations with others. Lasch's major point is that the decline of a parental authority that is the source of both love and discipline impoverishes the part of the superego Freud called the ego ideal and also deprives the individual of the psychological resources acquired in the struggle to gain freedom from the control of the parents. The dissolution of parental authority does not eliminate the superego but fixates it at the pre-Oedipal stage, where the mother is unconsciously perceived as a devouring vampire and the father as a capriciously violent, threatening monster. (Lasch here draws on Klein.) The individual never establishes secure "object relations" by learning to cope with parents who discipline the child rather than indulging his or her every impulse. An enormous fund of unfocused hostility and aggressiveness accumulates, easily converted into a self-hatred that is warded off by self-aggrandizing fantasies.

I could not agree more with Lasch's claim for the general social and cultural significance of psychoanalytic evidence:

> By conducting an intensive analysis of individual cases that rests on clinical evidence rather than common-sense impressions, psychoanalysis tells us something about the inner workings of society itself, in the very act of turning its back on society and immersing itself in the individual unconscious. . . . Psychoanalysis best clarifies the connection between society and the individual, culture and personality, precisely when it confines itself to careful examination of individuals. It tells us most about society when it is least determined to do so. (1978: 34)

But Lasch scarcely resolves any of the difficulties that have long plagued efforts to relate personality and culture. On the issue of how or whether psychiatric patients are representative of the total population, Lasch confines himself to observing that "every age develops its own peculiar forms of pathology, which express in exaggerated form its underlying character structure." Patients, in short, suffer from ailments that are more widely prevalent in milder form. The discussions of sports, education, crime, and other subjects that make up the bulk of *The Culture of Narcissism* can therefore be regarded as diagnoses of expressions or manifestations of a general condition, although Lasch neglects to trace the exact links between these areas and underlying characterological dispositions. *The Culture of Narcissism* remains a collection of loosely related essays, in contrast to *Haven in a Heartless World*, a more coherent book in which originally discrete essays have been reworked into a unity.

In *The True and Only Heaven* (1991) Lasch returns to intellectual history, going back as far as the eighteenth century to seek out ancestors who repudiated the idea of progress and were dubious about the supposed benefits of technology without becoming nostalgic reactionaries mourning the disappearance of some *ancien régime*. Indeed, in a valuable early chapter Lasch treats nostalgia as the counterpart to belief in progress, the substitution of a self-indulgent fantasy of a past that never was for serious consideration of the bearing of the past on the present and future. Nostalgia, he notes, was originally coined to describe a psychological disorder with such physical symptoms as irregular breathing and gastroenteritis.

Lasch reviews an immense range of thinkers, political movements, and ideological currents critical of the major trends of industrial capitalism over the past two and a half centuries while remaining clearly distinct from its socialist opponents. Christian moralists anxious about the corruptions of luxury and affluence; early critics of wage labor as a form of slavery; celebrants of individual heroism and striving for excellence fearful of the enervating effects of the conformist pressures of urban society; adherents of the sociological tradition of communitarianism afflicted with what Lasch dubs *Gemeinschaftsschmerz*; syndicalists and guild socialists who wanted the workers to run industry themselves, dispensing with both capitalist and state managers; nineteenth-century agrarian populists affirming individual proprietorship and bitterly opposed both to the "wage system" and the manipulations of money men; the "new labor historians" since the 1960's who have discovered that independent artisans offered stronger revolutionary resistance to early capitalist exploitation than proletarians—all are included in Lasch's story. He also subjects a number of individual thinkers to detailed examination in a sympathetic spirit: Jonathan Edwards, William Cobbett, Tom Paine, Orestes Brownson, Thomas Carlyle, Ralph Waldo Emerson, William James, Georges Sorel, G. D. H. Cole, Reinhold Niebuhr, and Martin Luther King Jr. and he does not neglect the positions taken by their political and intellectual adversaries.

Underlying the obvious diversity of the movements and thinkers surveyed in *The True and Only Heaven*, Lasch finds some common emphases. All of them valued individual responsibility, devotion to work, the primacy of the concrete, moral realism about human nature, a sense of limits, anti-utopian skepticism. These qualities are, Lasch maintains, particularly characteristic of "the sensibility of the petty bourgeoisie," although he repudiates Marxist and sociological reductionism that treats culture and morality as mere reflections of economic interest or social position. In the face of the almost universal contempt expressed by intellectuals for the petty bourgeoisie, Lasch's claim resembles that of E. P. Thompson in *The Making of the English Working Class* (1963) in wishing to rescue certain social groups and political movements from "the enormous condescension of posterity." However, in contrast to Thompson's preoccupation with nascently class-conscious manual workers, Lasch wants to defend the small producers who lost out to the emerging industrial order. He also wants to associate their outlook with the present values of the lower middle class, including those of blue-collar workers who have experienced *embourgeoisement*, against their liberal and socialist detractors. He identifies these values with "populism," a label he is anxious to salvage by ridding it of its vague and usually pejorative overtones. Populists view with suspicion not only big business but also the cultural elitism of liberal intellectuals, the historical vanguardism of Marxists, and the centralizing thrust of social democrats eager to extend the welfare state.

The continuity between these views and the decentralist, antibureaucratic communitarianism of the early New Left is obvious. In his introductory chapter Lasch gives an account of his own political history—his midwestern Progressive and pro-New Deal background, his movement to the left in opposition to the cold-war stasis of the 1950's, his disillusionment with the "revolutionary histrionics" of the New Left. (Although he does not say as much, a good deal of old-fashioned isolationism has always been part of his political makeup—foreign policy has never been one of his strong points.) The experience of parenthood, he claims, led him in the mid-1970's to studies of the family and socialization and eventually turned him against a liberalism that "now meant sexual freedom, women's rights, gay rights; denunciation of the family as the seat of all oppression; denunciation of 'patriarchy'; denunciation of 'working-class authoritarianism'" (1991: 34).

But Lasch did not become a conservative rhetorically upholding "traditional values." Seeking a historical lineage for populism, he was influenced by the tradition of "republican virtue" recently revived by a few theorists anxious not to cede the entire heritage of the Enlightenment to the "possessive individualism" of bourgeois liberalism. Lasch observes, however, that these writers have often presented "a caricature of liberalism"; he even speaks up for "the wise Locke," as Rousseau called him, noting that recent Locke scholarship has shown that Locke himself had severe reservations about boundless acquisitiveness and big as opposed to small capitalism. Lasch's wide scholarship in intellectual history joined to his social criticism endows *The True and Only Heaven* with its distinctive flavor.

Lasch extols what he calls "producerism" over the passive "consumerism" of contemporary capitalism, which promotes "the shift from a work ethic to a consumption ethic." "The politics of the civilized minority," as he entitles his penultimate chapter, both reflects and helps create this new passivity. The inveterate elitism of the intellectuals is an additional expression of increasing acceptance of universal dependence on professional experts and commodities marketed by large enterprises relying on advertising. The radicals of the 1960's are part of this trend: it is easy to imagine Lasch recoiling in disgust after hearing just one too many callow graduate student pronounce that millions of his plebeian fellow-citizens are victims of "false consciousness" (today it would be "hegemonic ideology"). He says he was surprised to find that more moderate left-wing intellectuals were still, after all the terrible events of this century, believers not only in material but in moral progress. And, of course, they saw their own political and cultural beliefs as enlightened anticipations of the future, thus entitling them to make use of such nondemocratic agencies as the courts and the federal bureaucracy to implement policies unlikely to win popular support.

Doubtless there is a sense in which H. L. Mencken and his admirers in the 1920's, New Deal social planners, social scientists such as Robert Lynd and Gunnar Myrdal engaging in foundation-sponsored research, political psychotherapists diagnosing "authoritarianism," the Camelot mythologists of the Kennedy years, student radicals of the 1960's, the "suburban" neoliberals of the 1970's and 1980's, and judicial supporters of busing and affirmative action share a common "elitism" and belief in progress. But Lasch paints with too broad a brush. He telescopes together earlier and later tendencies and overlooks the ferocious controversies within and between them: power elitists against pluralists, Marxists against liberals, cold-war supporters against peace advocates. For example, he lumps together contributors to the theme of the *em-*

bourgeoisement of the working class in the 1950's, ignoring the sharp debate between liberal supporters of the Keynesian–welfare state consensus and socialists who still regarded the workers as a potentially radical force. By the end of the 1960's, to be sure, the New Left had for the most part dismissed the working class as politically indistinguishable from the despised lower middle class. But this came after the *embourgeoisement* controversy among sociologists, superseding the briefly revived Marxism of a large segment of the postwar intelligentsia. In general, Lasch alludes too infrequently to the chief countertendency to the elitism he condemns: the idealization of oppressed groups, whether workers, blacks, or Third World peasants, imputing to them primitive vigor, innocent virtue, and natural solidarity. The disdain for the petty bourgeoisie of which Lasch makes so much owes a lot to this disposition of bourgeois intellectuals to romanticize classes that are still lower in status than those just below them.

In his preface Lasch insists, "I have no intention of minimizing the narrowness and provincialism of lower-middle class culture; nor do I deny that it has produced racism, nativism, anti-intellectualism and all the other evils often cited by liberal critics" (1991: 17). He finally turns to a consideration of these negative qualities in his last chapter, "Right-Wing Populism and the Revolt Against Liberalism." After a fairly conventional analysis of the ambiguity of the concept "middle class," he reviews the "cultural class war" over patriotic symbols, busing, abortion, affirmative action, pornography, homosexuality, and other so-called social issues. The revolt against liberalism and the Democratic party at the polls and in some lower-middle- and working-class communities represents a defense of a way of life threatened by politicians, bureaucrats, and professionals who do not themselves experience the effects of the policies they devise. This has by now become a fairly familiar diagnosis; Lasch draws on the useful work of such sociologists as Jonathan Rieder, Kristin Luker, Lillian Rubin, E. E. LeMasters, and Herbert Gans and the journalists J. Anthony Lukas and Kevin Phillips. He rightly observes that the blatant anti-Americanism of the movement protesting the Vietnam War may have had the effect of strengthening support for the war among people who might otherwise have opposed it.

Nor does Lasch overlook the excesses of the resistance to liberal social policies, remarking of the antibusing movement in Boston that it "seldom rose above the level of resentment, self-righteousness, and self-pity" (1991: 502). He is aware that his defense of right-wing protest movements, though qualified, brings him close to the standard neoconservative polemic against liberal intellectuals. He perceptively criticizes the neoconservatives, however, for striving to deflect blame for the hedonistic "permissiveness" they denounce from consumer capitalism by charging it to a "new class" of intellectuals whose influence they grossly exaggerate. Left-wing new-class theories, on the other hand, go in for the reverse operation. *Both* consumer capitalism and the educated classes (whether or not they constitute a truly new class) are jointly responsible for our plight, in Lasch's view.

But if the neoconservatives obfuscate a political disagreement in identifying as their adversary a vaguely defined new class, is not Lasch guilty of a similar error in socially grounding the morality he wishes to defend in the petty bourgeoisie? The values of hard work, self-discipline, frugality, personal independence, family loyalty, and local pride have a long history and were not always peculiarly characteristic of the lower middle class. They were part of a general bourgeois outlook with roots in Puritanism and even earlier peasant traditions before the transformations that have shaped contemporary capitalism. Lasch's own intellectual heroes—Emerson, James, and Niebuhr—were hardly of petty-bourgeois origins.

If the cultural class war has often twisted these values into ugly forms of racial bigotry and intolerance, it may also have deformed the antitraditionalism of the liberal intelligentsia, which has hardly been politically ascendant in recent decades. That people should have as wide a range of choice as possible in personal and family life may as a principle lend itself both to abuse in practice and to conversion into a smug nihilistic relativism that preens itself on its superiority to those who live by more restrictive codes. Lasch often includes feminist beliefs in the roster of "enlightened" liberal attitudes that he condemns, although he never directly confronts feminism. Feminism has produced its share of rigid ideologues, but it is surely an idea whose time has come. Lasch thinks that damage to the natural environment puts an end to the prospect of perpetual material progress, but if so, it also rules out continued population growth, which has obvious and weighty implications for the traditional roles of women. Lasch himself recognizes that new-class intellectuals, though a diversified group, share an admirable critical, empirical, and cosmopolitan outlook that need not degenerate into snobbery and cynicism. Perhaps all values assume unattractive dogmatic forms when they are selectively upheld by different classes and social groups locked in bitter political and ideological conflict.

In *The Minimal Self* (1984) Lasch complains that his critics have pigeonholed him in the categories of old and familiar debates such as those over mass culture or pluralism in American life, whereas it has been his purpose to say something new and more radical. This turns out primarily to be the suggestion, developed more fully in *The True and Only Heaven*, that our dependence on technology is the cause of our psychic debilitation, that modern civilization may be a dead end and the Industrial Revolution a wrong turn in human history. "What if technological progress is an illusion?" he asks, and he concludes that "at this point in history, it is essential to question the boundless confidence in human powers that acknowledges no limits, which finds its ultimate expression in the technology of nuclear warfare" (1984: 222).

Yet on Lasch's own evidence, boundless confidence in human powers hardly seems to be the dominant mood of our culture. Nor are his doubts especially new. Even before nuclear weapons, Freud in *Civilization and Its Discontents* voiced skepticism about the human value of the technical marvels of the modern age as well as forebodings about the invention of even more destructive weapons in the future. Freud assumed that sexual repression and strict paternal authority were part of the price we must pay for civilization. Lasch thinks that our "liberation" from these constraints has only made things worse by undermining our capacity for self-control and creating an abject dependence on a host of therapeutic experts, many of whom claim to be Freud's heirs. Lasch refuses to settle for the even-handed conclusion that these and other spiritual deficiencies are simply unavoidable costs of the material comforts we enjoy. This is much too balanced a judgment to suit him.

His rejection of modernity is scarcely new either. I was brought up intellectually to think that belief in progress was a nineteenth-century illusion shattered by the fateful sequence of events that began in 1914. Oswald Spengler's *The Decline of the West* was a bestseller after that first disastrous world war and Spengler regarded preoccupation with what he called "technics" as a major symptom of decline. A few years later, the century's most famous poem declared the modern world to be a "waste land." If T. S. Eliot had little interest in psychoanalysis, his description in a later poem of contemporary city dwellers "distracted from distraction by distraction / filled with fancies and empty of meaning" sounds a lot like Lasch's account of today's narcissistic personalities.

But Lasch is a historian, not a poet or a Teutonic philosopher. His case against modernity draws on concrete evidence, though it is sometimes challengeable. In *The Minimal Self* he accepts without qualification, for example, the recently revived claim that industrialism downgrades the occupational skills of the labor force, an idea resting on the comparison of machine tenders with an idealized image of preindustrial craftsmen. Lasch's major authority for this, Harry Braverman, has been called a neo-Luddite even by some of his fellow Marxists. Moreover, there was a much larger underclass of people lacking *any* secure means of livelihood in preindustrial societies, consisting of both the landless rural poor and an urban *Lumpenproletariat*. V. S. Naipaul, hardly someone given to cheery optimism, is surely right that "Indian poverty is more dehumanizing than any machine." Perhaps, if we have lost faith in inevitable progress, it is not wildly Panglossian to suggest that we might also give up the counter-belief in inevitable decline. Lasch himself deplores the promiscuous invocation of Auschwitz as a symbol of our condition.

Although he may not appreciate the comparison, there are striking similarities between Lasch's general argument and that of Daniel Bell in *The End of Ideology* nearly forty years ago. Their very language is often identical. Both writers begin by claiming that old political ideologies are "exhausted." Both men admire and say they have learned from Reinhold Niebuhr. Lasch thinks the crisis of the environment negates the belief in progress still affirmed by both left and right. Bell thought that the experience of world wars and totalitarian regimes must necessarily moderate

the intensity of ideological conflict. Both men deplore the sacrifice of the living to utopian visions of the future.

Lasch concludes his immensely long book with the insistence
that "limits and hope: these words sum up the two lines of argument I have tried to weave together" (1991: 530). Bell chose as an
epigraph to his title essay Machiavelli's statement, "Men commit
the error of not knowing when to limit their hopes." I was one of
the first critics of the end-of-ideology thesis, arguing that a sense
of limits needed to be balanced by recognition of the indestruc-
tibility of hope. Lasch makes a distinction between hope as basic
trust in the possibilities of life, and optimism, which he links to
belief in progress and the lack of a sense of tragedy in history.

Bell limited the end of ideology to the West and noted the continuing appeal of revolutionary apocalypticism in the underdeveloped countries. Lasch asks on the first page of his opening chapter, "Who would have predicted, twenty-five years ago, that as the
twentieth century approached its end, it would be the left that was
everywhere in retreat?" (1991: 21–22) Obviously, the query applies
also to the Third World, where faith in state-directed rapid modernization has largely waned. Although Lasch nowhere so much
as mentions the collapse of Communism, it clearly strengthens
his case against progress toward a "true and only heaven" that will
completely transcend the past. Bell may have overestimated the
stability of the transitory consensus of the 1950's and failed fully
to anticipate the brief revival of radicalism in the 1960's, but he
was right about the long-run trend, as he argued in a new after-
word to a reissue of his book in 1989.

Lasch would clearly welcome a new populist revolt in American politics centered on the economic interests of the hard-pressed
lower middle and working classes while bypassing the divisive
cultural issues. Unlike Kevin Phillips, however, he wisely declines
to predict the occurrence of such a revolt. Nevertheless, in addition to its historical scope and depth, *The True and Only Heaven*
provides valuable new understanding of the curious political inter-
regnum that now prevails in *fin de siècle* America.

CHAPTER 16

Allan Bloom: The Paperbacking
of the American Mind

Much wondering comment has been aroused by the enormous and quite unexpected success of Allan Bloom's *The Closing of the American Mind: How Higher Education Has Failed Democracy and Impoverished the Souls of Today's Students*. Its appearance in a paperback edition will earn it renewed attention and almost certainly, judging by past experience, sales two or three times greater than those of the hardcover original, which was on the bestseller list for almost a year.

What accounts for the popularity of a book by a previously unknown academic political philosopher, much of it consisting of commentaries on difficult texts by canonical Western thinkers who have long been dead? *The Closing of the American Mind* is by no means the first book apparently dealing with an arcane scholarly subject to have surprised its author and publisher by becoming a bestseller. In recent years such books have cropped up with fair regularity. The postwar paperback revolution has made difficult academic works available at reasonable prices to a large readership. Some books originally published in modest hardcover printings by small elite publishers or university presses have taken off when reissued in paperback. Others, moderately successful in their first printings, have reached a much wider public and become famous only in paperback, sometimes in abridged form. The assignment of paperback books to college and even to high school classes is a central channel through which ideas are rapidly disseminated. Higher education has become an important mass medium, as is taken for granted as a major premise in Bloom's ferocious assault upon it.

Bloom's book has already equaled or exceeded the sales of similar hardcover titles by reaching 475,000 copies in print (it has gone through twenty printings), so the paperback sales are likely to be impressive despite the increasingly harsh critical attention it has been receiving. The book, however, is far from being an exercise in strictly scholarly exegesis; as its title and subtitle suggest, its philosophical themes are linked to urgent contemporary concerns over the decline of American power and influence in the world. It resembles in this respect previous successful books by academics that have tapped into some vein of anxiety or alarm in the educated public.

In 1978, Christopher Lasch's bestselling book *The Culture of Narcissism* made many of the same critical observations about American life as Bloom's book—especially in a chapter entitled "Schooling and the New Illiteracy"—despite Lasch's very different intellectual and political outlook. At the end of the 1960's, *The Greening of America*, by a Yale University professor of law, Charles Reich, also brought unanticipated fame and fortune to its author. A cluster of books of the same genre had comparable success in the early 1960's and managed to establish for at least a few years the terms of public discourse on their subjects: there was Paul Goodman's *Growing Up Absurd*, *The Other America* by Michael Harrington, Herbert Marcuse's *One-Dimensional Man*, and Norman O. Brown's *Life Against Death*, which is Wesleyan University Press's biggest seller in both hardcover (13,000 copies sold) and paperback (93,700 sold).

A bit over a decade earlier, in 1950, Yale University Press printed just 3,000 copies of *The Lonely Crowd* by David Riesman (written in collaboration with Reuel Denney and Nathan Glazer), only to be forced to thirteen additional printings (and 35,000 copies in print) even before the abridged paperback edition became one of the most popular titles ever in Doubleday's Anchor Books series. And Yale's own paperback edition, published in

1961, has gone through forty printings, with some 486,000 copies sold to date.

What these books have in common is their diagnosis and condemnation of some widespread condition in American society revealing rapid recent deterioration or, at the very least, long-standing neglect. *The Lonely Crowd* was something of an exception, for its aim was primarily to analyze rather than to point with alarm, but it was widely read as deploring the rise of the psychological disposition it called "other-direction" at the expense of "inner-direction." The combination of urgent warning and manifest learning displayed by these authors came across as a trumpet call to some sort of remedial action.

At one extreme, specific reforms such as the anti-poverty programs of the Kennedy and Johnson administrations were partly inspired by Harrington's book. At the other, the authors resembled prophets of old calling for nothing less than the total intellectual or spiritual transformation of their errant fellow citizens. Bloom is obviously closer to the latter pole. Yet his conviction that the classics of Western culture are losing their proper central place in American higher education has provided ammunition for conservative educational reformers, such as Secretary of Education William J. Bennett, calling for a return to basics and the restoration of a privileged canon of texts and authors.

Bloom writes as a declared conservative, although most of the books I have mentioned were critical of American life from a broadly left position. It would be a mistake to make too much of this difference, treating Bloom as a reflection of the Reagan era, the authors of the early 1960's as harbingers and shapers of that decade's later radicalism, Charles Reich as a full-fledged expression of the ethos of the counterculture, and Christopher Lasch as a voice of the disillusion of the Carter years. For one thing, their complaints about the shallowness and philistinism of American culture are much the same.

The major count in Allan Bloom's indictment of contemporary students is their relativism about values, their bland acceptance of any and all "life styles" as morally permissible. They are so open-minded that their brains have fallen out, although Bloom avoids such a vulgarly colloquial way of putting it. Yet his major thesis is the deliberately paradoxical one that the "closing of the American mind" results from an abysmal openness that destroys the very capacity to make firm moral or intellectual judgments. The affinity between this claim and Herbert Marcuse's oxymoronic conception of "repressive tolerance" is evident, although Bloom predictably regards Marcuse as a baneful influence. Nearly fifty years ago, Riesman's contrast between inner- and other-direction anticipated in a much more nuanced way Bloom's polarity between firmly internalized moral standards and easygoing adjustment to the fluctuating expectations of others. Yet Riesman is a particular bête noire of Bloom's, disparaged on eight separate occasions in the book on the basis of an entirely erroneous equation of inner-direction with the "do your own thing" ethic—or anti-ethic—of the 1960's counterculture.

The opposition of Bloom and Charles Reich, who as a latecomer reflected rather than helped shape the ideology of the countercul-ture, is, on the other hand, salient and unambiguous. It is startling to recall that less than thirty years ago Reich's book drew the same kind of attention now being received by Bloom's.

The major subject of both authors is university students, but Reich saw the youthful rebels of the late 1960's as bearers of a new consciousness destined to redeem us all, whereas for Bloom precisely the remnants of that consciousness in the 1980's have immunized contemporary students against intellectual enlighten-ment and growth. Reich wrote when the protest movements of the 1960's were beginning to fade away. After the initial éclat fol-lowing the appearance of his book, it became the subject of sav-age derision and tends to be remembered today, by Bloom himself for one, as a particularly extreme and silly effusion of 1960's uto-pianism.

Despite their opposite evaluations of the young, the popularity of Reich's and Bloom's books probably have owed something to the note of personal intensity conveyed by both. Reich later pub-lished an autobiography, *The Sorcerer of Bolinas Reef*, in which he revealed the enduring loneliness and unhappiness, including re-pressed homosexuality, that had led him to the total rejection of conventional life espoused in *The Greening of America* and to his later "dropping out" by resigning his professorship and embracing the bohemian life in San Francisco (facilitated, no doubt, by the size of his royalty checks). *The Greening of America* communicated an almost erotic charge in its rhapsodical descriptions of so-called liberated young people. It was this that powerfully moved first readers of the excerpts published in *The New Yorker*, many of whom later suppressed their original responses when the book became generally ridiculed by leading intellectuals.

Bloom's book, on the other hand, is free of obvious undertones of strongly personal emotion. Although there are many reports of the author's encounters with students and teachers, the dominant tone is drily ironic, abstract and pedagogic. Yet the book conveys the unmistakable sense of an *apologia pro vita sua*, recounting Bloom's long love affair with the University of Chicago, fake Gothic and all, and the lofty notions he first encountered and now expounds there, especially the ideas of Plato and Aristotle. He also dwells repeatedly on a single shattering experience that has become the focus of his contempt for the youth culture and dismay over the state of higher education: the events in 1969 at Cornell University, where Bloom was then teaching, when armed black student militants occupied a campus building and the faculty voted to accede to their demands for the sake of averting violence.

The behavior of the Cornell administration and faculty was widely seen as cowardly even at the time, and Bloom and a handful of other dissidents were viewed as courageous men of principle. Today Bloom regards the whole episode as the ultimate betrayal by the university of its own professed principles and compares it without qualification to the capitulation of the German universities to the Nazis in the 1930's. The student radicals of the 1960's often made the same comparison in reverse, denouncing the university's complicity with the Department of Defense and what they called its "institutional racism." How long will it be, one wonders, before deep political differences can be argued without the invocation of the *argumentum ad Hitlerem*, usually by both sides?

Bloom's negative appraisal of the student radicalism of twenty years ago is unremarkable. He is right to insist that the student left's much-vaunted contribution to the civil rights movement was marginal and that its commitments to equality and democracy, far from being its own "autonomous creations," were borrowed entirely from the liberal university. But the claim that the student radicals eventually "bankrupted" that institution and "abandoned the grand American liberal traditions of learning" is hyperbolic. It attaches vastly too much importance to the transitory and largely inconsequential *Sturm und Drang* of the late 1960's, amounting essentially to no more than a mirror image of the nostalgia of aging leftists who look back on the 1960's as a shining moment and credit the student movement with improving race relations and making possible the ultimate ending of the Vietnam War. Like the neoconservatives, Bloom wants to see the 1960's as a momentous fall from a lost state of grace.

The expansion of higher education after World War II when Bloom was a student was certainly attended by much hopeful idealism. Indeed, the frustration of excessive expectations helped cause the angry outbursts on the campuses of the 1960's. Bloom surveys, for the most part accurately and often perceptively, the heterogeneous offerings of the university and the quite different states of morale prevailing in the three major divisions—the natural sciences, the social sciences, and the humanities. He bewails the absence of any center or even of a minimal coherence that might unify a diversity that is intellectually chaotic. Most of what he says could have been said with equal justification at any time in the present century. In fact, it *was* said in 1917 by Max Weber, with the German university primarily in mind, in his famous essay "Scholarship as a Vocation." Nor does Bloom, who passionately deplores the abandonment in the 1960's of core curriculums requiring students to take some courses in all three divisions, seem to have noticed that most major universities have restored such requirements.

Bloom's attack on relativism also continues an old tradition. In the confrontations of the past with fascist and Communist enemies abroad, ethical relativism was often blamed for undermining the American capacity to resist the appeal of those absolutist ideologies. In the years just before Pearl Harbor, liberal interventionists like Archibald MacLeish and Lewis Mumford assailed American intellectuals for failing to rally their countrymen against Hitler. They placed the blame not on German philosophies but on Deweyan pragmatism, the purely provisional beliefs of those committed to science as the sole source of truth, and the negativism of avant-garde writers who dwelt on the more squalid aspects of modern life.

The failure of a skeptical, latitudinarian mentality to mount an effective moral opposition to militant Communism became a standard theme at the height of the cold war. William F. Buckley Jr.'s *God and Man at Yale* (1951)—perhaps the book that, though less intellectually sophisticated, most closely resembles Bloom's in its conservative point of view and its assault on liberal academia for encouraging relativistic tolerance—was a product of that period. Neo-Thomist and neo-Aristotelian schools of thought criticized more systematically that same liberalism and were a major intellectual presence in academia for several decades before the 1960's. They were strongly represented at the University of Chicago, where the Robert Hutchins–Mortimer Adler Great Books program, centering education on the reverential study of the classics of Western civilization, flourished from the early 1930's until the 1950's. Some of these conservative antimodernist systems of thought sought to revive the traditional grounding of morality in religion; others, like the doctrines of Bloom's teacher, the refugee political philosopher Leo Strauss, affirmed classical conceptions of natural law discoverable through reason.

I have mentioned these recent precursors of Bloom's general outlook because it is surprising that some of his critics have evidently forgotten them in expressing shocked surprise at his views. "Why, this is reactionary stuff, this fellow is an elitist, even an authoritarian!" they have exclaimed. Taking note of Bloom's veneration of Plato, they have accused him of harboring an antidemocratic hankering for the rule of philosopher kings. On this count, however, there is less to Bloom than meets the eye. He goes so far as to claim that *The Republic* is actually an antiutopian tract intended to warn against efforts to create any ideal political regime and even against its own apparent advocacy of the education of women and the abolition of the family in the interests of equality.

This is a convenient claim for a conservative (and antifeminist) to make, consistent with the insistence of followers of Leo Strauss that the great thinkers of the past usually meant the opposite of what they seemed to be saying, but it finds no support from contemporary classical scholars, as one of them, Martha Nussbaum, has pointed out. Bloom proceeds to argue that his beloved Greek philosophers favored aristocracy and even plutocracy over democracy, not on principle but solely because only "gentlemen" "despise necessity" and "have money and hence leisure and can appreciate the beautiful and useless." Not the ancients but the philosophers of the Enlightenment, the fathers of our modern democracy, really believed that philosophers should rule. Bloom wants to sever theory from *any* practice, to build a high wall between thought and action, because he agrees with Socrates that "the greatest good for a human being is talking about—not practicing—virtue (unless talking about virtue is practicing it)." What a gloriously self-enhancing opinion for a bookish professor to uphold!

The modern university is, Bloom writes, the contemporary equivalent of the "free lunch" Socrates demanded "with ultimate insolence" that Athens should provide him. Is this not at the very least a prescription for an educational dictatorship, for taking St. John's College of Annapolis, Md., where education consists solely of reading a selected list of largely premodern great books, as the model for all higher education?

That may be Bloom's ideal, but he proposes little more than that philosophy courses based on the ancients should be restored to a central place in the liberal arts curriculum. Moreover, he is surprisingly admiring of Enlightenment thinkers, calling Hobbes, Locke, and Rousseau "Columbuses of the mind." He is also shrewd enough to recognize that Marx is an old-fashioned and derivative Victorian progressive who today poses much less formidable a challenge to a morality based on natural law than more recent and subtler Germanic savants like Nietzsche, Heidegger, Freud, and Weber. He refers with great respect even to these men, except for a few trite anti-Freudian remarks.

Since followers of Leo Strauss are given to arguing that no really means yes in the texts they peruse, they may also write that way themselves, especially when they feel threatened by a hostile public opinion, as Bloom manifestly does by surviving echoes of the 1960's and "the guns at Cornell." So it could be argued that a hidden political agenda underlies Bloom's sour reflections on contemporary education. But few of his readers are likely to probe beneath the surface of his argument instead of taking it at face value. Nor is the argument itself a very dense and rigorous one, free of contradictions. The personally expressive, even self-indulgent quality of the book is revealed by the adjectives reviewers have affixed to it: grumpy, pettish, cantankerous, crabby, cranky, crotchety, crusty. (Why do so many of these words begin with "c"?)

The success of *The Closing of the American Mind* is partly to be accounted for by the current wave of concern over the recently publicized ignorance of the young, which also precipitated E. D. Hirsch Jr.'s quite different *Cultural Literacy: What Every American Needs to Know* onto the best-seller lists for almost six months. Its popularity is probably also a response to anxieties over the decline of American international competitiveness combined with a traditionally American disposition to view education as the solution to or the agent responsible for major problems. *The Closing of the American Mind* looks in this perspective like a classier 1980's counterpart of Rudolf Flesch's *Why Johnny Can't Read*, the alarmist manifesto published at the time of the shock of Sputnik in the 1950's. Today the Japanese rather than the Russians are seen as our main competitors. The belief that world power is shifting away from America to the Pacific rim has created a general climate of opinion that has helped both *The Closing of the American Mind* and *The Rise and Fall of the Great Powers* by Paul Kennedy to become bestsellers. Bloom, to be sure, is hardly an advocate of improved scientific and technical education, and the Japanese are not, one supposes, profound students of Plato and Aristotle; but the book-buying public is moved by vague hopes and fears, and it often does not know what it's getting.

AUTOBIOGRAPHICAL CODA

✌

CHAPTER 17

"As we grow older the world becomes stranger"

As one grows older, one is always surprised—and sometimes depressed—to realize the truth of "in my beginning is my end" and "in my end is my beginning." T. S. Eliot was, of course, thinking of personal identity in its deepest and fullest sense, but his words also apply to "merely" intellectual beginnings and ends, the more so when reading, writing, and thinking have from a fairly early age been central to one's self-definition.

I decided more or less consciously that I wanted to become an "intellectual" at a moment of abrupt and unwelcome transition in my life several months before my sixteenth birthday. After living for two years in Geneva, Switzerland, where my father was Canadian delegate to the League of Nations, I was sent by my parents to board at a prominent preparatory school in Toronto. The school was not altogether strange to me, for I had been a boarder in its junior division the year before we moved to Europe after living in Washington, D.C., for most of my early life. Until now I had always identified myself entirely, indeed overeagerly, with my peers and had in fact been bitterly unhappy over the move to Europe. Twice my parents had dragged me, in a sulky and sullen mood, across the Atlantic. This time I was not only older but, feeling that my European sojourn had made me more refined and cosmopolitan than my schoolmates, I resisted making yet another readjustment to an environment I had not chosen.

We returned in the summer of 1939, and the coming of the war removed all possibility of my going back to Switzerland. It lessened my anger at my parents, but it made me, if anything, more inclined to idealize my years at school in Geneva and more determined than ever not to become a hearty, provincial, prep-school philistine. Since I laid claim to a personal relation to Europe, where the great events of the war were unfolding, I decided that I ought to be more fully informed about them. So I started to follow the world news and tacked maps of the battlefronts from the Sunday *New York Times* "Week in Review" section on the wall of my dormitory room, which my schoolmates regarded as a pretentious affectation.

I bought my first "serious" book, *Fallen Bastions*, by a British newspaper correspondent in Central Europe, to learn about the events preceding the war, especially the Munich crisis, which had the year before impinged on even our self-centered adolescent concerns at school in Geneva. The author, G. E. R. Gedye, passionately denounced the appeasement of Hitler and wrote favorably of "socialism." The leading Toronto bookstore—Britnell's, incredibly still there and looking much the same more than fifty years later—carried other British Left Book Club publications; I bought a few and was quickly converted by a John Strachey pamphlet entitled *Why You Should Be a Socialist*. In the next year I read books, many of them British Pelicans that still sit on my shelf, by Strachey, H. G. Wells, George Bernard Shaw, G. D. H. Cole, and Harold Laski on socialism, politics, and world affairs. (In Canada, incidentally, one had easy access to British as well as American publications, including books and journals that were not available for sale or distribution in the United States, such as many Penguins, Pelicans, and Left Book Club books and pamphlets.)

I also exchanged long, nostalgic letters with my closest Geneva friend, the late Stuart Schulberg, son of pioneer Hollywood movie magnate B. P. Schulberg and younger brother of the novelist Budd Schulberg, who later was for a long time the producer of the NBC *Today* show. I was astounded by his opposition to American entrance into the war, for at school we had all declaimed against the wickedness of Hitler. I wrote a letter to *Life* magazine denouncing the American isolationists—my first appearance in print—

and Stuart wrote a letter disagreeing with me. His opinions, as I began to grasp, reflected those of the Communist Party, to which he had been exposed through his brother, who had been a leading figure among the Hollywood Communists of the 1930's. Stuart had always been the older, dominant figure in our friendship, so I wavered in the direction of his views. I bought and read International Publishers' editions of the shorter writings of Marx, Engels, and Lenin, as well as *Capital*, managing to plow through at least the first (and most difficult!) chapters. The war maps on my wall were replaced by cut-out pictures of Marx, Lenin, and Trotsky, though some vague, intuitive wisdom kept me from including Stalin among them.

Never one to do things by halves, I offered my services—at the suggestion of a teacher who claimed to be a secret sympathizer—to the Canadian Communist Party newspaper just before it and the party itself were banned, for Canada was at war and it was, of course, the period of the Stalin-Hitler pact. The editor, who was elected a few years later to the Ontario legislature after the Soviet Union had become our ally, asked me to proofread a huge manuscript, so I carried galleys of *The Socialist Sixth of the World* by Hewlett Johnson, the "Red Dean" of Canterbury, back to my dorm room. Even at my tender age, I found it hard to believe that there could possibly be a land of such milk and honey as the contemporary Soviet Union in the Dean's description of it. Still, I rather cherish the memory of sitting in my room at Upper Canada College, identified by recent Canadian Marxist sociologists as the seedbed of the Canadian corporate elite, reading tracts for the soon-to-be-outlawed Communist Party.

I sometimes wonder if I am perhaps not the only person in the world who became a Communist sympathizer *after* the Stalin-Hitler pact and was disillusioned within a few weeks by the Soviet invasion of Finland. In my case, at least, the time at which I became politically conscious—which almost invariably meant adopting left-wing views—was undoubtedly crucial in shaping my later outlook. I began to read, even subscribe to, *The Nation*, *The New Republic*, and *The New Statesman*, which during the 22 months of the Soviet-German alliance were firmly anti-Stalinist, printing articles, often by former Communists, that were highly critical not only of Stalinism but even of Marxism. All these journals reverted to pro-Soviet apologetics and at times outright fellow traveling after Hitler invaded Russia, but I was immunized forever against the illusion that truth and virtue are always to be found on the left. I also picked up an occasional copy of the Trot-skyist monthly *New International*, which provided crucial "anticipatory socialization" for my later encounter in New York with former or near Trotskyists associated with Dwight Macdonald's *politics, Partisan Review, Commentary*, and, a bit later, *Dissent*. I continued to think of myself as at least a qualified Marxist and an ardent democratic socialist, generally sympathetic to the Co-operative Commonwealth Federation (CCF), the Canadian party modeled on the British Labour party, in which I was later active as an undergraduate.

The political weeklies also contained cultural "back of the book" sections, which were resolutely highbrow, drawing their reviewers and authors from the most advanced Bloomsbury and Greenwich Village circles. Here I gleaned an idea of the proper preoccupations and values of the bona fide intellectual, a label that, as Daniel Bell has shown, scarcely predates this century and has today acquired a much looser, vaguer, and doubtless less "elitist" meaning than it used to have. I took up smoking cigarettes, cultivated less plebeian tastes in classical music, and plunged into modern literature. In the course of my two years at Upper Canada I read the poetry of Eliot, Auden, Spender, and Jeffers and the fiction of Hemingway, Fitzgerald, Dos Passos, Steinbeck, the early Joyce, Lawrence, Malraux, Romains, Silone, Isherwood, Saroyan, Thomas Wolfe, and Richard Wright. (I did not read the great Russians or the more "difficult" writers, except for some of the poets, until later.)

I decided, as many did in those days, that I wanted to be a writer. I wrote about a dozen sketches and short stories, very much in the vein of William Saroyan, most of them full of wide-eyed adolescent romanticism about the wonder and glory of it all. Several were printed in the school literary magazine and won me a prize on graduation for the best prose fiction. I also wrote political articles, especially in a short-lived school newspaper that I edited, exhorting my contemporaries to build a new, more just social order after the war and liberally quoting Marx, Lenin, Eugene V. Debs, Big Bill Haywood, and other left-wing luminaries.

I first encountered sociology in V. F. Calverton's 1937 Modern Library anthology. Calverton was hardly a sociologist or even an academic, but an independent, "premature" anti-Stalinist Marxist who included selections by, among others, Lao-tze, Augustine, Machiavelli, Locke, Darwin, Lenin, Hitler, Mussolini, Max Eastman, and Sidney Hook as well as such unambiguous sociologists as Spencer, Durkheim, Weber, and Cooley. When Robert Bierstedt revised the book more than twenty years later, he dropped many of the original choices, complaining that V. F. Calverton's "predilections" were "Marxian" and that he included too much "social philosophy." Accurate enough, but it occurs to me that my own sense of sociology may have been permanently formed—or, if you like, deformed—by Calverton's comprehensiveness. I would love to have possessed the wit and self-confidence, or perhaps the chutzpah, that led Daniel Bell as a fledgling graduate student to describe himself as a "specialist in generalizations" (though Dan says he spoke "without wit or irony"). I was, in any case, voted by my graduating class at Upper Canada the member "with the most opinions on the most subjects."

Although I acquired strong later interests, world politics and international relations, ideological politics centering on the left and Marxism, and literature have somehow stubbornly remained my bedrock intellectual concerns, perhaps helping to explain why I have never been able to embrace fully the identity of sociologist. Often enough I have tried to set aside and resist the claims of the first two—never, never, never those of the third! Politics was a kind of family heritage—obviously so in the case of international relations because my father was a diplomat and I lived for two years at an impressionable age in Geneva on the eve of the most terrible war in history. I thought of my radicalism as a rebellion against my family, Upper Canada College, and my class. But I grew up in Washington, D.C., and later spent much time there visiting my parents, who lived in Washington for a total of eighteen years in three separate periods from the 1920's to the 1950's. I lived more briefly in Ottawa but regularly visited my parents and my sister there and vacationed at a family summer cottage nearby for more than thirty years. Washington and Ottawa are notoriously one-industry towns dominated by the business of government and politics. I hardly needed to be instructed about the significance of the state, solemnly declared to be "relatively autonomous" by recent sociologists, having spent so much of my youth in capital cities as well as in the Geneva of the ill-fated League of Nations, where conflicts among states loomed so large.

It hardly seems surprising that I can't remember seriously contemplating attending any university other than the University of Toronto or that I should have gone on to become a professor. My family line includes professors going back four generations, all of the first three associated with the University of Toronto. A great-grandfather on my mother's side was a classicist, a Protestant immigrant from Ireland, who became the second president of the university. He even has a Toronto street named after him, although McCaul Street has been in a shabby, deteriorated downtown neighborhood for as long as I can remember. Both of my grandfathers were prominent professors at the U. of T. One was a classicist recruited from Oxford by McCaul, who married McCaul's daughter, became principal of University College, the largest liberal arts college, served briefly as acting president of the university, and has a building, Hutton House on the University College campus, named after him. My paternal grandfather, George Wrong, was the founder of the university's history department and the creator of Canadian history as a scholarly discipline. He wrote the textbooks on Canadian and British history that were used for many years in the Ontario high schools. I remember as a small child tradespeople recalling this, not always fondly, and making the inevitable hackneyed jokes about the Wrong name.

George Wrong's oldest son married one of the four daughters of a famous Master of Balliol College, Oxford, and himself became a don at Magdalen College, publishing several books on Canadian history before dying young, when still in his thirties, though not before fathering six children. My father taught history at the University of Toronto for several years before joining the newly created Canadian Department of External Affairs along with a fellow junior member of the University of Toronto history department, Lester Bowles ("Mike") Pearson, who won the Nobel Peace prize in 1956 and became prime minister of Canada in the 1960's. My father and his siblings produced a total of eleven children. Of the four males, two became history professors, one (me) a sociology professor, and the other a medical doctor and professor who retired recently from the chair in internal medicine at the University of London. Of the seven women, one became a history professor in Scotland, one a private school teacher of Latin and Greek in Washington, D.C., and one a teacher in women's studies with a doctorate in history at a Quebec community college. Another of the seven, my sister, is a psychotherapist with a doctorate in psychology, two others are medical doctors, and one is a journalist in Montreal.

All this is rather daunting, not to say humbling, if one fancies that one has struck out on one's own in independent fashion. Perhaps I was fated to become a professor no matter what, but in choosing the identity of "intellectual" when still in high school with no thought of turning it to occupational advantage I had embraced a secular "calling" or "vocation" that was universalistic in reach and aspiration, even though it is now evident that in its combination of left political concerns and literary modernism it was very much a unique product of the fourth, fifth, and sixth decades of the twentieth century.

In enrolling at the University of Toronto I did make a point of separating myself from my Upper Canada College classmates by entering the large nondenominational arts college, a third of whose students were Jewish. I had already acquired a veritable philosemitic outlook, for in Geneva most of my friends had been American Jews from New York City or German Jews on the first leg of permanent migration from Nazi Germany. There was an awful lot of anti-Semitism of the genteel variety in Toronto at this time, against which I rebelled.

During my freshman year I stumbled in my own reading on various mystical ideas, chiefly in the writings of Aldous Huxley and Henry Miller, and turned to philosophy in search of answers — to popularized accounts by C. E. M. Joad and even Will Durant, Schopenhauer, the essays of William James and Bertrand Russell, and some writings of Bergson, Dewey, and Whitehead. All of this reading knocked me for a loop, because I wanted to think of myself as a hardheaded, atheistic scientific materialist. I didn't know what was happening to me and thought I might be having some kind of mystical experience or that I had been unlucky enough to hit on the ultimate secret, hidden from, or suppressed by, others, that nothing had any meaning. I babbled incoherently to a few people, including teachers and my father, and obtained a psychiatrist's certificate that I was suffering a nervous breakdown so as not to flunk out. In spite of doing little or no studying for my courses, I wrote and passed all my exams, achieving respectable grades.

I realize now that I was undergoing an acute anxiety attack. The discovery of so much that I didn't know and couldn't understand, of so many books that I hadn't read, overwhelmed me. I had never been any good at sports; I was not very successful with women, usually vainly pursuing popular, good-looking girls a bit older than me; and I had turned my back on wanting to be "one of the boys" in a passive, conforming spirit. My sense of personal worth depended totally on my intellectuality. I thought that I was nothing if I could not sound like the supersophisticated characters in Huxley's novels, or like Jallez and Jerphanion, the Parisian students of Jules Romains's endless "Men of Good Will" series of novels (utterly forgotten, it seems, today). Pathetic and juvenile, as I even half knew, but it was a long time before I fully recovered from this experience, which often recurred in milder forms for years afterward, usually at the beginning of the new academic year, and was the main cause of the writing block that I suffered in graduate school and for some time after.

The best students at Toronto enrolled in the honors program, requiring higher grades and an additional year of study to earn the degree. The program was designed as the opposite of Harvard's general-education curriculum, providing three years of fairly intensive specialized study in a particular field. I was tempted by a philosophy and English literature combination, but feared it after my "breakdown." Why did I choose sociology? Partly for no better reason than that my first girlfriend had chosen it, but also because it seemed relevant to my socialist beliefs and, the status of sociology being a lowly one, we were required to take courses in political science, economics, and philosophy as well as others chosen from an array that included history, psychology, and anthropology. My choice of sociology was also a rebellion against the family association with history. Several onetime colleagues of my father and grandfather even sought me out to try to dissuade me from wasting my time on such an unsound, newfangled, and disreputable pseudodiscipline.

Despite a small teaching staff, sociology was a popular honors subject, partly because an undergraduate degree in it entitled one to credit for a full year's work toward a degree in social work. This advantage attracted many women, who in my year outnumbered the four males by more than three to one. One of us was an older man who had already begun a career as a social worker, but the other two and I became close friends; with the addition of a few women, including several from the psychology program, with which we shared many courses, we formed a kind of nucleus of serious and interested students. In my senior year we were joined by a short, articulate young man named Erving Goffman. I had met him on a summer job for the government in Ottawa; on learning that he planned to resume his interrupted studies by coming to the University of Toronto to obtain the remaining degree credits he needed, I urged him to try sociology. (It may well be the only thing I am remembered for in future histories of sociology!)

Goffman stories are legion among those who knew him at all well, although mine go back farther than just about anyone else's. I shall confine myself to a few recollections about his intellectual outlook. The widespread notion that Erving was an inspired naïf, a novelist manqué with unusual powers of social observation, is utterly wrong. He already had an acute and far-ranging theoretical mind when I met him. He was much more intellectually advanced than the rest of us; I remember him rebuking us for reading textbooks and popularizations instead of tackling the originals. Once he defended Freud's emphasis on the body and the priority of infant experience against the more congenial neo-Freudian culturalists we all favored. His later antipathy to psychoanalysis is well known, but he created in me the first small twinge of doubt as to whether there was not perhaps more truth and profundity in the vision of the founder than in all the Erich Fromms, Karen Horneys, and Gordon Allports who were so ready to revise him. Erving

had studied philosophy and had actually read in full Whitehead's
Process and Reality. He argued in Whiteheadian language that
reality should be conceived "along the lines on which it is naturally articulated," a rule he obviously followed in his later work.

All of us, including Erving, were most attracted by the cultural anthropology that strongly shaped the sociology we were
taught. Its chief purveyor was the senior sociologist C. W. M. Hart,
an Australian anthropologist who had been a student of A. R.
Radcliffe-Brown. Some of us also took anthropology courses from
Reo Fortune, Margaret Mead's second husband, and in our senior
year from a young anthropologist out of Chicago with whom we
mixed a good deal socially. But Hart was the most inspiring of
teachers and undoubtedly deserved major credit for the surprising
number of Toronto students from this period who went on to become professional sociologists or anthropologists. He was a large,
saturnine man, resembling depictions of Simon Legree. He had a
reputation for being something of a reprobate; it was rumored that
he had been banned for drunken brawling from several local tav-
erns. This reputation, in conjunction with his witty mockery of
conventional pieties in the classroom, led the Catholic college to
forbid its students from studying sociology and another denomi-
national college to discourage such study. Hart was a convinced
functionalist. He gave us a year-long course (all Toronto courses
ran for both semesters, with an exam at the end of the year) on
Durkheim, especially *Le Suicide,* sections of which I translated
since it was not yet available in English.

I missed the theory course offered by S. D. Clark, the other
senior sociologist and later the dean of Canadian sociology, because he was on leave one year, but I first learned of the importance of Max Weber in his course on the development of Canada,
in which he discussed religious movements. We thought of Clark
as a historian rather than a sociologist, and unlike more recent
students we were not very interested in Canada, whoring, rather,
after universal generalizations. In many ways Clark was ahead of
his time—not, as we thought, behind it—in his historicist conception of the atemporality of functionalist community studies.
But he failed to enchant us with new vistas like those apparently
opened up by functionalism and the study of culture and person-

ality. In common with others at this time, my sense of the potentialities of sociology was strongly awakened by Erich Fromm's *Escape from Freedom*, which tried to synthesize three of my own
major interests: an interpretation of fascism and the rise of Hitler,
a version of psychoanalysis that was culturally relevant, and left-
wing political sympathies.

Both Hart and Clark introduced us to Talcott Parsons's *The
Structure of Social Action*, and Parsons himself visited us for several public lectures. I remember Goffman and me infuriating our
classmates by asking him questions that gave him the impression
that all present had read and understood his book as thoroughly
as we had, with the result that his later remarks were over the
heads of most of the audience. Robert Merton also came and gave
us his famous discussion of manifest and latent functions. I was
enthralled by his clarity and rigor after the rather fuzzy, organicist
anthropological functionalism to which I had been exposed and
decided then and there to do graduate work at Columbia instead
of following the usual path of Canadian students to Chicago. To be
sure, I was also excited by New York, where I had visited Geneva
school friends several years before, and looked forward to the prospect of finding congenial literary and anti-Stalinist left political
circles there.

In my senior year I read George Orwell and Arthur Koestler (including *Darkness at Noon* and his essay collection *The Yogi and
the Commissar*) and discovered *Partisan Review*. I was fully aware
that the political views I formed from these sources were far from
popular in the university community. It was the last year of the
war, and I could not know that in the passionate debate among
intellectuals over Communism and the Soviet Union that lay just
ahead, the side I had chosen would be confirmed by world events
before the end of the decade and was already attracting the most
able and independent writers and thinkers. But the guest speaker
at my graduating class banquet was a Soviet Embassy official re-
splendent in a Red Army uniform. (Less than a year later he was
expelled from the country when it was revealed that he was the
coordinator of Soviet espionage in Canada. Fifteen years later the
same man became the first Soviet ambassador to Cuba after Anas-
tas Mikoyan's famous visit had secured Fidel Castro's alignment

with the Soviet bloc.) I was aware of the efforts of the Communists to penetrate the CCF, including the student CCF club of which I was president, and of their insistent demands for a new popular front. They were firmly resisted on grounds of principle by David Lewis, the CCF national secretary, later leader of the New Democratic Party, its successor party, and a former Rhodes scholar whom I knew and respected. When they failed, Communist candidates ran in several Toronto federal and provincial constituencies, in which I campaigned arduously for the CCF. Two of my teachers who were Americans took me aside and solemnly warned me to be sure in New York to shun the "pro-fascist" followers of Trotsky and the Norman Thomas socialists. I silently resolved to do just the opposite and in due course acted accordingly. I recall that my very first week in New York I picked up a copy of Dwight Macdonald's *politics* at the newstand in front of the 116th Street subway station at Columbia, encountering in it the names of people I would later meet: Macdonald himself, Irving Howe, Louis Clair (Lewis Coser), C. Wright Mills, Paul Goodman, Lionel Abel.

Robert S. Lynd was the left-wing voice in the Columbia sociology department at this time. (Mills had only recently joined the department and was not full-time.) Under Lynd's auspices, a graduate student Socialist Club was organized and I became its first, and it turned out only, president. Our very first public meeting in early 1946 was a panel discussion of the proposition that the Soviet Union was a true socialist society and therefore the only hope for peace and progress in the world. Lynd's son Staughton, a precocious high school senior who later was prominent in the New Left of the 1960's, affirmed this statement and I opposed it, insisting that the Soviet Union was a totalitarian and imperialist despotism little if at all better than the just-defeated Nazi Germany. The audience, including Lynd Senior, didn't much like my view, with one exception who spoke up for me from the floor— Nathan Glazer. Politically involved graduate students were split between the largest group, which upheld the prevailing pro-Soviet views of most American liberals and looked to Lynd on the faculty for support, and a smaller, much more intellectual, anti-Stalinist, neo-Trotskyist group that included Glazer, Rose Coser, Morroe Berger, and myself, rather drawn to Mills, who published fairly often in anti-Stalinist left journals like *politics, Commentary,* and *Partisan Review.*

Merton's lectures did not disappoint me, but my first year at Columbia (1945–46) was frustrating. I found that I already knew more sociology than most of my fellow students and, needing less time to study, was eager to explore the New York scene but could find no companions to join me. Merton and Paul Lazarsfeld were just beginning in 1945–47, my years of full-time residency, to establish their ascendancy over the sociology department. The "unity of theory and research" that was the goal of the sociology they promoted, with research meaning survey research in the tradition Lazarsfeld established at the Bureau of Applied Social Research, was not yet as dominant as it became in the 1950's. This was not at all the kind of sociology, needless to say, that appealed to my sort of intellectual. I had little or no interest in becoming a specialized expert or a technician in possession of various certified research skills or even an academic man confined to a limited field of knowledge. I felt, consequently, more and more identified with the political and cultural world of the "New York intellectuals," as they have now come to be labeled, and alienated from the positivistic or science-building claims of sociology in general and sociology at Columbia in particular.

Years before, when I had first aspired to be an intellectual, I had been much impressed by the declaration of a character in André Malraux's *Man's Hope* that the way to "make the best of one's life" was "by converting as wide a range of experience as possible into conscious thought." (Still a pretty good definition of the intellectual's vocation, I think.) I was acutely conscious of the narrowness of my own experience and strongly regretted (I still do) not serving overseas in the war. So I jumped at the chance to work as a temporary seaman on a ship out of Montreal carrying a United Nations relief cargo to Europe. I enjoyed a proletarian-style Mediterranean cruise, stood the graveyard watch from midnight to four A.M., and caught at least a glimpse of the underside of postwar Europe when we docked for long stays in Venice and Trieste. Two summers later I repeated the experience, this time to the Baltic, docking at Gdynia, Hamburg, Rotterdam, and Antwerp. I was able to arrange to leave the ship and spent most of the summer in Paris, with shorter visits to Geneva, London, and Oxford. It turned out, alas, to be sixteen years before I again set foot in Europe, so these summers were much valued. I also cherish the memory of having worked and lived at close quarters—and played, on visits ashore in port—with a lively group of men from a working-class background quite different from my own. I have the impression that such an experience is less common among young people today than it was in my generation.

Back in New York, I fell in with a group of young literary bohemians in Greenwich Village. They were considerably more highbrow and self-consciously intellectual than the Beats who became famous a few years later. Essentially, they were a kind of junior auxiliary to *Partisan Review*, toward which, although they were occasional contributors, their attitude was highly ambivalent. I was much influenced by this circle for nearly a decade. They were scornful of academic life and particularly contemptuous of sociology, which did not strengthen my own far from robust self-confidence. I felt guilty for lacking the nerve to emulate them by burning my bridges to an academic career, although I was also sensibly restrained by the unstable, *Luftmensch* traits I sensed in several of the group whom I knew best.

Thanks to Nathan Glazer, I began to review books for the old Menshevik organ *The New Leader*, and for *Commentary*, of which Nat was a junior editor and to which several of my literary friends were also contributors. My first two published articles, on family sociology and on demography, eventually appeared in the "Study of Man" section created by Nat, who was himself its most brilliant contributor. I wrote regularly for *Commentary* for more than twenty years until the early 1970's, when its editor, Norman Podhoretz, turned the journal in an increasingly strident and monolithic anti-left direction, and I switched to *Dissent* as my major place of publication.

At Columbia I was inevitably drawn to Mills, who was a link between the sociology faculty and the larger New York intellectual world. His conception of sociology was more to my taste than that favored by most of the Columbia department in this period of strenuous discipline building. Ten years later his *The Sociological Imagination* was a book I would dearly love to have written

myself—certainly my favorite of Mills's works, most of which I
commented on in print at the time of their appearance, applaud-
ing their vigor and scope while criticizing the rhetorical radicalism that later made Mills a founder and hero of the New Left.
As Irving Louis Horowitz has correctly stressed in his biography,
there was more to Mills than his politics. His later work suffered,
I think, from his rupture with the New York intellectuals and,
more specifically, with his Columbia colleagues Merton, Richard
Hofstadter, and Lionel Trilling (as reported by Horowitz).

I completed my course work and passed my written and oral
comprehensives within two years but avoided writing any papers
with the single exception of a long one, for Mills, on bureaucracy
in the novels of Franz Kafka. I wistfully considered the possibility
of becoming an editor or an intellectual journalist connected to
one of the general political-cultural periodicals in the ambience of
the New York intellectuals. In the meantime I spent another two
years in New York teaching part-time at New York University in
the Bronx and fiddling with several abortive dissertation projects.
All of them were on political and literary subjects close to my
"real" interests, but I succeeded only, or so I thought, in convincing Merton, Mills, and Leo Lowenthal in succession of my hopeless inadequacy as a prospective scholar or social scientist. Then I
got married and took my first full-time teaching job at Princeton
but was let go after a year. The experience was repeated the next
year at the Newark branch of Rutgers University. The pay was low
and the teaching hours long by today's standards. The main reason
I lost both jobs was the shrinking enrollment caused by the small
college-age cohorts born in the worst years of the Depression, but
my confidence was shaken, and I still had not even settled on
a dissertation topic. Partly to appease my parents' anxieties over
my career vacillations, partly to show them that I was capable on
their terms, I twice took the examinations for the Canadian foreign service and was one of the dozen or so out of several hundred
candidates who qualified on both occasions. But at the point of
decision I drew back from the only serious alternative to an academic career that I have ever contemplated.

I was, however, much more influenced during those years than
I then cared to admit by the world of my father. He was appointed

the first Canadian ambassador to the United States and served for all but the opening eighteen months of the Truman administration, remaining in Washington for such a long time because old friends going back to the 1920's were now top State Department people, most notably Dean Acheson, the secretary of state. I visited my parents often, not only because the luxurious comforts of the embassy were welcome after drab graduate-student living conditions, but also to get the feel of official Washington and enjoy at least a worm's-eye view of history in the making. The succession of international crises and major decisions in the six years from the Truman Doctrine to the Korean peace settlement is surely unparalleled in American peacetime history. Canada, more than ever before or since, was involved in nearly all of them, and my father, always a tremendously hard worker, wore himself out. He died in his sixtieth year only seven months after finally leaving Washington.

In addition to what I had learned at second hand, I had chances to hear Acheson and other leading figures—among them Lester Pearson (often), Oliver Franks, Felix Frankfurter, Hubert Humphrey, and Christian Herter—discuss informally world (and also domestic) events. The decisions of those years were improvised under intense pressures, as is true, to be sure, of most political decisions. Acheson in 1969 entitled his memoirs *Present at the Creation*, but twenty years earlier neither he nor anyone else could have imagined that they were laying the foundations of an American foreign policy that stayed in effect for over forty years. I learned enough to *know* that the attacks of the "nationalist" Republican right were mostly nonsense, as were the charges of American imperialism still heard at the time in my own liberal-left milieu and revived in the 1960's by the revisionist historians of the cold war. Realism about the cold war and foreign policy in general has perhaps more than anything else isolated me from the conventional pieties of academic liberalism.

I had one year of systematic education in the field of international relations. After losing my second teaching job, the opportunity came through my father to work as a research assistant to George F. Kennan on problems of American foreign policy at the Institute for Advanced Study in Princeton. Few, if any, graduate programs could possibly have matched this experience. Most important, Kennan tried out his own developing ideas on his small staff. J. Robert Oppenheimer, then director of the Institute, and several top Princeton professors often participated in our group discussions. Several State Department officials and foreign diplomats visited us, as did Isaiah Berlin and Hans Morgenthau. It was an unforgettable year.

A result of these experiences and exposures was that I was from the very beginning of the cold war a bona fide example of what Mills with invidious intent labeled a "cold war liberal." And I remained one until the cold war ended in 1989–91. Ultimately, I think my attitude toward the cold war had roots going back to my two years of early adolescence spent in Geneva on the eve of the Second World War, when the Munich crisis became the first historical event that I remember as having an impact on my own life. I recall vividly my mother's outrage over the abandonment of Czechoslovakia—my father almost certainly shared her view, but his official position obliged him to keep his opinions to himself. What I acquired was the firm belief that resisting aggression by expansionist dictators was right in itself and was more likely to avoid all-out war than acquiescing in it. My support of the United States and NATO in the cold war kept me from joining the New Left radicals in the 1960's and my liberalism kept me from becoming a neoconservative in the 1970's. I did not, to be sure, support the war in Vietnam, but I never regarded it as an inherently immoral enterprise and I was inclined to dislike the antiwar protest movement as much as or more than the war itself. I always regarded Soviet power as the adversary, not some noxious ideology of "communism," and I agreed with Kennan's view of the necessary limits to the policy of "containment" to which he gave a name.

My work for Kennan ended when President Truman unexpectedly appointed him ambassador to the Soviet Union. Seven years after having entered graduate school, I found myself unemployed, with a record of having been fired from—or, as Bob Bierstedt would prefer to say, non-reappointed to—two academic jobs, still with no dissertation even under way, and rumored to have left the field by working for Kennan. The time had come to fish or cut bait on the dissertation. Kennan had hired me to work on population problems, although I had merely taught one undergraduate course on the subject without ever having formally studied demography. But I had learned quite a bit and had overcome my block by writing reports for Kennan, one of which I had revised for publication in *Commentary*. Kingsley Davis had recently joined the Columbia faculty, and several friends were writing dissertations in demography under his direction. Davis gave me welcome encouragement, and, with some financial help from my father and a little part-time teaching, I was able to spend most of the next two years completing the first draft of a dissertation in demography.

With revisions yet to make, I returned to my old undergraduate department at the University of Toronto for a year of research on Canadian voting patterns. I was moving into political sociology as a research field, but I also managed to write a short introductory book on the study of population (which has gone through six editions and is still in print). The next year I joined the regular teaching staff. I was happy in Toronto, surrounded by old friends, but my wife, a New Yorker to the bone, was not. So after two years I reluctantly returned to the States, accepting a position at Brown University, where in time I was granted tenure.

I continued to write fairly regularly for journals associated with the New York intellectuals, *Commentary*, *Dissent*, *Partisan Review*, and *The New Leader*, through the 1950's and 1960's. Before I had tenure, at least two chairmen urged me to desist from this writing, assuring me that it would do my career no good at all and perhaps even prejudice my chances for tenure. I did not follow their advice. My view of the reigning tendencies in sociology, both empirical and theoretical, continued to be highly critical. In common with a few others, I saw the work of Mills and David Riesman in the 1950's as a beacon of what sociology might be, but, alas, wasn't.

Although I was past thirty, the five years at Brown through the quiet late 1950's were for me years of incubation. I became a father. My major ideas and areas of interest within sociology crystallized. Brown was developing a graduate program in demography, but many faculty members in the program knew so little else that I ended up teaching broad undergraduate courses in theory and social organization, with the result that I taught, thought, and wrote myself—the three have for me always been closely connected—right out of demography. I retain, however, much respect for that craftsmanlike discipline; a field whose basic subject matter is natural quantities, it never offended my sensibilities by artificial quantification or by forcing human reality into the mode of what Mills called "abstracted empiricism."

At Brown I buried myself in the growing literature on the Holocaust to the point where I sometimes thought it not only the most significant thing that had ever happened but the only significant thing. I also read Freud more widely and deeply, partly to accommodate students disappointed by a behavioristic psychology department and a quantitative sociology department. The article for which I am best known to sociologists, "The Oversocialized Conception of Man in Modern Sociology," was conceived and written at this time. I was powerfully affected by the utopian Freudian writings of Herbert Marcuse and, especially, Norman O. Brown some years in advance of the rise of the counterculture of the 1960's to which their vision contributed. Their influence on me was not only intellectual, for it played a part in the ending of my first marriage when I fell in love with a woman to whom I have now been happily married for over thirty years.

The crisis in my personal life took me back to New York as a member of the graduate faculty of the New School for Social Research. I became editor of the New School's social science journal and learned much from having as colleagues the exiled German scholars who were still well represented on the faculty in the early 1960's. But financial problems, aggravated by alimony and child-support obligations, induced me to move in 1963 to New York University, where I have remained ever since except for short visiting and summer-session stints at various places, including interesting ones at the University of California at Berkeley, the University of Nevada–Reno, Trinity College in Connecticut, and Oxford. Our department at N.Y.U. has since the turmoil of the late 1960's been extraordinarily stable and harmonious; truly collegial relations among people of widely varying interests and backgrounds have prevailed there to an unusual degree. Although I live in Princeton, I have become, I suppose, a full-fledged New York intellectual, even serving on the editorial boards of *Dissent* and *Partisan Re-*

view. Of course, New York intellectual life is not what it once was—what is?—and I often wryly remember Goethe's advice to be careful of what you wish for in your youth because you will get it in middle age.

New York University is in the heart of Greenwich Village, where so many innovative cultural and political movements are born and their adherents live. The amorphousness of sociology as a field ensures that it will attract a probably disproportionate number of students attuned to *le dernier cri* in culture and politics, searchers for the true meaning of life, and *enragés* and *engagés* determined to change the world. Inevitably, we had more than our share of them in the N.Y.U. graduate sociology department. Until just a very few years ago one heard from the lips of students Marxist clichés that one had after a brief youthful flirtation rejected years before in the belief that one had outgrown them intellectually. I sometimes think that I have wasted far too much intellectual energy arguing with Marxists and about Marxism during at least two periods of my life separated by several decades.

The New Left struck me from the outset as the end of something rather than as a new beginning, a pathetic willed and thoroughly histrionic attempt to revive a set of political and ideological impulses going back to the nineteenth century that had no future. I recall seeing a student with a raised red fist stenciled on his canvas jacket worn over a T-shirt with "power to the people" emblazoned upon it. I burst out laughing—it seemed a species of play-acting that could not possibly be taken seriously. To me, the 1930's were to the 1960's as tragedy is to farce, in Marx's famous aphorism. Yet after all the sound and fury in 1968–71, I came to wonder whether I wasn't perhaps missing something, whether the huge shadows cast by Hitler, the Second World War, Stalinism, and the early cold war did not prevent me from seeing some vital historical meaning in the ferment of the 1960's. But, of course, I turned out to be right in my original reaction.

Mills's definition of the sociological imagination as the understanding of "the intersection of history and biography within society" has always appealed to me, though not, as for Mills, because it makes possible the redefinition of "private troubles" as "public issues," thereby providing a rationale for political action.

With age I have become not only more anti-ideological but more antitheoretical in general, and it now seems to me that historical knowledge is not just necessary but often sufficient to answer many of our most urgent questions. I remember my father arguing that sociology should only be a graduate subject studied after the acquisition of broad historical knowledge. That was also Sorokin's view when he was invited to head the first sociology department at Harvard, but he did not get his way. However, I am not prepared to capitulate completely to the shades of my father and those historians who long ago tried to dissuade me from studying sociology, for history as a discipline has since then enormously widened and deepened its concerns. To a considerable extent this expansion has been the result of enrichment by ideas, methods, and even subject matters—stratification, cultural *mentalités*, the family, demographic trends—taken over from sociology and anthropology. I was one of the first people to review at length Philippe Ariés's *Centuries of Childhood*; I suggested that because it deals with the lives of our own ancestors, archaic and distorted echoes of which still surround us, social history of its kind conveys more successfully to the reader than anthropological reports on primitive peoples both "the strangeness of time and change in the life of man and society" and, in Ariés's own words, "the tremor of life that he can feel in his own existence." But fifty years ago we were right to be excited by the subjects sociologists studied. And this was a more important source of its appeal than the chimera of creating a social science modeled on the natural sciences that played so large a role in sociology's drive for disciplinary respectability.

"As we grow older the world becomes stranger, the pattern more complicated." T. S. Eliot was the poet of my generation, and some of his lines have become so much a part of me that I scarcely know when I am quoting. There is the strangeness of the sheer pastness of the past: anything out of the 1930's is for me bathed in a special light, a distant glow from the lost country of childhood. Not only is there the further strangeness of realizing that one's memories have become history, or the awareness of "a lifetime burning in every moment," but I find myself reaching back before my own life to find continuity in "not the lifetime of one man only / But of old stones that cannot be deciphered." Here, too, history and biography intersect. "People are always shouting they want to create a better future," writes Milan Kundera in *The Book of Laughter and Forgetting*. "It's not true. The future is an apathetic void of no interest to anyone. The past is full, eager to irritate us, provoke and insult, tempt us to destroy or repaint it. The only reason people want to be masters of the future is to change the past." Un-American, that, but so be it.

What I have come to value most in a sociologist is not theoretical reach, logical rigor, empirical exactitude, or moral passion but a palpable sense of reality. It is not a unitary trait, and it is more easily pointed to than described. My old classmate Erving Goffman had it, which is why his work will live. But it is not limited to accounts of micro-interaction or everyday life. Raymond Aron had it too. Of the "classical" sociologists, it was preeminently possessed by Max Weber. When I first read Weber as a graduate student in the then-new Gerth-Mills translations, my response was the same as that of Ernst Topitsch: "In the midst of this twilight atmosphere of insidious intellectual dishonesty, the work of Max Weber shed a flood of cold hard light. Anyone who has once been thunderstruck by contact with him can never see the world in the same light again."

If one lives long enough, one sees history—the sequence of events, not the discipline that studies them—disaggregate many things that once seemed indissolubly connected. At least that is true of life in the present century. Here are a few examples, fairly obvious ones no doubt. In contrast to fifty years ago, protest against technological change and modernization comes today from intellectuals on the left rather than the right, although this may be further evidence that the left-right distinction itself is becoming obsolete. Who can believe any longer that the elimination of Victorian sexual repressions makes people more selfless, more loving, and less acquisitive? The association between modernist cultural tastes and political radicalism, virtually the hallmark of an intellectual when I "decided" to become one, clearly no longer holds. To understand the world, one needs a feeling for the peculiarity and fragility of the present historical moment to avoid the fallacy of both eternalizing the present and exaggerating its novelty. No abstract theoretical model identifying relevant variables, nor careful empirical charting of trends, can make up for the absence of such a sense of the present.

A keen awareness of the particularity of the historical moment, its precise location along the moving continuum of political and cultural events, was one of the most characteristic features of the New York intellectuals when I encountered them in the 1940's. Sometimes the striving for this awareness seemed labored, even ludicrous. I remember an intense, opinionated friend complaining after a woman had resisted his overtures that "women are taking the period badly." I thought this was a pretty classy way of easing the pain of sexual rejection, although even in those unenlightened days its unabashed male chauvinism seemed a bit raw. But this highly charged sense of the historical moment was not just a by-product of commitment to Marxism, for it reflected the truly apocalyptic events of the first half of the century. The theme of ceaseless change afflicting all of us with what has been called future shock has been rather overdone in recent decades. I liked to argue before 1989 that nothing really important had happened in the world since about 1950—nothing, that is, at all comparable to two world wars, the Russian Revolution, the Great Depression, the rise of fascism, the Stalinist terror, the Holocaust, the birth of new and powerful non-Western nations, the invention of nuclear weapons, and the beginnings of the cold war with the Soviet Union. A provocative exaggeration at best, at worst a half-truth. Despite the ever-changing surface, we still lived in a world that had assumed its shape in the first half of the century. All epochs—or generations—may, as Ranke said, be equal in the sight of God, but not all of them are equally consequential in history. The collapse of Communism and the end of the cold war have, of course, ended both the threat of world destruction through nuclear warfare and much of the stability imposed by the policies of deterrence of the two superpowers that averted such a disaster. Ancient tendencies as well as undeveloped potentialities kept in check by the cold war have asserted themselves. And all this has happened with symbolic appropriateness in the closing decade of both the century and the second millennium.

Important as a sense of reality is to a sociologist, he or she is also subject to stringent additional intellectual requirements.

For literature, however, the communication of a sense of reality through language is its very essence. I mean a sense of reality beyond the words on the page, the fashionable notions of structuralists and deconstructionists to the contrary notwithstanding. Because my intellectual generation had "literary sensibility," we had no need to develop the kinds of arcane and abstract theories of the primacy of the simple and concrete that have been so prominent in sociology since the antipositivist revolts of the 1960's.

I have never been to Dublin. I have sometimes been tempted to take one of those tours on or about June 16 to walk the streets that Leopold Bloom walked, peer at the facade of Number 10 Eccles Street, go out to the headland slope where Molly said yes, visit the Martello Tower, and perhaps even swim in the snotgreen sea. But I don't really need such a trip, for I can imagine well enough standing on the bridge over the Liffey where it flows into the harbor and listening to the water murmur, "And it's old and old it's sad and old it's sad and weary I go back to you, my cold father, my cold and mad father, my cold mad feary father, till the near sight of the mere size of him, the moyles and moyles of it, moananoaning, makes me seasilt saltsick and I rush, my only, into your arms."

I was once in northern Mississippi for little more than an hour when driving east across the country alone. It was January; I was slowed up in Memphis by school buses delivering children to their homes, and when I crossed the state line a pale, late-afternoon sun shone on light snow. But everything looked as it should, and the air was full of voices—Sartoris voices and Snopes voices, the voices of Ike McAslin and Lucas Beauchamp, of Addie Bundren and Rosa Coldfield—but most of all doomed Compson voices— Benjy saying, or rather remembering since he could not speak, "Caddy smelled like trees"; Mrs. Compson whining, "It can't be simply to flout and hurt me. Whoever God is, he would not permit that. I'm a lady"; Quentin insisting, "I don't hate the South. . . . *I don't hate it* he thought, panting in the cold air, the iron New England dark; *I don't, I don't!* I don't hate it! *I don't hate it!*" Clearest of all was the voice of Dilsey, walking home from the Negro church on Easter morning of 1928, tears rolling down her face, saying to her embarrassed daughter, "I've seed de first en de last. I seed de beginnin, and now I sees de endin." As I approached the next state line, I wondered how long I would have to live there before the voices would fade and it would become for me something more than Faulkner country. But the voices are not heard only in Mississippi. A few years ago a plaque was set in the wall of one of the bridges over the Charles between Cambridge and Boston commemorating the site where on June 2, 1910, Quentin Compson committed suicide by drowning himself in the river. But such an event never happened; Quentin Compson never existed, he is nothing but words on a page, the product of one man's fancy. The reality of the imagination and, inversely, the power to imagine the real lie at the root of all successful creations of the mind.

REFERENCE MATTER

Notes

Chapter 1

1. For a celebrant of capitalism who lauds the "invention" of the market, see Novak 1982: 65, 76–77, 88, 116; for a detractor who regards Adam Smith as the eulogist of "selfish" behavior and the virtual founding father not only of economics but of market capitalism itself, see Schwartz 1986: 57–68, 301, 308.

2. Nove made the remark at a conference on "market socialism" organized by the journal *Dissent* at the New School for Social Research, New York, May 12, 1990.

Chapter 2

1. This idea of objective reason should not be confused with the notion of action that "uses the objectively correct means in accordance with scientific knowledge" as distinct from action based on the actor's possibly erroneous belief that he/she has used effective means. The latter has been called "subjective rationality," connoting the actor's perception that he/she is acting rationally, whereas objective rationality refers only to actions for which it can be verified that the means-ends link is causally effective. See the valuable elaboration of this distinction by Rogers Brubaker in *The Limits of Rationality* (1984: 53–55). Both versions of rationality would be lumped together as "subjective reason" by defenders of the premodern conception of "objective reason." In his final chapter Brubaker identifies this classical conception of reason with "philosophical anthropology" or "the anthropological

perspective on reason" and discusses Weber's complex relation to it. See esp. pp. 91–101.

2. Parsons followed Pareto in identifying rational action as such with the effective (according to empirical science) use of means to attain a given end—the equivalent of "objective rationality" in the sense defined in note 1. Parsons wrote: "Action is rational in so far as it pursues ends possible within the conditions of the situation, and by the means which, among those available to the actor, are intrinsically best adapted to the end for reasons understandable and verifiable by positive empirical science" (1937: 58). Parsons considered action that involved a choice of means regarded as appropriate by the actor but not by the judgment of science to be irrational—he had no conception of "subjective" as distinct from "objective" rationality. This accounts for why, unlike Weber, he chose to identify as "nonrational" (as distinct from "irrational") action engaged in as an end-in-itself because it intrinsically embodied a norm or value. Rational choice theorists have clearly chosen not to follow such a highly restrictive view of rationality.

3. Coleman 1990: 18, italics in original. This view obviously differs from Parsons's in defining rationality entirely from the point of view of the actor independent of any "objective" scientific standpoint.

4. Horkheimer 1947: 6; Marcuse 1968: 201–26; Strauss 1953: 35–80.

5. Amitai Etzioni's *The Moral Dimension* (1988) is one of the fullest recent elaborations of this point of view.

6. Coleman 1990: 241. Coleman's massive work can be seen as a rejoinder over half a century later in defense of utilitarian individualism against Parsons's enormously influential rejection of it in *The Structure of Social Action*.

7. I discuss at some length the distinction between "Meadian" socialization, or the acquisition of language enabling the individual cognitively to "take the role of the other," and "Freudian" socialization, or the emotional identification with others leading to the eventual "internalization of social norms," in *The Problem of Order* (1994), chaps. 3, 5, and 6. See especially my discussion of Coleman and rational choice theory, of which these comments are a continuation (pp. 193–201).

8. Harrison C. White (1990: 785) notes that "Coleman, unlike Gary Becker, recognizes that self-interest cannot exist without a self."

9. Robert B. Edgerton (1985: 4–16) contrasts the "normative model" with the emphasis, in reaction against it, on "strategic interaction," which involves the manipulation of norms by individual actors for self-interested purposes.

10. As Elster writes, "There can be no society in which people *as a*

rule knowingly refuse to choose the best means to realize their goals" (1989: 98, n. 3; italics in original).

11. I am echoing the late William Barrett's memoir *The Truants* (1982). Barrett took his title from Philip Rahv, who, Barrett reports, sadly so described their erstwhile associates in the circle around the journal Rahv founded and Barrett for a time coedited, *Partisan Review*.

12. The quotation is actually from an unnamed "wise French critic" whom Barrett (1947: 5) cites as epitomizing Dostoyevsky's argument in *Notes from Underground*.

Chapter 4

1. See, for example, Clegg 1989: 72–75. For a particularly lucid objection to intentionality, see Gasky 1995.

2. Wrong 1995: chap. 9, first section. I have also discussed it at even greater length in *The Problem of Order* (1994: chaps. 4 and 5).

3. J. G. Merquior uses the term *pancratism* to refer to "a systematic reduction of all social processes to largely unspecified patterns of domination" in *Foucault* (1985: 115).

4. See my elaboration of this conception in chap. 3 of *The Problem of Order* (1994).

Chapter 5

1. See, e.g., Schacht 1970, Israel 1971.

2. Schacht suggests the separation of "self-alienation" from the use of the concept as a relation in *Alienation* (1970: 256–59). See also Tucker 1972: 148–49.

Chapter 6

1. Excluding, of course, a few categories of persons (other than minors) that are nowadays limited in size in most constitutional democracies.

2. The best-known references are Marx's "Amsterdam speech," partially reported in Gerth 1957: 236–37; and Friedrich Engels, "Introduction" to Marx's *Class Struggles in France*, quoted in Wolfe 1965: 219–23. The controversial translation history of Engels's text is summarized by Wolfe, pp. 222–23, n. 8. Wolfe is highly informative on the attitude of Marx and Engels to universal suffrage and parliamentary democracy.

3. For broad reviews and summaries, see Lenski 1966: 308–433; Parkin 1972.

4. See Stein Rokkan's valuable comparative survey of progress towards full democratization in Western Europe (1966: 101–31).

5. I have in this section drawn on and revised an earlier article, "The Rhythm of Democratic Politics," which has been reprinted in *Skeptical Sociology* (1976c: 226–41). This paragraph is adapted from my contribution to a symposium in *Commentary* (Wrong 1976b).

6. The blurring, of course, is in accordance with Anthony Downs's expectations in his well-known *An Economic Theory of Democracy* (1957).

7. For an excellent argument developing the partial mutual entailment of liberty and equality, see Walzer 1974: 107–23; see also Lukes 1977: 96–117.

8. The combination of the *content* of a movement's ideology with its *social base* leads Lipset to use the unfortunate, apparently oxymoronic phrase "extremism of the center" to characterize fascism (1960: 132–33).

9. A case in point was the defeat in Alberta in 1935 of the agrarian socialist United Farmers of Alberta by the Social Credit Party, which at the time was widely perceived as one of several radical movements responding to the economic distress of the depression, although its doctrines were upheld elsewhere by thinkers and political sectarians on the extreme right. The Canadian and Albertan parties ultimately moved to the far right after World War II.

10. See the arguments of Popper 1964; Gellner 1964: 15–20; Nisbet 1969: 160–88.

11. See the old but still valuable account by Adolf Sturmthal (1943: 35–97, 129–43).

12. The Canadian Conservative Party renamed itself the "Progressive-Conservative" Party in order to increase its appeal to an electorate favorable toward social reform immediately after World War II.

13. President Eisenhower used the label "moderate Republicanism" to distinguish his outlook from that of the traditional anti–New Deal Republicans shortly after his election in 1952.

14. I owe the suggestion of this image to Robert L. Heilbroner.

15. I have drawn on Raymond Aron's valuable account of how democracy generates both a Left and a Right Opposition (1954: 241–61).

16. See the impressive attempt to support this with comparative evidence by Robert A. Dahl (1971: 105–23). See also Tom Nairn's brilliant argument (1977) concerning the oldest capitalist nation, Britain; also Ernest Gellner's searching discussion of Nairn (1978: 103–11).

17. See the useful brief discussion by Martins (1971: 60–63); also Gellner 1964: 66–172.

18. Arthur Schlesinger Jr., in addition to using his father's "tides"

metaphor, described the movement of American politics as similar to "the systole and diastole" of the beat of the heart (1980: 42–43, 70–73, 79). Schlesinger Jr.'s fullest statement of the cyclical theory is in his *The Cycles of American History* (1986: 23–48).

19. See Wrong 1981b, Lipset 1982, and Schlesinger Jr. 1982. I confess that I am possibly vulnerable to Schlesinger's point that sociologists are always explaining things as owing to "deep" structural trends, and I am enchanted by his quotation from Emerson: "In analyzing history, do not be too profound, for often the causes are quite superficial." See Wrong 1982b. I had tried to combine in my original formulation of the rhythm theory Lipset's "democratic class struggle" with the Schlesingers'—*père et fils*—view of a cyclical spiral movement over time.

20. An excellent discussion of the implications of the spatial metaphor and of alternatives to it may be found in Bobbio 1996: 40–51.

Chapter 7

1. For an especially lucid criticism of Benedict's psychiatric relativism, see Wegrocki 1948: 551–61.

2. Gitlin 1995: 166–99. See the inept and superficial effort of Roger Kimball to "trash" Gitlin's book, arguing as if there could be no genuine liberal or left-universalist Enlightenment-based rejection of ideological multiculturalism and the identity politics based on it (1996).

3. Gitlin criticizes the loose invocation of questionable demographics in *The Twilight Of Common Dreams* (1995: 107–25).

4. The distinction has been most fully developed by Liah Greenfeld (1992).

Chapter 8

1. This paragraph is chiefly based on Ladd 1979: 101–22. For surveys on "life-styles," see also Yankelovich 1981: 59–62.

2. For a short but incisive account of Labour and SDP sources of support, see Williams 1982.

3. The most detailed and cogent argument to this effect that I know is Turner 1981: 289–317; see also Abercrombie, Hill, and Turner 1980: 102–5, 138, 180–85.

4. As indicated by Glazer 1979: 89–100; see also Bazelon 1979.

5. Hacker does this, most fully, in "What Rules America?" (1975); also see his "Cutting Classes" (1976).

6. Hacker 1979; also Parkin 1982: 576–78.

7. In 1819, Henri de Saint-Simon suggested that the instantaneous loss of all of France's courtiers, state officials, and church dignitaries

would do little permanent damage to French society. By contrast, the sudden elimination of the country's leading craftsmen, scientists, and artists would transform the nation into a "lifeless corpse" that would require at least a generation to revive.

8. Statistic from Hacker 1976: 15.

9. See Wrong 1982a: 899–905. See also my earlier review of Gouldner's *The Two Marxisms* (1980) in *The New Leader* (1980: 16–18).

Chapter 9

1. See my discussion of "competent authority" in Wrong 1995: 52–60. See also Wrong 1976a: 262–72.

2. Parkin distinguishes between "individualist" and "collectivist" criteria of discrimination or exclusion (1979: 65–71).

3. See the discussion by Peter Steinfels (1979: 216–18) of the 1965 Moynihan Report. Senator Moynihan recalled (1986: 24) that he borrowed the phrase "equality of results" from Nathan Glazer in his 1965 report. For an even earlier statement of the principle of reverse discrimination by Daniel Bell, see his "Reflections on the Negro and Labor" (1963: 18–20).

4. The term "situs," meaning sphere of institutional or organizational activity, is Daniel Bell's (1980: 159). See Chapter 14 for a further discussion of the term, and see Chapter 8 for my critique of the new class concept.

5. I have drawn considerably in the next few paragraphs on Daniel Bell's "The 'Intelligentsia' in American Society," in Bell 1980: 119–37.

6. I am citing Louis Menand's humorous query at a conference on the centennial of Edmund Wilson's birth held at Princeton University on Nov. 17–18, 1995.

7. Brombert's remarks are explicitly confined to "the French concept of the intellectual," but since he himself shows that the word if not the concept is of French invention, I have not hesitated to apply his observation more broadly.

Chapter 10

1. Merton (1961: 21) wrote: "One of its [sociology's] principal functions is to subject popular beliefs about man and his works to responsible investigations."

2. One of the best discussions of the epistemological issue and its larger implications that I have seen is in Apel (1977).

3. Ned Polsky contends that, although he borrowed the term from Alfred Adler, he himself is responsible for its spread through his book

originally published in 1967 and later widely excerpted in anthologies for college courses. I remain unpersuaded that Weber was not the original source. Polsky (1985: ix), incidentally, properly notes that "'lifestyle' has been horrendously overworked and indeed become a cliche of the adman [and] should now be avoided by any serious writer."

4. The phrases in quotation marks are drawn from Yankelovich (1981) and from Bellah et al. (1985).

Chapter 13

1. Riesman was kind enough to send me a copy of his talk at the 1987 meeting of the Eastern Sociological Society, at which he made this comment. The talk was published in *Society* in 1990.

Bibliography

Abercrombie, Nicholas, Stephen Hill, and Bryan S. Turner. 1980. *The Dominant Ideology Thesis*. London: Allen and Unwin.

———. 1986. *Sovereign Individuals of Capitalism*. London: Allen and Unwin.

Apel, Karl Otto. 1977. "Types of Social Science in the Light of Human Interests of Knowledge." *Social Research* 44 (Autumn): 425–70.

Arendt, Hannah. 1951. *The Origins of Totalitarianism*. New York: Harcourt, Brace.

———. 1964. *Eichmann in Jerusalem*. New York: Viking.

———. 1968. *Between Past and Future*. New York: Viking.

Aron, Raymond. 1954. *The Century of Total War*. Garden City, N.Y.: Doubleday.

———. 1984. *Politics and History*. New Brunswick, N.J.: Transaction.

Barrett, William. 1947. *What Is Existentialism?* New York: Partisan Review Series.

———. 1982. *The Truants: Adventures Among the Intellectuals*. Garden City, N.Y.: Doubleday.

Bazelon, David T. 1979. "How Now 'the New Class'?" *Dissent* (Fall): 443–49.

Bell, Daniel. 1960. *The End of Ideology*. Glencoe, Ill.: Free Press.

———. 1963. "Reflections on the Negro and Labor." *New Leader* (Jan. 21): 18–20.

———. 1973. *The Coming of Post-Industrial Society*. New York: Basic Books.

———. 1976. *The Cultural Contradictions of Capitalism*. New York: Basic Books.

———. 1979. "The New Class: A Muddled Concept," in B. Bruce-Briggs, ed., *The New Class?* New York: McGraw-Hill.

———. 1980. *The Winding Passage: Essays and Sociological Journeys 1960–1980.* Cambridge, Mass.: ABT Books.

Bellah, Robert N., et al. 1985. *Habits of the Heart.* New York: Harper and Row.

Bellow, Saul. 1970. *Mr. Sammler's Planet.* New York: Viking.

Bendix, Reinhard. 1978. *Kings or People: Power and the Mandate to Rule.* Berkeley: University of California Press.

Benedict, Ruth. 1934. *Patterns of Culture.* Boston: Houghton Mifflin.

Berger, Peter L. 1966. "Response." *New Left Review* 35 (Jan.–Feb.): 76.

———. 1967. *The Sacred Canopy.* Garden City, N.Y.: Doubleday Anchor Books.

———. 1986. *The Capitalist Revolution: Fifty Propositions About Prosperity, Equality, and Liberty.* New York: Basic Books.

Berger, Peter L., and Thomas Luckmann. 1966. *The Social Construction of Reality.* Garden City, N.Y.: Doubleday Anchor Books.

Berlin, Isaiah. 1992. *The Crooked Timber of Humanity: Chapters in the History of Ideas.* New York: Vintage.

Bloom, Allan. 1987. *The Closing of the American Mind.* New York: Simon and Schuster.

Bobbio, Norbert. 1996. *Left & Right: The Significance of a Political Distinction.* Chicago: University of Chicago Press.

Braudel, F. 1986. *The Wheels of Commerce: Civilization and Capitalism 1500–1800.* Vol. 2. New York: Harper and Row.

Braunschweig, Max. 1946. "The Philosophic Thought of the Young Marx," in William Phillips and Philip Rahv, eds., *The Partisan Reader.* New York: Dial Press.

Brombert, Victor. 1983. "Toward a Portrait of the French Intellectual," in Edith Kurzweil and William Phillips, eds., *Writers and Politics: A Partisan Review Reader.* Boston: Routledge and Kegan Paul.

Brown, Norman O. 1959. *Life Against Death.* Middletown, Conn.: Wesleyan University Press.

Brubaker, Rogers. 1984. *The Limits of Rationality: An Essay on the Social and Moral Thought of Max Weber.* London: Allen and Unwin.

Bruce-Briggs, B. 1979a. "An Introduction to the Idea of the New Class," in B. Bruce-Briggs, ed., *The New Class?* New York: McGraw-Hill.

———. 1979b. "Conclusion: Notes Toward a Delineation of the New Class," in B. Bruce Briggs, ed., *The New Class?* New York: McGraw-Hill.

Clegg, Stewart R. 1989. *Frameworks of Power.* Newbury Park, Calif: Sage.

Cohen, Jean L. 1983. "The New Class: Does It Exist? 2. Skeptical Thoughts from Another Direction." *Dissent* (Fall): 499–504.

Coleman, James S. 1990. *Foundations of Social Theory*. Cambridge, Mass.: Harvard University Press.

———. 1993. "The Rational Reconstruction of Society." *American Sociological Review* 58 (Feb.): 1–15.

Collingwood, R. G. 1942. *The New Leviathan*. Oxford: Clarendon.

Coser, Lewis A. 1965. *Men of Ideas*. New York: Free Press.

Dahl, Robert A. 1971. *Polyarchy: Participation and Opposition*. New Haven: Yale University Press.

Dahl, Robert A., and Charles E. Lindblom. 1953. *Politics, Economics and Welfare*. New York: Harper and Row.

Diggins, John Patrick. 1992. *The Rise and Fall of the American Left*. New York: Norton.

Dobriner, William L. 1963. *Class in Suburbia*. Englewood Cliffs, N.J.: Prentice-Hall.

Downs, Anthony. 1957. *An Economic Theory of Democracy*. New York: Harper and Row.

Edgerton, Robert B. 1985. *Rules, Exceptions, and Social Order*. Berkeley: University of California Press.

Eliot, T. S. 1963. *Collected Poems, 1909-1962*. London: Faber and Faber.

Elster, Jon. 1989. *The Cement of Society: A Study of Social Order*. Cambridge, Eng.: Cambridge University Press.

Etzioni, Amitai. 1988. *The Moral Dimension*. New York: Free Press.

Finkielkraut, Alain. 1995. *The Defeat of the Mind*. New York: Columbia University Press.

Freidson, Eliot. 1968. "The Impurity of Professional Authority," in Howard S. Becker, Blanche Geer, David Riesman, and Robert S. Weiss, eds., *Institutions and the Person*. Chicago: Aldine.

Gans, Herbert J. 1988. *Middle American Individualism*. New York: Free Press.

Gaski, John F. 1995. "'Volume' of Power: A New Conceptualization of the Power Construct." *Sociological Spectrum* 15 (3): 257–76.

Geertz, Clifford. 1988. *Works and Lives: The Anthropologist as Author*. Stanford, Calif.: Stanford University Press.

Gellner, Ernest. 1964. *Thought and Change*. London: Weidenfeld and Nicolson.

———. 1974. *Contemporary Thought and Politics*. London: Routledge.

———. 1978. "Nationalism, or the New Confessions of a Justified Edinburgh Sinner." *Political Quarterly* 49 (Jan.–Mar.): 103–11.

Gerth, Hans, ed. 1957. *The First International: Minutes of the Hague Congress*. Madison: University of Wisconsin Press.

Gerth, Hans, and C. Wright Mills. 1953. *Character and Social Structure*. New York: Harcourt, Brace.

———, eds. 1946. *From Max Weber: Essays in Sociology*. New York: Oxford University Press.

Giddens, Anthony. 1985. *The Nation-State and Violence*. Cambridge: Polity Press.

Gitlin, Todd. 1995. *The Twilight of Common Dreams: Why America is Wracked by Culture Wars*. New York: Metropolitan Books.

Glazer, Nathan. 1975. *Affirmative Discrimination: Ethnic Inequality and Public Policy*. New York: Basic Books.

———. 1979. "Lawyers and the New Class," in B. Bruce-Briggs, ed., *The New Class?* New York: McGraw-Hill.

Gouldner, Alvin. 1979. *The Future of the Intellectuals and the Rise of the New Class*. New York: Seabury Press.

———. 1980. *The Two Marxisms*. New York: Seabury Press.

Greenfeld, Liah. 1992. *Nationalism: Five Roads to Modernity*. Cambridge, Mass.: Harvard University Press.

Gutman, Robert, and Dennis Wrong. 1961. "David Riesman's Typology of Character," in Seymour Martin Lipset and Leo Lowenthal, eds., *Culture and Social Character: The Work of David Riesman Reviewed*. Glencoe, Ill.: Free Press.

Hacker, Andrew. 1975. "What Rules America?" *New York Review of Books* (May 1): 9–13.

———. 1976. "Cutting Classes." *New York Review of Books* (Mar. 4): 15–18.

———. 1979. "Two 'New Classes' or None?" in B. Bruce-Briggs, ed., *The New Class?* New York: McGraw-Hill.

Hardwick, Elizabeth. 1954. "Riesman Considered." *Partisan Review* 21: 548–56.

Hechter, Michael. 1987. *Principles of Group Solidarity*. Berkeley: University of California Press.

Hirschman, Albert O. 1970. *Exit, Voice and Loyalty*. Cambridge, Mass.: Harvard University Press.

Hollander, Paul. 1973. "Sociology, Selective Determinism and the Rise of Expectations." *American Sociologist* 8 (Nov.): 147–53.

Horkheimer, Max. 1947. *Eclipse of Reason*. New York: Oxford University Press.

Horkheimer, Max, and Theodor W. Adorno. 1972 (1944). *Dialectic of Enlightenment*. New York: Seabury Press.

Hout, Michael, Clem Brooks, and Jeff Manza. 1995. "The Democratic Class Struggle in the United States, 1948–1992." *American Sociological Review* 60 (Dec.): 805–28.

Howe, Irving. 1968. "The New York Intellectuals: A Chronicle and a Critique." *Commentary* 46 (Oct.): 29–51.

Howe, Irving, and Lewis Coser. 1957. *The American Communist Party: A Critical History (1919–1957)*. Boston: Beacon Press.

Israel, Joachim. 1971. *Alienation from Marx to Modern Sociology: A Sociological Analysis*. Boston: Allyn and Bacon.

Jacoby, Russell. 1987. *The Last Intellectuals: American Culture in the Age of Academe*. New York: Basic Books.

Kimball, Roger. 1996. "Whose Enlightenment Is It?" *The New Criterion* 14 (Apr.): 5–8.

Kolakowski, Leszek. 1978. *Main Currents of Marxism*. Vol. 3. Oxford: Oxford University Press.

Konrad, George, and Ivan Szelényi. 1979. *The Intellectuals on the Road to Class Power*. New York: Harcourt Brace Jovanovich.

Kundera, Milan. 1980. *The Book of Laughter and Forgetting*. New York: Knopf.

Ladd, Everett Carll, Jr. 1979. "Pursuing the New Class: Social Theory and Survey Data," in B. Bruce-Briggs, ed., *The New Class?* New York: McGraw-Hill.

Lasch, Christopher. 1977. *Haven in a Heartless World: The Family Besieged*. New York: Basic Books.

———. 1978. *The Culture of Narcissism: American Life in an Age of Diminishing Expectations*. New York: Norton.

———. 1984. *The Minimal Self: Psychic Survival in Troubled Times*. New York: Norton.

———. 1991. *The True and Only Heaven: Progress and Its Critics*. New York: Norton.

Lenski, Gerhard. 1966. *Power and Privilege: A Theory of Social Stratification*. New York: McGraw-Hill.

Lipset, Seymour Martin. 1960. *Political Man*. Garden City, N.Y.: Doubleday.

———. 1968. *Revolution and Counterrevolution*. New York: Basic Books.

———. 1982. "Comments." *Dissent* (Winter): 107–10.

Lukes, Steven. 1974. *Power: A Radical View*. London: Macmillan.

———. 1977. *Essays in Social Theory*. New York: Columbia University Press.

Malraux, André. 1941. *Man's Hope*. New York: Modern Library.

Mannheim, Karl. 1946. *Ideology and Utopia*. New York: Harcourt, Brace.

Marcuse, Herbert. 1955. *Eros and Civilization*. Boston: Beacon Press.

———. 1968. "Industrialization and Capitalism in the Work of Max Weber," in *Negations: Essays in Critical Theory*. Boston: Beacon Press.

Martins, Herminio. 1971. "Portugal," in Margaret Scotford Archer and Salvador Giner, eds., *Contemporary Europe: Class, Status, and Power*. New York: St. Martin's.

McInnes, Neil. 1972. *The Western Marxists*. New York: Library Press.

Merquior, J. G. 1985. *Foucault*. Berkeley: University of California Press.

Merton, Robert K. 1961. "Now the Case for Sociology." *New York Times Magazine* (July 16): 14, 19–21.

Mills, C. Wright. 1952. *White Collar*. New York: Oxford University Press.

———. 1956. *The Power Elite*. New York: Oxford University Press.

———. 1959. *The Sociological Imagination*. New York: Oxford University Press.

Moynihan, Daniel Patrick. 1986. *Family and Nation*. New York: Harcourt Brace Jovanovich.

Nairn, Tom. 1977. *The Break-Up of Britain: Crisis and New Nationalism*. London: New Left Books.

Nisbet, Robert A. 1969. *Social Change and History*. New York: Oxford University Press.

Novak, Michael. 1982. *The Spirit of Democratic Capitalism*. New York: Simon and Schuster.

Nove, Alec. 1983. *The Economics of Feasible Socialism*. London: Allen and Unwin.

Nozick, Robert. 1974. *Anarchy, State, and Utopia*. New York: Basic Books.

Page, Charles. 1985. "The Decline of Sociology's Constituency." *History of Sociology* 6 (Fall): 1–10.

Parkin, Frank. 1972. *Class Inequality and Political Order*. London: Granada.

———. 1979. *Marxism and Class Theory: A Bourgeois Critique*. New York: Columbia University Press.

———. 1982. "System Contradiction and Political Transformation," in Anthony Giddens and David Held, eds., *Classes, Power, and Conflict*. Berkeley: University of California Press.

Parsons, Talcott. 1937. *The Structure of Social Action*. New York: McGraw-Hill.

Pells, Richard H. 1984. *The Liberal Mind in a Conservative Age: American Intellectuals in the 1940's and 1950's*. New York: Harper and Row.

Perrow, Charles. 1972. *Complex Organizations: A Critical Essay*. Glenview, Ill.: Scott, Foresman.

Polsky, Nelson. 1985. "Preface," in *Hustlers, Beats, and Others*. Chicago: University of Chicago Press.

Popper, Karl. 1964. *The Poverty of Historicism*. New York: Harper Torchbooks.

Redfield, Robert. 1953. *The Primitive World and Its Transformations*. Ithaca, N.Y.: Cornell University Press.

Reich, Charles A. 1970. *The Greening of America*. New York: Random House.

Rex, John. 1961. *Key Problems of Sociological Theory*. London: Routledge and Kegan Paul.

Riesman, David (in collaboration with Reuel Denney and Nathan Glazer). 1950. *The Lonely Crowd*. New Haven: Yale University Press.

———— (in collaboration with Nathan Glazer). 1952. *Faces in the Crowd*. New Haven: Yale University Press.

———— (in collaboration with Reuel Denney and Nathan Glazer). 1969. *The Lonely Crowd*, abridged ed. New Haven: Yale University Press.

Rokkan, Stein. 1966. "Mass Suffrage, Secret Voting, and Political Participation," in Lewis A. Coser, ed., *Political Sociology*. New York: Harper and Row.

Sartre, Jean-Paul. 1946. *Réflexions sur la Question Juive*. Paris: Paul Morihien.

Schacht, Richard. 1970. *Alienation*. Garden City, N.Y.: Doubleday.

Schlesinger, Arthur, Jr. 1980. "Is Liberalism Dead?" *New York Times Magazine* (Mar. 30): 42–43, 70–73, 79.

————. 1982. "Comments." *Dissent* (Winter): 110–12.

————. 1986. *The Cycles of American History*. Boston: Houghton Mifflin.

Schlesinger, Arthur, Sr. 1949. *Paths to the Present*. New York: Macmillan.

————. 1963. *In Retrospect: The History of a Historian*. New York: Harcourt, Brace and World.

Schrecker, Ellen W. 1986. *No Ivory Tower: McCarthyism and the Universities*. New York: Oxford University Press.

Schwartz, Barry. 1986. *The Battle for Human Nature*. New York: Norton.

Searle, John R. 1995. *The Construction of Social Reality*. New York: Free Press.

Shils, Edward A. 1982. "The Intellectuals and the Powers," in *The Constitution of a Society*. Chicago: University of Chicago Press.

Smelser, Neil. 1990. "Can Individualism Yield a Sociology?" *Contemporary Sociology* 19 (Nov.): 778–83.

Smith, Adam. 1970. *The Wealth of Nations*. Books 1–3. Harmondsworth, Eng.: Penguin.

Steinfels, Peter. 1979. *The Neo-Conservatives: The Men Who Are Changing America's Politics*. New York: Simon and Schuster.

Stern, Fritz. 1987. *Dreams and Delusions: The Drama of German History*. New York: Knopf.

Stone, Lawrence. 1983. "An Exchange with Michel Foucault." *New York Review of Books* (Mar. 31): 44.

Strauss, Leo. 1953. *Natural Right and History*. Chicago: University of Chicago Press.

Sturmthal, Adolf. 1943. *The Tragedy of European Labor, 1918–1939.* New York: Columbia University Press.

Sumner, William Graham. 1940 (1906). *Folkways.* New York: Mentor Books.

Sweezy, P., and C. Bettelheim. 1971. *On the Transition to Socialism.* New York: Monthly Review Press.

Thompson, E. P. 1963. *The Making of the English Working Class.* New York: Vintage.

Thurow, Lester C. 1983. *Dangerous Currents: The State of Economics.* New York: Random House.

Trilling, Lionel. 1950. *The Liberal Imagination.* New York: Viking.

Tucker, Robert C. 1972. *Philosophy and Myth in Karl Marx.* 2d ed. Cambridge, Eng.: Cambridge University Press.

Turner, Bryan S. 1981. *For Weber.* London: Routledge and Kegan Paul.

Utis, O. (Isaiah Berlin). 1952. "Generalissimo Stalin and the Art of Government." *Foreign Affairs* 30 (Jan.): 197–214.

Walzer, Michael. 1974. "In Defense of Equality," in Lewis A. Coser and Irving Howe, eds., *The New Conservatives: A Critique from the Left.* New York: Quadrangle.

Weber, Max. 1930. *The Protestant Ethic and the Spirit of Capitalism.* New York: Scribner's.

Wegrocki, Henry J. 1948. "A Critique of Cultural and Statistical Concepts of Abnormality," in Clyde Kluckhohn and Henry A. Murray, eds., *Personality in Nature, Society, and Culture.* New York: Knopf.

White, Harrison C. 1990. "Control to Deny Chance, but Thereby Muffling Identity." *Contemporary Sociology* 19 (Nov.): 783–88.

Whitfield, Stephen J. 1980. *Into the Dark: Hannah Arendt and Totalitarianism.* Philadelphia: Temple University Press.

Williams, Philip M. 1982. "The Rise—and Possibilities—of Britain's Social Democrats." *Dissent* (Winter): 70–79.

Wilson, James Q. 1993. *The Moral Sense.* New York: Free Press.

Wolfe, Bertram D. 1965. *Marxism: One Hundred Years in the Life of a Doctrine.* New York: Dial Press.

Wrong, Dennis. 1956. "Riesman and the Age of Sociology." *Commentary* 21: 331–38.

———. 1976a. "Competent Authority: Reality and Legitimating Model," in Lewis A. Coser and Otto N. Larsen, eds., *The Uses of Controversy in Sociology.* New York: Free Press.

———. 1976b. Contribution to symposium "What Is a Liberal—Who Is a Conservative?" *Commentary* 62 (Sept.): 111–13.

———. 1976c. *Skeptical Sociology.* New York: Columbia University Press.

————. 1980. Review of Alvin Gouldner, *The Two Marxisms*. *New Leader* (May 19): 16–18.

————. 1981a. "The Rise and Fall of Neoconservatism." *Partisan Review* 47, no. 1: 102.

————. 1981b. "How Critical Is Our Condition?" *Dissent* (Fall): 414–24.

————. 1982a. "A Note on Marx and Weber in Gouldner's Thought." *Theory and Society* 11: 899–905.

————. 1982b. "Dennis Wrong Replies." *Dissent* (Winter): 112–14.

————. 1994. *The Problem of Order: What Unites and Divides Society*. New York: Free Press.

————. 1995. *Power: Its Forms, Bases, and Uses*. 3d ed. New Brunswick, N.J.: Transaction.

Yankelovich, Daniel. 1981. *New Rules*. New York: Random House.

Zeitlin, Maurice. 1982. "Corporate Ownership and Control: The Large Corporation and the Capitalist Class," in Anthony Giddens and David Held, eds., *Classes, Power, and Conflict*. Berkeley: University of California Press.

Sources

Chapter 1. "Disaggregating the Idea of Capitalism." *Theory, Culture & Society* 9 (1992): 147–58.

Chapter 2. "Is Rational Choice Humanity's Most Distinctive Trait?" *American Sociologist* 18, no. 2 (Summer 1997): 73–81.

Chapter 3. "Into the Dark: Hannah Arendt and Totalitarianism." *Society* 18, no. 4 (May/June 1981): 68–71.

Chapter 4. "Introduction to the Transaction Edition," in *Power: Its Forms, Bases, and Uses*, pp. vi–xvii. Reprinted by permission of Transaction Publishers. © 1995 by Transaction Publishers; all rights reserved.

Chapter 5. "Myths of Alienation." *Partisan Review* 52, no. 3 (1985): 222–35.

Chapter 6. Adapted from "The Bases of Power: Numbers and Political Democracy," chap. 8 of *Power: Its Forms, Bases, and Uses*, pp. 197–216. Reprinted by permission of Transaction Publishers. © 1995 by Transaction Publishers; all rights reserved. Also includes several paragraphs from "How Critical Is Our Condition?" *Dissent* 28, no. 4 (Fall 1981): 419–21; several paragraphs from "The End of Ideology?" *Dissent* 32, no. 2 (Spring 1985): 146, 149; and several paragraphs from "Swing Politics," *Dissent* 44, no. 4 (Fall 1997): 100–102.

Chapter 7. "Cultural Relativism as Ideology." *Critical Review* 10, no. 4 (Spring 1997).

Chapter 8. "The New Class: Does It Exist? 1. Skeptical Thoughts About a Fashionable Theory." *Dissent* 30, no. 4 (Fall 1983): 491–99.

Chapter 10. "The Influence of Sociological Ideas on American Culture," chap. 1 of *Sociology in America*, ed. Herbert J. Gans, pp. 19–

30. © 1990 by SAGE Publications. Reprinted by permission of SAGE Publications.

Chapter 11. "Professional Jargon: Is Sociology the Culprit?" *University: Academic Affairs at New York University* 2, no. 3 (Mar. 1983): 5–8.

Chapter 13. "*The Lonely Crowd* Revisited." *Sociological Forum* 7, no. 2 (June 1992): 381–89.

Chapter 14. "A Specialist in Generalizations." *New Republic* (Nov. 15, 1980): 23–28.

Chapter 15. Adapted from "Progress as Delusion?" *Dissent* 38, no. 2 (Spring 1991): 305–8. Also includes several paragraphs from "Bourgeois Values, No Bourgeoisie? The Cultural Criticism of Christopher Lasch," *Dissent* 26, no. 3 (Summer 1979): 308–10; and several paragraphs from "The Case Against Modernity," *New York Times Book Review* (Oct. 1984): 7.

Chapter 16. "The Paperbacking of the American Mind." *New York Times Book Review* (Apr. 17, 1988): 1, 20–24.

Chapter 17. Adapted from "Imagining the Real," chap. 1 in *Authors of Their Own Lives: Intellectual Autobiographies by Twenty American Sociologists*, ed. Bennett Berger. Berkeley: University of California Press, 1990: 3–21. Used with the permission of the University of California Press. Also includes paragraphs from "Fated to Be a Professor?" *American Sociologist* 28 (1997).

Library of Congress Cataloging-in-Publication Data

Wrong, Dennis Hume
    The modern condition : Essays at century's end / Dennis Wrong.
        p.   cm.
Includes bibliographical references and index.
ISBN 0-8047-3239-6 (cloth) — ISBN 0-8047-3241-8 (pbk.)
1. Political sociology.   2. Sociology—Philosophy.   3. Social
classes.   4. Intellectuals.   I. Title.
HM33.W76   1997
306.2—dc21   97-37687
                                                                    CIP

⊛ This book is printed on acid-free, recycled paper.

Original printing 1998

Last figure below indicates year of this printing:

07   06   05   04   03   02   01   00   99   98